Praise for *While America Sleeps*

Publishers Weekly Pick of the Week

"In *While America Sleeps*, Russ Feingold takes us behind the scenes in the Congress in the time leading up to and following 9/11. In thoroughly analyzing the good decisions and the many dangerous mistakes that were made after the attacks, Senator Feingold gives us insights that should help Americans support policies that keep us and our liberties secure. This book will alarm you, entertain you, enlighten you, and prepare you as citizens to engage in the national debate about a crucial part of our foreign policies." —**Former senator Bob Kerrey**

"While we hail from different political parties and most often disagree about the issues of the day, I have never met a more decent or honest public servant than Russ Feingold. We don't often hear about members of Congress with the courage of their convictions, but Russ lived that quality every day in the U.S. Senate. We waged many battles together for campaign finance reform, and I am honored to call him my friend. In his new book, *While America Sleeps*, Russ illuminates some of the challenges our nation faces in the post-9/11 era with his trademark integrity and independence." —**Senator John McCain**

"Great senator! Great book!" —**Lorrie Moore**, author of *A Gate at the Stairs*

"Feingold offers a thoughtful prescription for elected officials and voters alike, and he invokes a passionate plea for every American to realize the momentous connections between ourselves and others around the world so that our nation is better able to proactively meet future challenges." —*Booklist*

"Sage, sensible words by a leader who can now point to how right he was." —*Kirkus Reviews*

"[Feingold's] shockingly reasonable and carefully considered responses, as well as his respect for, and collaboration with, such Republican colleagues as John McCain and John Ashcroft, will make progressives, Wisconsinites, and other frustrated Americans nostalgic for the days of a more thoughtful, productive Congress." —*Publishers Weekly*

WHILE AMERICA SLEEPS

A Wake-up Call

for the

Post-9/11 Era

Russ Feingold

Broadway Paperbacks
New York

Published in the United States by Broadway Paperbacks, an imprint of the Crown Publishing Group, a division of Random House, Inc., New York.

www.crownpublishing.com

Broadway Paperbacks and its logo, a letter B bisected on the diagonal, are trademarks of Random House, Inc.

Originally published in hardcover in the United States by Crown Publishers, an imprint of the Crown Publishing Group, a division of Random House, Inc., New York, in 2012.

Library of Congress Cataloging-in-Publication Data
Feingold, Russ, 1953–
   While America sleeps/Russ Feingold.
      p. cm.
Includes bibliographical references and index 1. United States—Foreign relations—2001–2009. 2. United States—Foreign relations—2009– 3. September 11 Terrorist Attacks, 2001—Influence. 4. Terrorism—Government policy—United States—History—21st century. 5. United States—Politics and government—2001–2009.
6. United States—Politics and government—2009– 7. Progressivism (United States politics)—History—21st century. 8. Political culture—United States—History—21st century. I. Title.
   E903.F45 2011
   327.73009'05—dc23   2011051735

ISBN 978-0-307-95253-0
eISBN 978-0-307-95254-7

PRINTED IN THE UNITED STATES OF AMERICA

Illustration on page 100: copyright © 2010 the *Record*. Reprinted by permission of Jimmy Margulies.

Map illustration by Laura Hartman Maestro
Cover design by Daniel Rembert
Cover photography: Stephen Crowley/The New York Times/Redux (front);
Mandel Ngan/Getty Images (back)

10 9 8 7 6 5 4 3 2 1

First Paperback Edition

For CYF, JFL, and ERF

Contents

Contents

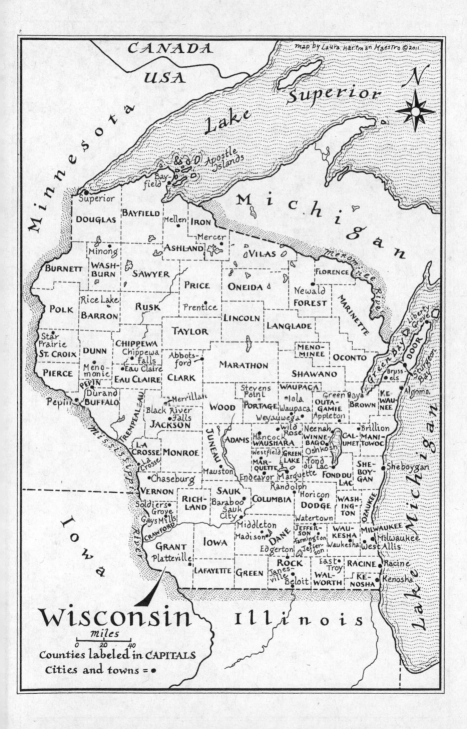

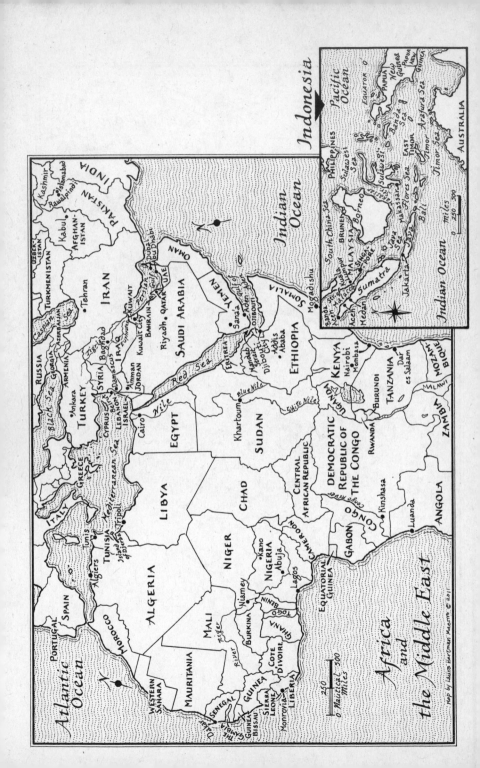

Indonesia

Pacific Ocean

Equator 0

PHILIPPINES

Papua
New
Guinea

AUSTRALIA

South China Sea

Sulawesi Sea

Sulawesi

Banda Sea

East
Timor

Papua
New
Guinea

Arafura Sea

Kuala Lumpur
BRUNEI
MALAYSIA
Borneo

Makassar
Strait

Timor Sea

Banda Aceh
Aceh
Medan
SINGA-
PORE

Java Sea

Flores Sea

Sumatra

Jakarta
Java

Bali

Indian Ocean

0   250   500
miles

Indian Ocean

UZBEK-
ISTAN
Kashmir
•Islamabad
•Rawalpindi
Kabul•
AFGHAN-
ISTAN
TURKMENISTAN
PAKISTAN
INDIA

RUSSIA
GEORGIA
AZERBAIJAN
ARMENIA
Caspian Sea
Tehran•
IRAN
OMAN
•Dubai
•Abu Dhabi
UAE
YEMEN
Indian Ocean

Black Sea
Ankara•
TURKEY
GREECE
CYPRUS
LEBANON
ISRAEL
SYRIA
•Damascus
Tigris
Baghdad•
IRAQ
Euphrates
KUWAIT
Kuwait City•
BAHRAIN•
QATAR•
•Riyadh
SAUDI ARABIA
Persian Gulf
Gulf of Oman
Sana'a•
Aden
Gulf of Aden
Mogadishu•
SOMALIA

ITALY
Mediterranean Sea
Tunis•
TUNISIA
Tripoli•
Island of Djerba
Algiers•
Red Sea
ERITREA
Asmara•
DJIBOUTI
Djibouti City•
Addis Ababa•
ETHIOPIA
Hamadi

SPAIN
PORTUGAL
MOROCCO
Atlantic Ocean
Cairo•
EGYPT
Nile
Khartoum•
SUDAN
Blue Nile
White Nile
UGANDA
KENYA
Nairobi•
Mombasa•
TANZANIA
Dar es Salaam•
MOZAMBIQUE
MALAWI

WESTERN SAHARA
MAURITANIA
ALGERIA
LIBYA
CHAD
NIGER
MALI
Niger River
CENTRAL AFRICAN REPUBLIC
DEMOCRATIC REPUBLIC OF THE CONGO
Kinshasa•
•Luanda
RWANDA
BURUNDI
ZAMBIA
ANGOLA
Congo River

SENEGAL
THE GAMBIA
GUINEA-BISSAU
GUINEA
SIERRA LEONE
Monrovia•
LIBERIA
COTE D'IVOIRE
BURKINA
GHANA
TOGO
BENIN
Niamey•
NIGERIA
•Kano
Abuja•
Lagos•
CAMEROON
EQUATORIAL GUINEA
GABON
CONGO

0   250   500
Nautical Miles

Africa
and
the Middle East

Map by Laura Hartman Maestro © 2011

WHILE AMERICA SLEEPS

Introduction

It may be hard for our island people, with their long immunity, to realize this ugly, unpleasant alteration in our position. . . . All our outlook for several generations has been influenced by a sense of invincible, inexpugnable security at home. That security is no longer absolute or certain, and we must address our minds courageously, seriously, to the new conditions under which we have now to dwell . . .

In the weeks before September 11, 2001, I was in the throes of trying to nail down the final votes in the House of Representatives that John McCain and I needed to pass the McCain-Feingold campaign finance reform legislation. The Senate had finally passed it in April, six years after we had started working together on the bill. Senator McCain loved telling audiences that we had worked on it for so long that people in Wisconsin now thought my first name was McCain. We had run into a snag in the House, though, in part because certain members of the key Congressional Black Caucus felt that some of the provisions in the bill could have a negative impact on their activities during local elections.

In this delicate situation, the great civil rights hero Congressman John Lewis of Georgia and Tennessee Congressman Harold Ford stepped up to the plate to help us. They arranged to have the four main legislative leaders on campaign finance reform—Congressman Marty Meehan of Massachusetts, Congressman Chris Shays of Connecticut, John McCain, and myself—join them and several civil rights leaders at the National Civil Rights Museum in Memphis, Tennessee, to highlight the importance of the legislation. John could not attend because of a brief medical problem, but on Friday, September 7, the three of us made a pilgrimage to this historic spot where Martin Luther King Jr. had been assassinated. John Lewis gave a moving tour of the museum, where some of the photographs actually show Lewis bleeding after being beaten during a civil rights march. Later we were treated to what Harold Ford dubiously described as a kosher barbecue lunch catered by the famous Rendezvous restaurant of Memphis. After lunch, we met with one of the ministers who had been with Dr. King at the Lorraine Motel in April 1968. We then all joined hands in prayer on the very spot on the balcony where Martin Luther King had been killed. It was powerful, helped us resolve the issues with the Congressional Black Caucus, and could not have been more unrelated to what we would all experience only four days later.

In fact, on that next Tuesday morning around nine, I was doing a telephone interview from my Washington apartment, a few hundred yards from the US Capitol. The interview was with a reporter from *Newsweek* magazine who was writing a big story on the rising prominence of the same Harold Ford who had hosted us in Memphis. In the middle of the interview, my deputy press secretary, Trevor Miller, who was listening in from our office in the Hart Senate Office Building, directly across the street, interrupted us to say, "Senator, I'm sorry, but the second tower has been hit." I couldn't help blurting out, "Holy sh**!"

After the Friday visit in Memphis, I spent just a few hours in Wisconsin before returning to Washington. I was accompanied by my longest-serving staff member, Nancy Mitchell. She had been my legal secretary at the Madison office of the Foley & Lardner firm since the day in 1979 when, fresh out of law school, I began practicing. I had always wanted to take Nancy to the annual White House congressional picnic as my guest. She had waited patiently as various family members had staked their legitimate claims to these rare White House events over the years. I was so pleased that the person who almost literally had been at my side for every day of my professional career could finally attend. The event had been scheduled for the evening of Tuesday, September 11. If you look at the photographs and video of the White House on the day of the attacks, you can see the big white tent that had been erected for the picnic, a picnic that didn't happen.

On this trip, Nancy Mitchell stayed at the home of my chief of staff, Mary Irvine, in Alexandria, Virginia. I had taken that Monday afternoon off to golf with some friends of mine, including one from my hometown of Janesville who has sadly since passed away. Dan Roach was one of the most gregarious guys I had ever known and for years I had urged him to come out to DC for some golf and a personal tour of the Capitol. The weather was perfect as we passed Dulles Airport on the way to the golf course. That night Mary and her husband, John Irvine, hosted an evening of outdoor grilling and political gossip. I remember how hard and long we all laughed as John and Roach, both of them pretty big-headed, argued about whose head could hold more nickels. Roach won. In retrospect it seems almost as though we didn't have a care in the world. When John Irvine gave some of us a ride back to Capitol Hill, I remember seeing an odd sight a few yards away from the Capitol. The Capitol Police had obviously asked a woman, who was wearing a burka, to open her car trunk, presumably so it could be searched. This type of security was still unusual near the Capitol on the evening of September 10, 2001. Within hours such a scene would take on a whole new meaning and would no longer seem unusual.

As anyone who was in the eastern part of the nation that day remembers, September 11 was an exceptionally beautiful, almost shimmering morning. At 6 a.m. I began my morning routine, starting (as always) with making coffee. After looking at the *New York Times* and the *Washington Post* and then reviewing the daily packet of memos that staff left at my door each night, I was getting dressed while casually watching the *Today* show. Like so many other Americans, I saw the initial story about a plane apparently flying into one of the two towers of the World Trade Center. Like just about everyone I've ever discussed this with, I naïvely assumed it was a little plane in a bizarre accident. Meanwhile, Nancy Mitchell and Mary Irvine were leaving Alexandria by car on their way to the Capitol. They were aware of the plane at the first tower but not of the attack on the second tower. En route, they passed the sun-drenched Pentagon.

Between the time that Nancy Mitchell got her coffee at the Hart Building and returned to our office on the fifth floor, she heard someone shout that the Pentagon had been hit. By that time I had spoken to Mary Irvine and instructed our entire staff to vacate the Hart Building and to go across the street to my apartment, directly across from the United States Supreme Court Building. I regarded my apartment as a haven, a place where I could be alone and relax after a day in the Senate constantly surrounded by others. Having even one federal staff member in my apartment—except to deliver something—was essentially unheard-of. Inviting some forty people, including new interns on their first week of the job, to come over right away was one indication that these rapidly unfolding events were completely beyond ordinary comprehension. After everybody had jammed into my place and we were handing out bottles of water, I looked out the window to see dozens of young students running away from the Capitol, going up Maryland Avenue Northeast, and scattering across the grounds of the Supreme Court. I had never witnessed anything like that before. We could hear police yelling but couldn't make out what it was they were shouting.

We soon knew. David Corn, a reporter for *The Nation* magazine, was based in the same place, the United Methodist Building. He ducked his head into the open door of my crowded apartment and said, "The Capitol Police say there is a plane headed toward the Capitol and they want everyone to get out." We were literally a stone's throw from the Capitol grounds, so another staff member, Mary Frances Repko, who lived about three blocks farther away on Maryland, suggested we retreat to her place. Most of us did exactly that. As we walked the short distance to her apartment, we found ourselves surrounded by thousands of confused pedestrians and drivers who simply had no idea what to do next. The rush hour traffic turned around and went back in the other direction, causing gridlock. Some were driving on the sidewalks and ignoring traffic lights. Those who were there recollect that "it got really vicious" or "it was anarchy." My longtime policy director, Sumner Slichter, described some people as having an "I don't care if I crush that old woman, I'm getting out of here sort of attitude. People figured, and I think with some justification, that there was a plane with their name on it headed at them."

We were lucky to be at Mary Frances's. She was a top-notch legislative aide with a wealth of practical knowledge that inspired her to fill her bathtub with water, which is apparently one of the things you are supposed to do in an emergency. Even in this context, this amused some of us. Things were fast breaking, confusing, and difficult to process. At one point we were told, incorrectly, that the State Department building had also been hit. There was no system in place that allowed for directly communicating with senators in a situation like this. The Senate leadership had been whisked away to a secure location almost immediately, but the rest of us were in the same boat as everyone else, trying to contact family members to let them know we were all right. Many of us had cellphones but they didn't work for hours, and there was no email system or warning device telling us where to go or what to do. As we huddled together at Mary Frances's, we and much of the rest of the world watched as the towers tumbled to the ground in New York and smoke billowed from the Pentagon, just across the Potomac River.

Even in a moment like this, however, some politicians will be politicians. My deputy press secretary, Trevor Miller, lived a few blocks away with a Republican staff member who worked for Wisconsin Congressman James Sensenbrenner. Trevor had chosen to go home instead of being with the mob at Mary Frances's and found the hulking form of Jim Sensenbrenner lurking in his modest apartment. Now, Jim and I simply didn't do joint press releases or joint anything else, but in the middle of this chaos, he proposed to Trevor that he and I do a joint press release on the unfolding events. Somehow Trevor got through on my cellphone and I said, "What in the hell are we going to say? That we're in charge here, like Alexander Haig after the Reagan assassination attempt?" Senator Orrin Hatch of Utah was already on television, touting his membership on the Intelligence Committee and blurting out information about the attackers and who he thought they were.

His comments seemed ill-advised, at odds with the confidentiality rules that I later became familiar with as a member of the same committee.

My younger daughter, Ellen, who was only a few days into her first semester at the University of Wisconsin–Madison, was the next to reach me on the phone. Soon after, my older daughter, Jessica, called from the University of Wisconsin–Eau Claire, where she was an upperclassman. She was sobbing and said, "Dad, just come home." Every American, especially those in the most directly affected cities, had similar conversations as the nation tried to grasp something for which there was no context or precedent. Mary Irvine, Sumner Slichter, Michelle Gavin, my foreign policy aide, and I decided that we had to do something to connect to whatever was going on in emergency response. We walked the couple of blocks from Mary Frances's home to the headquarters of the Capitol Police, located below the Hart Building parking lot close to Union Station. When we got there we witnessed what has to be one of the oddest, largely unknown meetings in recent American history. As we all knew, and as President Bush had been told earlier in the morning as he read to grade school children in Florida, America was under attack and we were smack in the middle of one of the newly minted war zones. But you couldn't tell it from the crowd that had assembled at the Capitol Police building. The leadership of the House and Senate were somewhere safe, and although we all fancied ourselves leaders of sorts in Congress, this was one of those moments when you realize why we do elect leadership. We were left to our own devices and it wasn't pretty. This was a completely random group of members from both houses and both parties who happened to show up at the station. Normally the mores of Congress, which define everything from seniority to party differences to the distance between the houses, prevent people like Senator Mark Dayton of Minnesota and Congressman Dana Rohrabacher of California from coming into too-close proximity to each other. And that's a good thing, having less to do with their radically divergent political views and more to do with the toxic mix of their personalities. As we gathered for a briefing from Senate Sergeant at Arms Alfonso Lenhardt and other congressional officers, I thought Dayton was going to tackle Rohrabacher as he droned on and on about "what we're going to do to these guys when we get ahold of them." I remember catching the eye of the always calm Senator Joe Lieberman and, while we were certainly not amused, it was clear that we agreed on the absurdity of the moment.

This uninformed parrying was mercifully interrupted by a briefing on what had already happened that morning. It is interesting that the sergeant at arms, who had been appointed only a week before, listed the missing and unaccounted flights, including the two that turned out to have struck the World Trade Center and the one that had hit the Pentagon. He added the now-famous Flight 93, but I don't believe he knew its tragic fate at that time. What has surprised me since this meeting is that Lenhardt listed a fifth flight number, suggesting it had gone down in or was flying somewhere over West Virginia. Later in the day, this fifth plane was no longer mentioned and there was never any real explanation of why it had been included in the list. We were interrupted at this point, because the president was going to address the nation. He had been flying around the country, apparently for safety reasons, after being told by Vice President Dick Cheney not to come back to the White House. The broadcast was not good: The picture quality was as bad as the old UHF channels in a storm; the president, frankly, looked just plain freaked out, and his words were uncertain. This was the first time I really started to feel that sense of vulnerability to which our nation, the most powerful on earth, had suddenly been subjected.

We stayed near the Capitol Police station for a while and learned that there would be a conference call for all senators with our cloistered leadership later in the day. When we reassembled at the station, there were many of the same Congress members who had been there before. We were crowded into a small conference room that featured a poorly functioning speakerphone in the middle of the table. It was hard to hear either Majority Leader Tom Daschle or Minority Leader Trent Lott. It got so bad that a frustrated Senator Barbara Boxer of California crawled up onto the table and lay down next to the speakerphone so she could hear—and be heard. Senator Lieberman had proposed that the Senate meet that night, on the actual day of the tragedy, to pass a resolution so we could "speak with one voice." A brief discussion ensued about whether we should go into session that same night, but it was quickly batted down by the faceless leadership. Lieberman said to Daschle, "You're our leader. We want to hear what you want us to do basically." Then Senator Mary Landrieu said more pointedly, "We need, Tom, we need someone in charge here. Who's in charge here? If you're not here, who's in charge?" This was a legitimate question, but Daschle laughed and said, "I don't really think we need to deal with this sort of chain of command issue right now. We'll all be back tomorrow."

There was a foreboding sense that this was merely the beginning, and other attacks could happen at any time. The prevailing question was "What are they going to do to us next?" We left the building knowing little more than we did going in. But then we started to receive a few updates and notices from the Senate communications system on our beepers (as they were called at the time). I remember reuniting with Mary Irvine and Nancy Mitchell, who was naturally worried about how she was going to get back to her children in Middleton. Mary, Nancy, and I walked over to a Mexican restaurant on Massachusetts Avenue to have dinner and a very welcome margarita. I remember that I was surprised to find the place was open. As we finished dinner, we got late notice that members of Congress were gathering on the Senate steps in the still beautiful, but now eerie fading daylight of this momentous day. This was to go down in history as the show of unity and resolve that Joe Lieberman had pressed for earlier in the day. We rushed there to find that we had missed whatever speeches or comments had been made. But just as we arrived, this gathering of about one hundred legislators broke into a rendition of "God Bless America." That moment came to be one of the symbols of America's intention to stand up to the cruelty and viciousness of Al Qaeda.

If there ever was a time to call it a day, this was it. Mary and Nancy went home and I walked the few hundred yards to my apartment. I knew it would be futile to try to make sense of all this too fast. I knew it would take far more information than we had and some emotional distance to play my role as a member of a Congress that faced one of the greatest challenges our nation had ever seen. That evening I watched the news reports and replays of those horrendous attacks—it was all I could do for hours. Like so many people, I woke up many times that night thinking this could not be real and didn't really happen. The next morning my staff and I reported for work at the Hart Building, and within minutes of my arrival Dan Roach came into my office. He had apparently been caught in the middle of the chaos on Tuesday morning in a park where police were desperately trying to clear the area. He said with the kind of look only Roach could give, "When's my tour of the Capitol?" Thinking that the Capitol might not even be there if not for the bravery of the passengers on Flight 93, I said to Dan, "There's not going to be a tour. Sorry. I have to go to caucus. And you need to figure out how to get home." So I went to the Democratic Caucus in the Lyndon Johnson Room in the Capitol. It was obviously a somber meeting but especially so when Senator Chuck Schumer announced that the loss of life from the twin towers could exceed twenty thousand people.

I often think about how quiet it was in America during the summer of 2001. After the frenzy and bitterness of the disputed election between Vice President Al Gore and Governor George W. Bush in 2000, the mood on Capitol Hill and, so it seemed, throughout the country, was relatively mild. But events in the Middle East and particularly in Israel were very violent, even for that region. At times during the summer, it seemed as if things could spin out of control there. In early August, my older sister, Nancy Feingold, whose son Dan lives in Jerusalem, called me from her place in Minnesota. She was in Grand Marais, the lights of which I could actually see as I was speaking with her. My vantage point was the most idyllic of Wisconsin settings—Devils Island in Lake Superior, the northernmost point in the state. I had just finished picking wild blueberries with some of my staff members as we were beginning a weekend as volunteer lighthouse keepers to highlight the Apostle Islands National Lakeshore. I could hear the jarring alarm in my sister's voice. Earlier in the day, August 9, fifteen people had been killed in a suicide bombing in downtown Jerusalem at a Sbarro restaurant. It was one of the first attacks of this kind in Jerusalem itself. Nancy sought whatever reassurance I could give on the Middle East situation, based on my knowledge as a member of the Senate Foreign Relations Committee. I remember thinking how comparatively invulnerable we usually felt in America, how removed from so many of the brutal conflicts and tragedies around the world.

The biggest news story of the early summer of 2001 had been the daily drumbeat concerning the investigation into the death of a young woman named Chandra Levy. Chandra, who had been an intern for California Congressman Gary Condit, had been found murdered along a jogging path in Rock Creek Park in Washington, DC. The incident had all the lurid qualities that usually sustain intense media focus on one story in modern America, and despite its truly sad content, it seemed amazing to me that it received almost more attention than all the other news stories put together. The only story that seemed to rival this was the spate of shark attacks all around the world at the same time. After September 11, the slow-news-summer quality that this story highlighted seemed more menacing to me. This is because of an incident that occurred as I visited Hawaii for the first time in mid-August 2001.

We had been warned not to be entirely flippant about the dangers of snorkeling near Kapalua on Maui. We ignored this, had a wonderful snorkeling adventure, and sure enough the next day the local paper printed a photograph of a twenty-foot-plus tiger shark that had entered the same alcove we had been swimming in the same day. I also had the opportunity during the trip to tour Pearl Harbor courtesy of one of the admirals stationed there. I was deeply moved by the honor of placing a wreath on the USS *Arizona* memorial, where hundreds of Americans had given their lives, victims of a surprise attack by the Japanese in 1941. It had been the last major attack on American soil by a foreign power. As the admiral gave me a tour from one of the navy's boats, including describing the plans for the upcoming sixtieth anniversary of Pearl Harbor on December 7, 2001, I distinctly remember how hard it was to imagine what a direct attack on America would feel like; I assumed that such a thing would never happen again. Later the juxtaposition of that harbor on Oahu and the shark off the shore of Maui became linked in my mind as harbingers of 9/11.

It would be absurd for me to suggest that I somehow foresaw the kind of events we were to experience on September 11, 2001. Ever since Black September at the Summer Olympics in Munich in 1972 and the bombing of the US Marine barracks in Lebanon in 1983, not to mention numerous airplane hijackings that often involved what were commonly referred to as "Arab terrorists," most Americans had a generalized sense that terrorism was especially likely to emanate from the Middle East. Yet the phenomenon of suicide bombings was not yet anticipated. Accordingly, when the first attack on the World Trade Center in New York City occurred in 1993, it seemed more like an isolated incident, rather than a warning or the first in a series of attacks against America. Many of us immediately assumed that the Oklahoma City bombing in 1995 must have been the work of terrorists connected with the first World Trade Center attack. I remember hearing about the Timothy McVeigh bombing in Oklahoma while traveling in Wisconsin's Fox River Valley to attend my listening sessions as a senator. When I learned the identities of the likely perpetrators, I was embarrassed that my first thought had been to blame foreign Arab or Muslim terrorists, rather than white men from Michigan. I think this incident made some of us a little less likely to see the pattern that was emerging from Al Qaeda's increasing series of attacks.

A sense that Al Qaeda itself, under the leadership of Osama bin Laden, was planning a sustained assault on the United States and Americans around the world slowly began to enter my thinking after our retreat, which I supported, from a miserable situation in Somalia in the early 1990s. As we extricated ourselves from what had been planned as essentially a humanitarian/military mission to prevent mass starvation, there were some suggestions that bin Laden or his operatives had been involved in the "Black Hawk Down" incident in Mogadishu in 1993. This took into account the public rejoicing at the humiliation of the corpses of fallen American soldiers. The possibility of a disturbing new pattern became more evident when Al Qaeda pulled off two simultaneous bombings of American embassies in two different African countries, Kenya and Tanzania, and apparently narrowly missed a third one in Uganda on the same day in August 1998. That was when I first felt a genuine sense of alarm.

This nascent feeling of dread intensified in October 2000, when the navy's USS *Cole* was brazenly attacked in a waterborne suicide attack in Aden harbor in Yemen. I happened to be in the Fox television studios in Washington, DC, the morning of that attack for an interview about the issue I was most associated with, campaign finance reform. Upon hearing of the attack right before going on the air, I remember feeling a chill. Later I learned that one of the seventeen Americans killed in the attack was a young fellow Wisconsinite, Engineman Marc Ian Nieto of Fond du Lac. Another time when I had this same distinct sense of foreboding about Al Qaeda was in a very different setting. Shortly after the contentious 2000 presidential election in the United States, I traveled to Nigeria in my capacity as the then ranking member of the Senate's Subcommittee on African Affairs. I recall a fairly light moment on the trip when I was meeting with a group of civil society leaders in the capital of Abuja. I was supposed to encourage them to demand free and fair elections in the upcoming rounds of balloting in this divided and complex country. Some of the Nigerian participants started to smile, and even laugh, as I spoke. I believe I blushed when I had to acknowledge that we had had some pretty serious problems with our most recent attempt to elect a president ourselves. The African participants in this meeting knew that a hanging chad had nothing to do with Chad, the unstable neighbor on their eastern border. The issues we had planned to focus on—and did focus on—during this trip had principally to do with governance, especially government corruption in western Africa and conflict resolution for the ongoing and brutal war in Sierra Leone.

A day or two after our Abuja meeting, we flew to the large and ancient Nigerian city of Kano. Somehow, despite this city's significance in this critical Islamic region of Nigeria and the use in Kano State of the controversial and revitalized sharia law, the United States had virtually no diplomatic presence there. The primary topic of conversation of the Nigerian-based American diplomat who accompanied us on this portion of the trip was his preference for a certain cut of steak from a butcher whose shop was in

Kano. As he made arrangements on the phone to get his next meat ship-ment, my staff member, Michelle Gavin, and I were puzzled to see children selling not only postcards and T-shirts featuring Muammar Qaddafi but also ones showing a smiling Osama bin Laden. This was more than four thousand miles from bin Laden's headquarters in Afghanistan. There had already been enough subtle hints about Al Qaeda on the trip that Michelle and I briefly discussed how we might assess the breadth of the organization's influence in various parts of Africa. I asked her to set up a briefing for me in Washington, although I certainly cannot say I felt it was urgent. Michelle went through all the hoops to arrange the briefing; it was scheduled to occur on September 13, 2001. Needless to say, it was superseded, or perhaps oblit-erated, by events.

Finally, another incident in early 2001 seemed exceptionally ominous. What Al Qaeda's and bin Laden's direct involvement—if any—in this was, I don't know, and I am not sure anyone else does. At the same time that the United Nations, the United States, and many others in the world com-munity were pressuring the Taliban in Afghanistan to give up bin Laden, the Taliban announced their plans to destroy the ancient and magnificent Buddha statues carved into the entire side of a mountain in Bamiyan. Although I had seen pictures of them before, I had no idea what an amaz-ing feat this millennium-old sculpture was, a true international treasure. Upon hearing reports of the threatened destruction, I recall believing that the Taliban must be bluffing—no one would really commit such a barba-rous act. I thought about how some had speculated that Hitler had spared St. Paul's in London and the colleges of Oxford, apparently because he was looking forward to using these buildings himself. When the Taliban went ahead and blew up these monuments in early March 2001 it seemed to me to be an extraordinarily different sort of threat than anything we had witnessed before. This ostentatious cultural brutality, coupled with their harsh treatment of women, gave the Taliban in Afghanistan a reputation that equaled that of the Khmer Rouge as one of the most despicable regimes in modern history. Even so, most people still perceived the Taliban, like the Khmer Rouge, as a huge but localized mass violation of human rights rather than a direct threat to America. In retrospect, the willingness to destroy these treasures of humanity was a significant clue about the new kind of terrorism that was emerging from Afghanistan. The difference is reflected in the distinction between old-fashioned hijackings where everyone usually survived and the total destruction caused by suicide passengers.

While Al Qaeda was developing an international network and strategy during the late 1990s, America seemed to be focused on a contrasting set of priorities. The best example of our inadequate prioritizing skills has to be the energy and attention lavished on the full-scale impeachment trial of President Bill Clinton in early 1999. The Senate trial of the president dragged on in tedious six-day weeks (Monday through Saturday), when essentially we did nothing else. Senators were given only a short lunch break to catch up on other things and get something to eat. At the end of one of the breaks some weeks into the trial, we all started to gather in the chamber for what promised to be another tiresome afternoon, the titillating and interesting aspects of the trappings of this trial having long lost their luster. I was engaged in casual conversation with Paul Wellstone of Minnesota and Bob Kerrey of Nebraska at the back of the chamber. We became aware that Carl Levin of Michigan, one of the most senior and distinguished members of the Senate, was slowly making his way up the steps toward us. Carl is a meticulous, lawyerly member of the Senate who does a superb job of carefully examining both proposed statutory language and facts. Carl approached us and, as he lifted his ubiquitous "readers" from his face, said, "Listen, I am a little embarrassed to ask you guys this, but what's a thong?"

Wellstone and I couldn't contain ourselves. I was doubled over with laughter. I regretted that, because I have such respect for Carl's kind manner and great legislative skills, but the absurdity of the situation was too much. Wellstone, struggling for breath, managed to mutter something about not wanting to comment on the question because he had a young daughter. I turned to Bob Kerrey and said, "Bob, you do this," Kerrey being the obvious choice for this delicate mission and not because he had won the Congressional Medal of Honor. Suddenly, from the front of the chamber,

Chief Justice William Rehnquist in his flowing black robe with gold stripes solemnly intoned, "The Senate will come to order." As Wellstone and I staggered away, Bob Kerrey collegially placed his arm around a red-faced Carl Levin and calmly explained to him this key feature of modern attire.

This was amusing, of course, but when you consider what was going on with Al Qaeda, not to mention all the other issues that the leading nation in the world has to deal with, it has become a metaphor for me of just how complacent we had become. The senators engaged in that conversation at the back of the Senate chamber had an accumulated level of some forty years of seniority. For all of us to be spending that kind of time on that sort of topic—although considering the evidence was required by the Constitution once the trial was set in motion—was a clear sign of a government and a nation that was not only asleep, but having some pretty weird dreams to boot.

On May 28, 1938, Randolph S. Churchill wrote from Westminster Gardens, "My father has consented to a suggestion I made him some time ago that I should compile a volume of his speeches on Foreign Affairs and National Defense. This book is the result." The younger Churchill explains that the volume consists of some forty speeches and that "all except the first were delivered in the last six years, and all but two in the House of Commons." Originally published in England as *Arms and the Covenant,* its first American edition by G. P. Putnam's Sons was called *While England Slept: A Survey of World Affairs, 1932–1938.* Its author was described as "the Rt. Hon. Winston S. Churchill, C.H., M.P." I had often heard of this book but had never read it, although when I started thinking about the years before and then the years after 9/11, this title kept popping into my head.

Winston Churchill's book was not about a nation that was ignoring international affairs. Rather, in speech after speech Churchill doggedly declared his conviction that the government during that time, particularly under Neville Chamberlain, was mistakenly engaged in creating alliances and strategies that underestimated the growing strength of the German military. Many of the lectures were very detailed accounts of the German buildup and covered topics such as "The MacDonald Disarmament Plan," "Air Defense Research," and "Machine Tools." Only occasionally do these lectures speak in broader terms about the momentous British and world history that was unfolding. When he did, it was powerfully delivered:

> Now the demand is that Germany should be allowed to rearm. Do not delude yourselves. Do not let His Majesty's Government believe—I am sure they do not believe—that all that Germany is asking for is equal status. . . . That is not what Germany is seeking. All these bands of sturdy Teutonic youths, marching through the streets and roads of Germany, with the light of desire in their eyes to suffer for their Fatherland, are not looking for status. They are looking for weapons, and, when they have the weapons, believe me they will then ask for the return of lost territories and lost colonies, and when that demand is made it cannot fail to shake and possibly shatter to their foundations every one of the countries I have mentioned.

The speeches are full of diplomatic and military details and there are clever backhanded compliments for the prime minister and even some for Herr Hitler. But the passage that reminded me of America in this 9/11 era came in a speech titled "The Defense Loan," delivered in the Commons on March 4, 1937.

> We must remember that we are for the time being no longer entirely masters of our own fate. That fate no longer depends altogether on what we decide here or on what the Cabinet settle in Downing Street. It depends on what may happen in the world, on what other countries do, for good or for ill. It may be hard for our island people, with their long immunity, to realize this ugly, unpleasant alteration in our position. We are an undefeated people. Nearly a thousand years have passed since we were subjugated by external force. All our outlook for several generations has been influenced by a sense of invincible,

inexpugnable security at home. That security is no longer absolute or certain, and we must address our minds courageously,
seriously, to the new conditions under which we have now to
dwell. . . .

Obviously America is not literally an island but we are insulated by
two huge oceans, and geographical distance from the rest of the world has
allowed us to grow and prosper, like a remote island free of imminent dangers. We enjoyed the same sense of invulnerability to attack that Churchill
ascribes to the British at the time. And, on 9/11, we certainly experienced
an "ugly, unpleasant alteration in our position" when we watched in horror
as some of our most iconic buildings and the people in them were attacked
in the heart of two of our greatest cities. And, while this book is certainly
not a call for arming America as Churchill recommended for interbellum
Britain, it is a call for us to arm ourselves in other crucial ways. We were
asleep at the switch on 9/11 and during the ten years since, and we have
failed to stay alert and prepare ourselves properly for the future. We have
not addressed our minds "seriously to the new conditions under which we
now have to dwell."

This book is about our nation's collective failure to respond properly to
the challenges of the post-9/11 era. Negligent and willful oversimplification
of complicated new problems as well as a cynical exploitation of the fears
generated by 9/11 have undermined our ability effectively to adjust to a
new paradigm for America's place in the world. This has weakened our ability to protect American lives, our national security, and our constitutional
values. Too often we have made the wrong choices in confronting the issues
presented by the events of the last ten years. It is as if this country, after one
of the most dramatic wake-up calls in human history, has been induced into
a dangerous hibernation that prevents it from directly addressing the issues
that led up to and continue ten years after 9/11.

The goal here, however, is not merely to criticize the past. My dream
is that when the history of this era is written, it will be said that America
was taken off guard at the height of its power at the turn of the century; it
stumbled for a decade in an unfamiliar environment; but in the next decade

America found a new national commitment of unity and resolve to adapt to its new status and leadership role in the world. Accordingly, while much of this book focuses on the missteps of the last ten years, it concludes not only with hope but also with specific solutions to help us better connect with the world.

PART 1

LOSING OUR
FOCUS ON AL QAEDA

1

A Quiet, Almost Smoldering Determination

We are supported by the collective will of the world.

When I walked into the Democratic Caucus room just two days after September 11, I was entering well-known territory. Even after Senator Jim Jeffords of Vermont left the Republican Caucus to join ours in the spring of 2001, we Democrats continued to meet in the smaller of the two rooms used for Senate caucuses in the US Capitol building. Despite the Republicans' sudden loss of control of the Senate for the first time since 1994, the tenuous Democratic majority allowed them to continue to convene in the spacious Mike Mansfield Room, where the majority caucus traditionally gathered for the weekly party lunch meetings. This room is named after the mild-mannered but revered former Democratic majority leader from Montana, whose portrait dominates the room. Maybe Tom Daschle enjoyed the thought of the minority Republicans having to meet under the watchful eye of a looming Mansfield, informally posed, and holding his beloved pipe.

The much smaller Lyndon Johnson Room, where we had been meeting since our huge loss of majority in 1994, was certainly familiar by now. What was unfamiliar—and incongruous—was the whiteboard resting on an easel in the middle of this ornately old-fashioned, chandeliered room.

For a moment I assumed that someone had forgotten to remove the board from a previous meeting. As senators filed into the room, though, I read the words scrawled on it in green felt-tip pen:

> That the President is authorized to use all necessary and appropriate force against those nations, organizations, or persons he determines planned, authorized, harbored, committed, or aided in the planning or commission of the attacks against the United States that occurred on September 11, 2001, and to deter and preempt any related future acts of terrorism or aggression against the United States.

I had wondered whether our initial response to the shock of 9/11 would be measured or reckless and this was a first sign that it could be heartbreakingly reckless indeed. Despite the fact that we had a Republican House and, of course, a Republican president, Jeffords's switch made the Senate Democratic majority partly responsible for the critical post-9/11 choices that had to be made. This was the challenge for the Democratic Caucus. I believed that Tom Daschle's very determined and skillful luring of Jeffords could prove to be exceptionally fortunate timing, allowing the Senate Democratic majority to both check Republican excesses in response to 9/11 and provide bipartisan unity for good decisions that could be reached across the aisle.

Once I understood that the language on the easel was actually the proposal for our caucus to consider, I began to wonder if I was going to be placed in a very difficult position. I had already stated on the floor of the Senate the day after September 11 that there was no question in my mind that military action against Al Qaeda was not only warranted but necessary. It was fully justified under our own laws as well as under Article 51 of the United Nations Charter, which guarantees the right of self-defense to all nations—a time-honored principle of international law. I considered joining the queue to raise my objections to the imprecise wording, which I could do by slightly raising my hand until the majority leader noticed and wrote down my name. This proved to be unnecessary.

Almost immediately some of our most seasoned members, including Senator Joe Biden of Delaware and Senator Carl Levin of Michigan, chairmen of the Senate Foreign Relations Committee and the Senate Armed Services Committee, respectively, pointed out the obvious flaws in passing a resolution using open-ended terms like *terrorism,* rather than focusing the language on those who actually had attacked us. As justified as it was to pursue real terrorist organizations, either militarily or through law enforcement, for generations virtually every repressive regime in the world from Ethiopia to Uzbekistan has tried to demonize their political opposition by describing them as "terrorist organizations." I was not only relieved but proud to hear my colleagues successfully persuade a very nervous group of senators to carefully tailor the language into what ultimately became the Authorization for the Use of Military Force, or "AUMF." The wording was adjusted to read:

That the President is authorized to use all necessary and appropriate force against those nations, organizations, or persons he determines planned, authorized, committed or aided the terrorist attacks that occurred on September 11, 2001, or harbored such organizations or persons, in order to prevent any future acts of international terrorism against the United States by such nations, organizations or persons.

While this language came to be cited by the Bush administration (and to a much lesser extent by the Obama administration) to justify everything from certain illegal torture practices, to aspects of Guantánamo detention, to extreme claims regarding the power to wiretap without a warrant, the fact is that the comparatively narrow wording that ultimately passed rendered these arguments weak and almost bogus. As the caucus ended, amid all the sorrow and fear, I did feel proud of my Democratic colleagues and of the institution of the United States Senate, whose special role in issues of war and self-defense is enshrined in the Constitution. I was guardedly optimistic: If the Senate majority played a similar role as other key decisions were made, we would be able to pursue Al Qaeda and preserve fundamental constitutional principles. Unfortunately, the next major piece of legislation to follow the AUMF proved to be just the opposite—a rush to judgment and a capitulation to political fear: the USA Patriot Act. (A fuller discussion of the Patriot Act's passage follows later, in chapter 6.)

Given the intense divisiveness that characterized the George W. Bush era after the Iraq War began, it is easy to forget that it was not always so. For a brief period after September 11, 2001, it seemed to me that both the Washington political establishment and the public at large were resolved to put aside prior differences and agendas to get the response to this surprise attack right. Perhaps I was naïve, but I actually believed that the terrorist attacks would alter the post–Cold War political landscape for a sustained period of time. As Professor Theodore J. Lowi of Cornell University said to the *New York Times* on September 12, the attack had moved the political dynamic even beyond bipartisanship. "We will be operating as if we have a national unity party." That is exactly how I assumed things would evolve and this meant a significant change of emphasis for most members of Congress, including myself. In this vein, my policy director, Sumner Slichter, came into my office on the morning of September 12 and said wistfully but realistically, "There goes our agenda."

Sumner had been with me and advised me on every vote I had taken starting in the Wisconsin Senate in 1983, and he played this role throughout my legislative career. He's the guy you would turn to in a situation where somebody had to come up with the best answer in one minute. He was—and is—that quick to analyze things. I've often thought about Sumner's comment. I agreed with him in large part, for none of us felt that "our agenda" could begin to rival the new circumstances and challenges that now confronted us. At the same time, I was a legislator and these were highly professional legislative aides working with me on what we believed were very important issues for the state of Wisconsin and the nation as a whole. We had picked up significant momentum on efforts to legislate against racial profiling, a practice followed by some law enforcement officials of stopping motorists based on their race alone, an offense nicknamed "driving while black" or "driving while brown." We had had the first signs of positive movement on my goal of abolishing the death penalty throughout America, just as Wisconsin had done in 1851. In 2000, Governor George Ryan of Illinois had declared a moratorium on the death penalty in that state after DNA evidence led to the release of several death row inmates, and the national conversation was slowly moving our way. People at my listening sessions, from the neighborhoods of Milwaukee and Madison to the relatively unpopulated communities like the gorgeous Lake Superior town of Bayfield, were increasingly talking about the need for more affordable housing. When I brought this back to DC, I found that people like Senator John Kerry of Massachusetts and Senator Jack Reed of Rhode Island were hearing similar concerns, and we set out to work together to create a much-needed National Housing Trust Fund.

By the morning of September 12, 2001, all of this was stopped in its tracks. Ironically, the issue I assumed would most quickly be derailed was the one I was most associated with—campaign finance reform. Somehow, in the midst of all the tumult between September 2001 and the lead-up to the Iraq War, we were able to pass the McCain-Feingold bill and have it signed into law. But on September 12 that was the last thing I expected to happen. What I also can say is that as important as these matters were and still are, at the time I didn't care. I was completely consumed by the events of the previous few hours. And that's exactly how I found most other legislators felt for some weeks to come.

The battles over the budget and Social Security were suddenly pushed from the headlines. Instead we began to hear the initial reactions of members of Congress to the terrorist attacks. To be sure, some tried to outdo one another with tough talk. The Democratic senator from Georgia, Zell Miller, took the cake with "I say bomb the hell out of them. If there's collateral damage, so be it. They certainly found our civilians to be expendable." Others looked immediately for people to blame within the US government. It is not surprising that this contingent was led by the flamboyant Congressman Rohrabacher of California, who stated, "It's a day of disgrace. The president needs to clean house and wipe away the senior executives of the intelligence agency." But this was not typical. The focus was on measured expressions of unity and nonpartisanship led by the chairs of the two major political parties. Terry McAuliffe of the Democratic National Committee noted that "the budget debate and everything else is on the back burner now," while Virginia Governor James Gilmore of the Republican National Committee declared that "partisanship at this point is exactly the wrong approach."

This mood was reflected among the lawmakers most directly involved in working with the White House in the hours after 9/11. When a request for a doubling of the initial commitment of $20 billion for New York to $40 billion was assented to by President Bush, Senator Chuck Schumer of New York reported, with some emotion, "He said, 'I'm for it.' There was a lump in my throat." The negotiations that led to this outcome were actually interrupted on Thursday, September 13, because of a frenzied evacuation of the Capitol in response to a telephone bomb threat. In an example of goodwill and even humor at such a tough time, John McCain, standing with John Kerry on the Capitol lawn, quipped, as the negotiations continued outside, "I know I'm dying in bed. John and I have been through too much already."

Although I later became his leading congressional critic, the person I most credit for creating the tone and resolve that America evidenced in those first critical days after 9/11 is George W. Bush. His brief address on the evening of September 11 was a vast improvement over the hurried and fuzzy attempt to broadcast earlier in the day, when he was still far away from the White House. His tone was measured as he said, "These acts shatter steel, but they cannot dent the steel of American resolve." His manner was firm as he reassured us. "Our military is powerful, and it's prepared." In the following days the president made repeated and strong statements warning all Americans "not to discriminate against or retaliate against Arab Americans and Muslims in our nation." His performance when touring the World Trade Center with Mayor Rudy Giuliani of New York heartened virtually all Americans.

For many Democrats, the president's reaction and manner were more surprising for their skill than their restraint. After the bitter election of 2000, when many felt that he had gained the presidency only by virtue of an abysmal decision of the United States Supreme Court, the most common criticism of Bush was that he was not up to the job or that he was not really interested in the substance of the work. He was not expected to be an extremist in foreign policy any more than his relatively moderate father, President George H. W. Bush, had been, and he was not likely to go off the deep end even in the cataclysmic environment in the days and weeks after 9/11. I shared this view of George W. Bush and indeed thought that both Vice President Dick Cheney and Secretary of Defense Don Rumsfeld were of a similar persuasion—not my cup of tea but still in the more moderate tradition of the Ford administration. (On the other hand, US Attorney General John Ashcroft was, at best, an archconservative in the Ronald Reagan line.) In fact, over the last twenty years Cheney and Rumsfeld had been frequently mentioned as possible Republican vice presidential candidates because of their business backgrounds and relative moderation compared to the Goldwater/Reagan wing of the Republican Party. All of this suggested an almost ideal combination going forward in response to 9/11: a Democratic Senate countering the extreme conservative tendencies of the remaining "Contract with America" House, refereed by a moderate and reasonably cautious administration.

This impression was not only confirmed but enhanced nine days after September 11, when, on the evening of September 20, the president addressed a joint session of Congress. This speech was perhaps the best I had ever heard by a president in my lifetime. At the time, one of my closest friends, John Sylvester (Sly), a progressive talk-radio host in Madison, was visiting me to see what was going on after the 9/11 attacks. I had had a brief moment with the president as he left the chamber after his speech. Sly recalls my coming back to my apartment and saying, "Did you see me with the president? I told the president 'we will get this done together. You will have my full support.' That was one hell of a speech." Of course, I had a seat right at the front of the House chamber and the emotion of the occasion made all of us susceptible to hyperbole, but I did feel Bush chimed perfectly with the tone of the country and truly led the nation this time.

He had reminded us that the only other attack like this on American soil in the entire 136 years since the Civil War had been Pearl Harbor. And, regarding the uniqueness of this attack, he said that "Americans have known the casualties of war—but not at the center of a great city on a peaceful morning." He accurately stated that "Al Qaeda is to terror what the mafia is to crime," but he immediately reminded all Americans that "the terrorists practice a fringe form of Islamic extremism that has been rejected by Muslim scholars and the vast majority of Muslim clerics, a fringe movement that perverts the peaceful teachings of Islam." He pointed out that "there are thousands of these terrorists in more than sixty countries." (Later we discovered that the list on which Bush based this comment did not include Iraq.) This carefully considered performance contrasted well with his subsequent "axis of evil" speech, not to mention his "crusade" and "wanted dead or alive" gaffes.

To be sure, there were comments in the speech that now appear ominous, precursors of future errors. "Our war on terror begins with Al Qaeda, but it does not end there. It will not end until every terrorist group of global reach has been found, stopped, and defeated." And "Either you are with us or you are with the terrorists. From this day forward, any nation that continues to harbor or support terrorism will be regarded by the United States as a hostile regime." On the evening of September 20, 2001, these comments seemed reasonable, though, and proportional to what had been done to us. On that evening I felt that this man truly was my president. He may be in way over his head in this situation, but who wouldn't be? He needed our support, because his job, and ours, too, had just radically changed. So I was not only relieved but intensely proud of my country at this hour when the president concluded:

> I will not forget the wound to our country or those who inflicted it. I will not yield; I will not rest; I will not relent in waging this struggle for freedom and security for the American people. The course of this conflict is not known, yet its outcome is certain. Freedom and fear, justice and cruelty, have always been at war, and we know that God is not neutral between them. Fellow citizens, we'll meet violence with patient justice—assured of the rightness of our cause, and confident of the victories to come.

I was eager to support this president and so were my constituents in Wisconsin. In fact, earlier on the same day of Bush's speech, I had held my first listening session since 9/11 in Rock County, my home county. The people there mirrored the president's resolve and combined it with very practical ideas about how some of them might be able to help.

There are two mid-sized communities in Rock County: my hometown of Janesville, where members of my family have lived since 1917, and Beloit, situated along the Illinois border. Normally I tried to fly to Washington through Madison or Milwaukee, hoping to avoid the uncertainties of traffic on the way to and within what is one of the busiest airports in the world, Chicago's O'Hare International Airport. For many who transited between Illinois and the University of Wisconsin–Madison, or, in the summer, to central and northern Wisconsin to their vacation homes, Rock County was just drive-through land on the Interstate 90 route to these supposedly more desirable places. But for me and for several of my staff members who had grown up in this county, this was home, the center of the universe for the first eighteen years of our lives. So it was both practical, given the very few flight options just after 9/11, and comforting to hold my first post-9/11 town meeting in our home county. We held the meeting in the public library in Beloit, right near the home of Janesville's traditional bitter rival, Beloit Memorial High School's Purple Knights. On this day, however, the usual joshing and jabbing about the relative merits of the two leading communities were absent. And the crowd was much larger than we had anticipated. We ran out of chairs.

I like to think I did a pretty good job of conducting these town meetings, trying to respond at least briefly to each speaker and also trying to make sure that everyone got a chance to talk no matter how large the crowd. Sometimes I might be a little abrupt encouraging one speaker to conclude so others could talk and we could still finish at or near the allocated time. On September 20, I was clearly feeling rushed. I was curious to hear what people would say or ask in their first encounter since 9/11 with a federally elected official, but I also wanted to make my plane and get to the president's speech on time. I canceled my usual media availability time prior to the meeting and launched into a brief statement about the preceding days and the challenges ahead. Everyone seemed calm but somewhat dazed to be listening to an account of such a bizarre series of events. Yet most of my constituents did not even refer to the terrorist attacks. Comments ranged from criticism of the way the federal government gives money back to the counties, and of air pollution standards in a county that had always relied on car building for jobs, to opposition to the NAFTA and GATT trade treaties, as well as one request for help to get a new Social Security office in Janesville, to be located on someone's property.

About ten of the twenty-three speakers did speak of the whole new era we had just entered. The Democratic sheriff of the county, Eric Runaas, asked, "can the CIA get a longer leash to get these guys?" And County Clerk Kay O'Connell from Edgerton said that she had heard there was a shortage of anthrax serum, because of some permitting process that the federal government required. This was a prescient remark in September, as we did not start experiencing the anthrax attacks until October. One of the major liberal activists in the county, John Graf, warned that a military response could spiral out of control and suggested that there is a "danger to innocent people" and to our civil liberties. Another progressive, Georgia Duerst-Lahti, a local political science professor, stressed the need to use other sources of energy rather than foreign oil in light of these attacks. And Donna Thorson of Janesville said that "there needs to be a system of checks and balances and Congress should be involved." What struck me about all this was that, although there were clearly different mindsets present in the room, all the comments were calm and civil.

What took me just a little off guard and so impressed me, however, was what was suggested near the end of the listening session. Given the size of the crowd, and my need to get back to Washington on time, I was considering asking some people who had signed up to speak to withhold their remarks, promising to hold a longer session in the county very early in 2002.

Then, as I was gathering up my papers near the end of the meeting, I called on the chief of police of Beloit, James Reseburg, who asked me why police and firefighters couldn't be registered prior to a flight so that they could be available as additional assistance in case of an emergency, even if a federal marshal were on board. In light of the heroism of the people on Flight 93 over Pennsylvania just nine days earlier, this seemed both very practical and smart but also a moving demonstration of how Americans in all walks of life wanted to help and work together in response to this threat to America. As I was leaving, the deputy police chief, Charlie Tubbs, an African American who some thought would have made a good chief himself, said he strongly supported his boss's idea.

We discovered that allowing this kind of participation by nonfederal first responders on an airplane would require legislation. It was introduced, passed, and became law within a matter of a couple of weeks, the fastest legislating I could remember since the resolution commending the annual Girl Scout cookie sales cleared the Wisconsin legislature in 1983. The Volunteer for Safe Skies Program allowed volunteer first responders to register with air carriers so they could assist in the event of an onboard emergency. Regrettably, it took five years for this program to be actually implemented as it became mired in bureaucracy. Nonetheless, it was a symbol of what I felt was a link between the helpful and unified spirit of the people of heartland America and the words of President Bush. Nobody in Beloit asked me, "When are we going to get these guys?" There was no clear certainty yet about how these attacks on America had happened. We all knew of the connections to Al Qaeda, Osama bin Laden, and the Afghan Taliban government, but people seemed comfortable with a careful, deliberate approach to our military response and wanted to get this right from the beginning.

On October 3, I was invited for the first time after almost nine years on the Foreign Relations Committee to visit the State Department with all the members of the committee for an off-the-record lunch conversation with the secretary of state and other top officials there. Colin Powell was already emerging as the administration's public face to America and especially the rest of the world as we prepared our response to Al Qaeda. He graciously and calmly greeted us as we entered the magnificent dining room on the eighth floor of the State Department building. I fleetingly thought about how September 11 would always rank high with the hundreds of other critical moments in American foreign policy that had been hashed over in that room.

This gathering did not seem to be a mere formality. Powell and his lieutenants were intently listening as each of us, in seniority order, was given an opportunity to speak. I was able to address the need to connect with the Muslim populations in so many African countries, such as Kenya and Tanzania, which had already been attacked by Al Qaeda. Given the incredible range of things that had to be on the secretary's mind, I was very pleased to hear his substantive agreement and obvious understanding of the relevance of the issues I was describing. What sticks in my mind from this lunch, however, was Powell's deputy Richard Armitage, who looked like a guy who could snap Osama bin Laden in two with his bare hands. He was bald and fearsome-looking, with a barrel-shaped physique, but his comments conveyed the opposite of blind belligerence. Even when he described the crucial "are you with us or against us" conversation he had already had with Pakistani President Pervez Musharraf, Armitage seemed the voice of reason and cool. Led by the Powell/Armitage team, our buildup to war seemed not just methodical but also sensitive to the powerful emotions that had been exposed by the events of September 11.

Indeed, by September 15, Pakistan had already agreed to open up its airspace for launching of possible US missile attacks and aerial bombardment in Afghanistan. This was despite the strong public support that the Taliban enjoyed in much of Pakistan. China soon agreed to share intelligence it had gathered on alleged terrorist groups, in what some called a show of support for America's campaign against Osama bin Laden. Reportedly, no quid pro quo was asked by the Chinese when they spoke to Secretary Powell. In fact, the Chinese were already referring to what they regarded as their own part of the war on terror, the bombings in the Xinjiang Uighur autonomous region north of Tibet. The administration expressed great satisfaction with the unanimous condemnation of the attacks by all African nations, including not only countries with significant Muslim populations but even those that had been largely unfriendly to us. Libya's Muammar Qaddafi offered condolences and called the attacks "horrific," and Secretary Powell's request of Sudanese Foreign Minister Osman Mustafa for cooperation received a promise of exactly that.

As this process unfolded, what meant the most, though, was the outreach to the Islamic and Arab countries of the vast Middle East. There were still raw feelings about the failure of some of these countries, particularly King Hussein's Jordan, to support our efforts against Iraq a decade earlier, in the Persian Gulf War. But they were all brought on board by Powell and his team. The US announcement that it would use Saudi Arabia as a headquarters for air operations strained already tense relations between our two countries. Yet this pivotal Middle Eastern nation, the original home of almost all of the 9/11 suicide bombers, made common cause with us as well.

There were some difficulties with close allies, too. Israeli Prime Minister Ariel Sharon complained at a news conference on October 4 about the ongoing communications with Arab countries, and blurted out, "Do not try to appease the Arabs at our expense!" The response of the president's press secretary, Ari Fleischer, was a rebuke: "The Prime Minister's comments are unacceptable." Later, in his executive suite in the State Department, Colin Powell smoothed over the situation. He told two reporters, "I don't think there is anything to that comment [Sharon's]. . . . From time to time we'll have little cloudbursts, but that doesn't affect the strength of our relationship."

Time magazine had just written a piece titled "Odd Man Out," saying "the most popular man in America," Powell, had become isolated in the new Bush White House and that his "megastar wattage looks curiously dimmed." London's *Observer* observed on September 30 that "*Time*'s timing was unfortunate. The current crisis has seen Powell, in his deceptively quiet way, gain ascendancy over his many rivals." I joined many Americans (and particularly political progressives) in breathing a sigh of relief at Powell's success. He had headed off a faction led by Don Rumsfeld and Undersecretary of Defense Paul Wolfowitz that, according to the *Observer,* was already agitating for wide-ranging military strikes not only in Afghanistan but also Iraq and perhaps Lebanon. Of course, the administration later took advantage of Powell's reputation for coalition building and credibility when it sold the country a bill of goods for the 2003 Iraq invasion, but at this point Powell seemed the ideal symbol of both American calm and resolve. As Anthony Lewis wrote in the *New York Times* on September 29:

> That we have not yet retaliated with force is frustrating to many, but wise. There was a real danger that we would strike back in anger, heedless of civilian casualties and their consequences for our cause. The President and his people now plainly understand the cost of getting it wrong.
>
> The sense of deliberateness in our decision-making carries its own power in the world. . . . as almost everyone else in the country has seen over these weeks, Colin Powell has been a strong, reassuring figure, giving crucial support to George W. Bush as he has grown into the presidency.

So when President Bush announced on October 7 that "on my orders, the United States military has begun strikes against Al Qaeda terrorist training camps and military installations of the Taliban regime in Afghanistan," he could add that our effort was joined not only by staunch and traditional allies such as Great Britain, Canada, Australia, Germany, and France but also forty other countries, including many in Africa and the Middle East, that had granted us landing or air transit rights. He could say credibly as Operation Enduring Freedom commenced, "We are supported by the collective will of the world."

Between that first post-9/11 listening session in Beloit and the beginning of our formal military response in Afghanistan to the 9/11 attacks, I was able to hold only four of these town meetings, given the huge range of issues that we were addressing in Washington. People understood and expected that we would be responding, probably with significant force, but they seemed willing to await details and the timing as the administration got its ducks in a row. I did hear the occasional "let's just bomb the hell out of them" remark in informal encounters back home. But the most outrageously reckless commentary was the proposal by the well-known former Iran hostage from central Wisconsin, Kevin Hermening, who has dabbled in conservative politics since not long after his release in 1981. On September 19, 2001, in a *Wisconsin State Journal* column titled "Hold Back Nothing in Avenging Terrorism," Hermening gave us the benefit of his ideas. He said we should immediately mount "a prompt and massive military response to include total physical destruction of the capitals of the following nations— Afghanistan, Iran, Iraq, Lebanon, Libya, Sudan, and Yemen (unless they agree unequivocally to support our efforts to kill Osama bin Laden)." This apparently was merely the opening gambit in Hermening's vision of this new "war on terror." He further reasoned:

> After the annihilation of each country's capitals, we make them the same kind of financial offers made to the leaders of Japan and Germany after World War II: Cooperate with us on the establishment of democratic governments, and we will assist you in every way possible; don't cooperate, and your people will perpetually suffer. For more than 30 years, we have heard how dependent our nation is on foreign oil. Perhaps now is the time to guarantee the United States the free flow of crude oil by outright occupation of enough land in the Middle East to assure our nation that we can continue our way of life.

Perhaps Hermening was taking his cue from the stuff of conservative talk radio at the time but I heard nothing of the kind even from conservatives who attended my listening sessions for the remainder of 2001. At a meeting in Horicon, Wisconsin, on October 1, only one of the fifteen speakers even referred to the events of 9/11 and even then it was only an inquiry about how I felt about the attacks. The discussion instead ranged from the milk marketing order system, to immigration concerns, to why in the world I didn't support a constitutional amendment to ban flag burning. Less than three weeks after what will certainly always be one of the most dramatic moments in American history, it sure didn't feel like a nation besieged; at least not in Dodge County, Wisconsin. There seemed to be even less attention directed to the attacks and to our imminent involvement in a major war from the thirty people who gathered and the seventeen who spoke in Sauk City in Sauk County that same day. Only one person obliquely referred to the situation by reminding people that crop dusting is safe, countering one post-9/11 fear that these small planes might be used to spread chemical toxins.

Given these muted reactions, I was intrigued to see how people would respond to the commencement of the Afghanistan War, which more than ten years later has now become our nation's longest. I found out just six days later as I held town meetings on Sunday, October 7, on the beautiful Door Peninsula. This is the promontory that gives our state its famous shape, like a hand (an image I exploited to get elected to the US Senate in 1992, as in "Russ Feingold knows Wisconsin like the back of his hand"). The Door County listening session was scheduled to begin at noon in the city council chambers in Sturgeon Bay. The mayor at the time, Colleen Crocker-MacMillan, reminded me at a private meeting beforehand that Sturgeon Bay was one of the few dry docks in the world that can handle one-thousand-foot ships and that more than two hundred thousand people passed through the town each summer. They desperately wanted federal money to help them build a new bridge, because the current one was outdated. I listened and offered to provide what help I could. I then shifted the topic to tell her that I had just been informed that the president was going to announce in a few minutes the commencement of direct hostilities against the Taliban regime in Afghanistan. She understood the gravity of the situation and allowed me to make a slight adjustment to my usual approach to town meetings—I asked that a television be set up and turned on so we could all watch President Bush's announcement. I also asked that the television be brought into the council chambers afterward so we could continue to monitor the ongoing coverage of the breaking news. The only other time I recall doing this in the course of 1,296 town meetings was to witness the sad moment in Green Bay Packer history known as "fourth and twenty-six," when the Packers blew a playoff game against the Philadelphia Eagles on January 11, 2004, to the groans of the crowd at the listening session in Black River Falls, Wisconsin.

There were no groans or cheers in Door County, however, as I spoke after the president's televised talk on October 7, 2001:

> I didn't anticipate being here at one of the most historical moments in any of our lives but it's good to be with you. And it's good to be able to hear from you in this context. Let me first say that I'm grateful for our country and for our commander-in-chief. He did a good job when he spoke to Congress and he did a good job there of indicating our resolve. We don't know the details yet. My staff called me and said it's an attack on the Taliban and I was told that it included bombing but I can't confirm that yet. This is simply what I was told. I literally heard about this as I walked in the door. . . . This is a listening session and they asked to leave this on [that is, a television] and I will take no offense if you find it more interesting to look at that than to listen to me because naturally this is of enormous significance.

I sat down and read the name on the first slip in my pile of possible speakers, curious to know how Wisconsinites would react to the news. After his name was called, Peter Glashauser spoke with conviction. "I've talked to you before about trying to get a stoplight by the exit down on 42/57 by the Marathon station. I had numerous meetings with the state people, DOT. They qualified to get a stop-and-go light plus they did the median strip going up and the people living on the south side of the street can't even cross the highway anymore. So that's my concern." Well, so much for my dramatic announcement and the attempt to convey the historic nature of the moment. In a true demonstration of the maxim that "all politics is local," I listened to him claim that one of my staff members had refused to call him back and offered that we write another letter to the state government to give the problem a fresh look. It wasn't until the eighth of twenty-one speakers that anyone even acknowledged the events of 9/11 or any of the issues pertaining to it, including the invasion that was commencing as we gathered that day.

I confess I was a bit surprised at the lack of reaction to the news. On reflection, however, it makes more sense. Instead of ignoring the big story, Mr. Glashauser had in some sense been on the right track. Indeed, when the mayor told me about their bridge issue, she seemed a bit chagrined to be confronted with the invasion announcement. I told her not to be; I wanted people to continue to pursue their pre-9/11 priorities, of course, and soon urged the entire audience not to be apologetic about it. "I know the phrase 'another victory for the terrorists' is overused, but surely if we don't solve our problems and run our lives and deal with the issues we need to deal with as Americans while we deal with this then we will be weakened." This is exactly what people in my state and most of the rest of the country were already doing. I still try to imagine what most people did, in the immediate aftermath of 9/11, to process this bizarre series of violent events that suddenly dominated our newspapers, televisions, radios, and computers. Intense fear was not evident, though at times people seemed anxious or confused by the new phenomenon, hoping it was a one-time occurrence. At other times it seemed more like denial and resistance to the aggravations that these lunatics had inflicted upon us. More likely was the possibility that people hesitated to draw major conclusions about what this all meant and were still trying to absorb it. My belief ten years later, however, is that both Peter Glashauser and Mayor Crocker-MacMillan were doing what Americans are particularly good at; that is, we face crises by doing our job whatever that may be. By focusing on a wide range of issues and not merely the 9/11 catastrophe, the people of Door County, Wisconsin, and America in general told us that they expected those in government likewise to walk and chew gum at the same time. It seemed America was not going back to sleep then; it was more like a quiet, almost smoldering determination.

So we worked our way through comments on reparations for African Americans, the future of Social Security, drilling for oil in the Arctic National Wildlife Refuge, and the need for legislation concerning toxic mold syndrome, until one constituent directly but politely confronted me with what

I had assumed would be the main question of the day. Ann Hippensteel of Sturgeon Bay rose and said, "I don't have a lot to say. I consider myself a pacifist. . . . Is it difficult to vote your heart and your mind in a time like this when it might look to be unpatriotic?" She cited with approval Representative Barbara Lee's lone vote in all of Congress to oppose the authorization for military force that was the legal foundation for the imminent attack on Afghanistan, and was intimating that was how I should have voted as well. I continue to believe that supporting the invasion was the right thing to do, but Ms. Hippensteel had a good sense of how I would feel many times in the coming months and years as the initial cautions and care fell away in the ascendancy of the neoconservatives in the Bush administration. My answer to her question was "You bet it is."

There was an intentionally long break between the Door County listening session that day and the one down the peninsula in Kewaunee County in Algoma, Wisconsin. The longer break was scheduled, naturally, to watch a Packer game at a main-street bar, since it was foolhardy and not very much fun to try to do a town meeting during one. In between the game and the town meetings I had a chance to do some cellphone interviews along the shore of Lake Michigan in Algoma. The water was roiling and beautiful but the sky was dark and blustery as I walked along the shore endorsing the commencement of the major public side of our war on Al Qaeda—and hoping for the best. I then joined Mayor Wayne Schmidt and a good crowd of some thirty-three people at the Algoma City Hall. The mayor presented me with some mints, a pin, and a coffee mug in honor of the community's sesquicentennial that year. There was a brief exchange. "I don't know if you drink any coffee," he asked. I said, "I certainly do," and the mayor answered, "We figured every senator does, right?" I responded, "You bet. Especially lately." With the briefest of laughs, he gave that comment the slightest acknowledgment and moved on, saying, "Lately, right. So at this time I would like to introduce Senator Russ Feingold and I basically turn it over to you and thanks again." In the course of the following hour or so only two of fifteen speakers made any reference to the range of issues that emerged on or after 9/11, including the new war that had commenced that very day.

In the remaining months of 2001, my constituents' attitude toward our new international situation remained fairly stable considering all the alert levels, the new security requirements at airports, and the talk about poisoning of water supplies. More and more Wisconsinites who had joined the National Guard were finding out that their role in the 2000s was to be something shockingly well beyond the traditional nickname of "weekend warriors." We had been attacked by a new kind of enemy, one whose limits we could not know at that point; nearly everyone thought that this new war on terror was exactly the reason we kept a standing military, the reserves, and the National Guard.

Some began to warn about the aftermath of the Afghanistan invasion. One Wisconsinite, Wayne Hyduke, cautioned us in Green Bay, the day after the invasion announcement, that "looking back at history, Afghanistan, for example, when we supported the Afghans against the Russians, we just left them with no help and it got even worse." This was even before there was a general awareness that one of the main forces we had helped in Afghanistan was Osama bin Laden and his allies. A few days later, in Walworth County, bordering Illinois, a World War II veteran, Everett Refior, spoke of how "we are all greatly saddened by what happened in New York and Washington on the eleventh, but we have to be careful that we aren't just playing into bin Laden's hands by going to war and dropping bombs against them because that's exactly what he wants, a holy war." Others began to raise the broader question of our general relationship to the Islamic and Arab worlds. The day before the invasion announcement, a central Wisconsin couple joined together at the Waupaca County listening session to inquire, "Are we going to address the reasons why some Arab states are so hostile to the US? What might have made us vulnerable to attack was the belief that we were immune to it." At that same meeting in Weyauwega, Wisconsin, Helene Pohl more pointedly stated that "we should be reaching out to men of peace in Afghanistan instead of men of war [the Northern Alliance] and respect all binding UN resolutions including 242" (relating to Israeli and Palestinian territorial disputes). These comments about the international crisis we were now facing were thoughtful and forward-looking but rare. What was notable, though, was not only their relative scarcity but their tone. The discussion was measured, not polemical, and usually in a spirit of understanding; nothing like the kinds of conversations that had torn domestic opinion apart during the Vietnam War.

We always tried to finish these town meetings before Thanksgiving and—even more important—before deer-hunting season, a vital Wisconsin tradition that goes for ten days in mid to late November. In 2001 we were close but couldn't get the last one in, number seventy-two, until two days after Christmas, a very unpopular time for my loyal staff. The timing certainly did not deter the people of the city of Appleton and of Outagamie County as a whole. The home county of both Harry Houdini and the late Wisconsin Senator Joe McCarthy is always lively politically with both liberal (the home of Lawrence University) and conservative (the home of the John Birch Society) and everything in between represented at these forums. Sixty-seven people abandoned or perhaps escaped their relatives to come to this listening session. Three months into a new war and just four months after the 9/11 attacks, only a few of the forty-four speakers mentioned anything relating to 9/11, and these were mostly comments about civil liberties and the USA Patriot Act. When the rest of the world was mentioned, it was about a sister-cities program a local group had established a while back with a Siberian community, about the problems with withdrawing from the ABM Treaty, opposition to most-favored-nation trade status for China, and the need to "take a closer look at Israel-Palestine relations." Only one person verbalized a position on the Afghan invasion or Al Qaeda, saying she was against "the bombing in Afghanistan and is concerned about what the future will bring." Jim Flading simply said "my son is currently fighting in Afghanistan" and wanted to thank me for doing my part "to protect the Constitution."

As this very historic year came to a close, the people of my state were indeed mostly focused on what had concerned them prior to 9/11, from affordable housing to Social Security. The people in Appleton and just about everywhere else refrained from assigning blame for 9/11 on a partisan basis. No one seemed particularly fearful of being attacked or of the future. There were even the first few hints of post-9/11 humor. My regional coordinator, Bob Schweder, was trying out some new material after having exhausted his well-worn jokes about my and everyone else's golf game. I usually countered by good-naturedly questioning Bob's work ethic, since he worked on his own for us in that area. So I started with "Bob, what are you going to be working on in the next few days?" An avid fisherman, he replied, "I'll be out in the middle of my lake looking for terrorists." It felt good to be able to laugh with Bob as 2001 ended. And, by the way, no one, and I mean no one, said one thing about Iraq or Saddam Hussein.

2.

A Growing Climate of Fear in the Capital

We're going to recommend the vaccine for everybody.

On January 30, 2002, I opened the double doors of my high-ceilinged private office in the Hart Senate Office Building to see the bow tie and owly glasses of the columnist who had asked to interview me. I walked out into the open area between my office and the reception area and extended my hand, saying, "Hi, I'm Russ Feingold," having read hundreds of his columns but never having met him. Looking as aloof as humanly possible, an unsmiling George Will didn't say hello. He just said dryly, "Well, it's the devil himself." And he had been the one to request the meeting! So I replied, "Okay, well, why don't you meet the devil's chief of staff," and introduced him to Mary Irvine. After this cordial exchange, I invited him to sit down in my office. With Mary as my witness to this odd encounter, we spoke for about forty-five minutes.

Will had spilled a fair amount of ink over the years attacking me either for my all-out war on the First Amendment (which most people knew as the McCain-Feingold bill) or for my support for women's reproductive rights, which he preferred to think of as baby killing. Apparently he wanted to size me up in person because of some rumor about my alleged presidential aspirations, a candidacy with which he surely would have great fun. I tried to connect with him at the personal level by mentioning his Cubs (I was raised a White Sox fan) and our common privilege of having attended at different times the stunningly beautiful Magdalen College at Oxford University in England. His responses to these attempts were grunts and the conversation was not particularly memorable. The nasty columns continued unabated for many years.

What was more memorable, however, was the way the meeting ended. I escorted George back into the common area, informing him at the same time that this was one of the very first meetings we had held in our office for more than four months. The October 2001 anthrax attack had driven everyone from two-thirds of the office space allocated to all one hundred senators and their thousands of staff members and support services. I looked at George as I told him, "The building just reopened. You're one of the lab rats to come in here after the anthrax. This office was totally contaminated. We're right next to Daschle's personal office and his mailroom." I then gestured to the two huge quilts that hung on each side of the doors to my own office. We loved these quilts. On the occasion of Wisconsin's sesquicentennial in 1998, I put out a request that the children in an elementary school in each of Wisconsin's seventy-two counties design a patch to highlight something special about their county. After I had personally received these creations at seventy-two very heartwarming presentations, the ladies at the senior center in Middleton, my hometown, held a quilting bee in the old tradition and lovingly assembled these patches into the two quilts. They were part of the traveling exhibition that toured the state in commemoration of the founding of Wisconsin in 1848. Some squares depicted eagles or badgers, others bragged of the hardest granite in the world, and of course some had cows. But no one had seen the quilts for almost four months, as no one could enter the contaminated Hart Building.

The quilts had fared badly; all the images the children had made had faded and some had almost entirely disappeared. This was because the anthrax microbe had inspired such fear that the slow remediation of the Hart Building had included pumping the entire structure with chlorine dioxide in the fervent hope that these tiny particles that had already killed two postal employees would be killed themselves. As I took a moment to explain all this to George Will, the usually pompous and methodical pundit turned noticeably pale and quickly repositioned himself for what could only be described as a "skeedadle." He was gone for good and we all had a weary laugh as we reacquainted ourselves with our desks and workstations.

Shortly after we invaded Afghanistan and just as the USA Patriot Act was being jammed through the Senate, this completely different type of terrorist attack was taking place in apparently random locations: From a newspaper building in Boca Raton, to the NBC News studios in New York, to the home of a ninety-four-year-old Connecticut woman. Letters or packages containing a deadly white powder—anthrax spores—were mailed to or left at these and other places. On the day after the vote on final passage of the Patriot Act, I flew back to Wisconsin to speak to the national Associated Press Managing Editors Conference in Milwaukee. They wanted me to discuss the Patriot Act and were especially curious to know why I was the only senator to oppose it. As I settled into my room at the Pfister Hotel on the afternoon of October 12, and just before I went over for the speech, I remember the intense television coverage of this sudden wave of anthrax attacks. There was a developing, frightening realization of how deadly this type of anthrax was, even in tiny quantities. Earlier that same day, a big company in Madison, Wisconsin, American Family Insurance, had been evacuated as people panicked at the sight of a "suspicious green powder." And in another part of Madison, a scare was reported at a state office building, two blocks from the capitol, when a "suspicious gray powder" was found at the bottom of a mailing tube. As I prepared coffee in my hotel room I realized the same kind of panic could be caused by a little bit of ordinary white nondairy creamer— the kind provided in hotel rooms to go with coffee in the absence of the fresh Wisconsin dairy product—if separated from its packaging. In less than one month, "suspicious substances" had joined "suspicious packages" left in buildings, speculation about "dirty bombs," and theorizing about contaminated food supplies as concerns of the fear-filled new post-9/11 world.

The conference that Friday afternoon was one of the first events of its kind since 9/11 and the editors were attentive. I explained my concerns about the failure to tailor the Patriot Act to the nature of the threat we faced. I detailed, for example, the provisions allowing the government to delve into the library, medical, and other records of individuals about whom there was no real suspicion of terrorist or even inappropriate activity. As I left the museum where the speech had been given, one editor pulled me aside, thanked me for speaking, and said pointedly, "I'm glad you're there; I'm just glad they're not fifty-one of you." That remark has stuck with me for more than ten years as an illustration of just how fundamentally many people's view of their security had been altered by the 9/11 attacks. And now a little bit of white powder in the wrong place could throw people into an understandable panic at the drop of a hat.

The next morning I was scheduled to attend a small-dollar fundraiser for my campaign at a supporter's home in Waukesha, a conservative city in one of the most conservative counties in the country. My host, a teacher and a good friend who was actually elected mayor of Waukesha a few years later, believed that the event should go ahead, even though we had shied away from normal political events since 9/11. Given that my lone vote against the Patriot Act was only two days before, I was concerned that my constituents had had little time to consider the complexities of the bill and why I found it dangerous. So I was more than surprised to find a huge crowd waiting for me at my host Larry Nelson's home. The place was packed and the response to my vote was tumultuously positive. This was certainly no crowd of hard-core conservatives but it was not an extremely liberal group of Democrats, either. For some reason, after a month of terror and mourning, these citizens were looking for some affirmation that American values and in particular our constitutional values were still honored. My vote against the act had struck a chord in a way that I could not have predicted. For years and years after that, whether I was being introduced to speak at a service club gathering in Rice Lake, Wisconsin, a political rally in Los Angeles, or a law school in Manhattan, when the master of ceremonies got to the part about my solitary vote against the bill, the crowd would invariably erupt in applause or sometimes even give me a standing ovation in the middle of the introduction. This reaction to my vote surprised me time and again, but unfortunately it also meant that my subsequent presentation was rarely able to generate anywhere near the enthusiasm that that one word *no* had done.

After this weekend, on Monday morning, I resumed my listening sessions. Before traveling back to Washington for votes that afternoon, I held a well-attended and fairly cordial town meeting in what was another of the most conservative counties in the state, Walworth County. This year it was held in East Troy, Wisconsin, the hometown of Congressman Mark Neumann, the Republican I had just barely defeated in my reelection battle in 1998. I particularly remember that a group of older veterans attended and participated without confronting me on what was by then a well-publicized vote. I was in a fairly comfortable mood when I jumped into the car to head to O'Hare. But then I received a call from Mary Irvine.

Everyone has their own way of getting information, and my longtime method, especially since cellphones became so prevalent, was to pick up nonurgent messages on an answering machine. With the amount of information coming at me on a daily basis in my position as a US senator, I didn't want to get a steady stream of phone calls. When I got a call directly on my cellphone from Mary Irvine, it was always something timely or urgent. She told me that a letter with white powder in it had been opened in Senator Daschle's mailroom, which was next to our office. I said, "What is going on? Is it anthrax like the Florida incident? Are people in our office okay?" She described the situation as it was known so far and said, "Everyone's okay, but we are not allowed to leave. The people who work in our sixth-floor office have all been taken up to the ninth floor of Hart and will have their noses swabbed with a Q-tip to see if they've inhaled anything." She told me that everyone was composed and she was working to get more information. "I think we are in for a long haul on this one," Mary said. "This could go on for a while." Calls were coming in to my staffers from their worried family members watching the breaking news coverage on cable stations. Mary remembers telling her sister, who called after hearing that Senator Daschle's office was in the Hart Building, "Yeah, it's us, too. Not just Daschle's staff."

By the time I arrived in Washington that Monday afternoon, it was clear that, after so many false alarms and harmless "suspicious packages" in the wake of 9/11, this was the real thing and frighteningly so. Knowing that some victims had already died from what we were told were weaponized anthrax packages, the confirmation that this packet in Daschle's office also contained anthrax set off one of the most intense emergency operations the nation's capital had ever seen. It was already understood that anthrax could be effectively treated with the powerful antibiotic ciprofloxacin (Cipro), but only if administered soon after exposure. It was useless after just a day or two. By the time I reached the Senate chamber in the Capitol, where I was to preside for an hour, I learned that only two members of my staff had not been in the Hart Building when the letter was opened. Everyone else who worked for me, including some interns who had just started that week, was at risk. When the thousands of people who were in the Hart/Dirksen complex were medicated and then tested for exposure, three of my staff members initially tested positive, the only ones apart from some of Senator Daschle's staff who did so. Thanks to the quick administration of the Cipro pills, they were all right, but this was clearly a very close call.

In fact, at the nearby Brentwood Post Office, two postal workers who had merely handled this letter before it was opened died from exposure to anthrax spores. I shudder to think how extensive this disaster might have been. Had the young woman in Senator Daschle's office who opened the letter been distracted, or unaware of the growing concern about anthrax, or had she discounted the possibility that this was the "real thing," thousands may have been poisoned and died before it was clear that everybody in both the Hart and Dirksen Senate office buildings had to be treated—the two buildings shared one HVAC system. Had Daschle's aide not been on the alert, one of the greatest mass murders in American history would have occurred within a few days, perhaps with even greater loss of life than on 9/11 itself. For this to occur so soon after 9/11 in a major federal government building not only was obviously unnerving but also created almost an expectation that there would be a series of different terrorist attacks directed at Capitol Hill. Al Qaeda, however, made no effort to take credit for the anthrax attack, and so the mystery of who did it and why began. In many ways it continues till this day.

What most surprised (and impressed) me about this incident, however, was how Senate staffers simply followed instructions about how to take care of themselves and just kept working, despite these terrifying and directly threatening events. Their work was often interrupted by meetings with health-care officials who were desperately trying to determine the effects of the attack. Our office had to be consolidated into a tiny room in the US Capitol that had served as my "hideaway" office until then. Other Senate offices had to move several blocks away. Somehow work went on as we had to deal with the hundreds of new issues with which the Congress was confronted. And while the term has sometimes been overused in the post-9/11 era, the response of these public employees—who had never volunteered to serve in a war zone—was actually *heroic*. In particular, there was the determined leadership of my own chief of staff, Mary Irvine. Her sensitive response to the individual concerns of our people, while she was relentlessly demanding answers from health officials and others who were handling the incident, was remarkable. And I use the word *remarkable* specifically because for years to come the people in my office who lived through this experience credited her for holding everyone together in one of the toughest moments of any of their lives. Murph (as my staff and I referred to her at work) had sometimes been feared because of her tough manner, but now everyone was grateful that that quality was blended with a caring nature. Everyone survived and the hard work continued without interruption.

Whenever I think about this bizarre incident, my first thought is one of gratitude that the perpetrator failed to kill any of my staff members. Then I think of the true bravery that all those federal employees showed each and every day as they calmly returned to the geographical bull's-eye of Al Qaeda's murderous fantasies. We may never know who really committed this terrible crime. As the years passed, however, the apparent lack of connection to Al Qaeda made this attack seem more of an aberration. In fact, in 2006, on the fifth anniversary of the anthrax attack, Tom Daschle wrote a column for the *Washington Post* titled "The Unsolved Case of Anthrax," in which he complained about the lack of progress in finding the killers who obviously had hoped to kill so many more. (The FBI's main suspect, a scientist who had worked at Fort Detrick, a US biodefense lab, committed suicide in 2008.)

One of my staffers at the time, Tom Walls, whose last week on the job and going-away party had coincided exactly with the anthrax attack, posted a blog item a few days after Daschle's piece was published, and cleverly titled it "I Keep Forgetting That I Was a Victim of Attempted Murder." He pointed out that he had to take Cipro, that he never got sick, and that it was hard for him to remember how jarring it was at the time. Quoting Winston Churchill that "there is nothing so exhilarating as to be shot at without result," Walls said, "Churchill might have felt differently about an attempt on his life with microscopic spores—it's too abstract, too slow." And Walls bemoaned the fact that "nobody in authority seems especially concerned about it."

I felt sorry for my staff and even a little guilty, since I managed not to be in Washington when this occurred. When the incident began to unfold, I called my friend John Sylvester back in Madison and said, "I've got my staff having to take Cipro. These people dedicate their lives to these jobs and they're having to take Cipro because someone's trying to make a greater statement. I'm back here. I'm protected. This isn't fair." My staff and thousands of others had to go through a simultaneously frightening and tedious process—from nose swabs, to blood tests, to heavy-duty medication—as the alarmed medical community on Capitol Hill scrambled to make sure no one got sick and tried to gather as much information as possible to respond to this and potential future attacks. Things got even scarier, though, when Mary Irvine got the call from Greg Martin, a naval doctor who was the chief of infectious disease at Bethesda National Naval Medical Center. "We're going to recommend the vaccine for everybody" (meaning all of the Feingold staff who had been in the building). Murph had a high regard for Martin, because he "was so all over everything and he was clued into everybody's situation and giving what I thought was reasonable advice," but when she heard him say that they were recommending the vaccine for everybody, for the first time this tough-as-nails administrator became truly upset. I asked her to take a break and to come with me outside the Capitol instead of talking in the building where she and all my staff were stuck in the temporary post-anthrax office. I tried to reassure her and thank her but also remind her that she didn't want to freak out in front of an already very edgy group. We sat on a bench across from the Capitol steps and she said,

"I'm really tired of this and I'm worried about people asking me for medical advice. All I can tell them is what I'm going to do. And that's not an easy answer for me."

What is particularly important about this anthrax incident is its central role in promoting an atmosphere of fear on Capitol Hill and in the greater Washington area. Government employees, including members of Congress as well as the many others working or living in the Capitol Hill neighborhood, had already been through the 9/11 attack on the Pentagon. Now there was a major biological attack in our midst just over a month later. In between these two events there had been several panic-button evacuations of the Capitol and the office buildings. My environmental aide, Mary Frances Repko, remembers one of the first of many "suspicious package" alerts and how one such alert just two days after 9/11 led to a very hurried exit from the Hart Building:

> On September 13th, there was the package scare and the fire alarm got pulled in the building and everyone was evacuating, the look on people's faces was sheer terror. I mean people were absolutely terrified. For myself, I was going down the stairs and people were rushing so much that I got knocked down a flight between four and three . . . and Bruce Lesley . . . to tell you how much people's adrenaline was flowing, he reached down and grabbed me by the lapel of my jacket and picked me up and stood me on my feet. And the guy is, I mean if he's 150 pounds I would be shocked. . . .

And then there was a growing belief among some of those affected that the anthrax attack and its aftermath had been mishandled at various points along the way.

And for so many who had been driven from their office buildings, these five weeks were only the prelude to spending months cloistered in cramped and inadequate office space while they advised senators on some of the toughest calls they would ever have to make. The combination of constant security fears with the weightiness of the responsibilities made this what had to be one of the most tense and frightening times on Capitol Hill since the Civil War.

The feeling of danger that permeated Washington in late 2001 and into 2002 was exacerbated by the unexpected consequences of terrorism or the fear that terrorism can generate. The evil genius that created an atmosphere of uncertainty, tentativeness, and knee-jerk reactions revealed itself in the nation's capital in a way that fighting our previous wars had not. To be sure, the horrifying losses of World War I cast a pall over so many American communities. World War II entailed the almost unspeakable fear that if the Nazis prevailed in Europe they could then overtake us at home as well. The Cold War, which was unfolding as I grew up, included the seemingly endless week of the Cuban Missile Crisis, when American families discussed with their children the possibility that the Soviet Union could launch a nuclear attack on our nation. As little kids we learned to do drills in the lower levels of our elementary schools where we had to sit down with our heads bowed against the wall in case of a nuclear attack. Yet somehow none of this had achieved an environment of such impending and immediate danger as the terrorist phenomenon did to Washington, DC, and its inhabitants at this time. Senators, congressmen, their staffs, and their families experienced a sense of heightened alert and security virtually all the time. The beautiful area around the Capitol began to resemble an armed camp with police and military roadblocks at every turn. As ground was broken for the new Capitol Visitor Center, which was to provide an entirely new system of Capitol security as well as new facilities for tourists, it created a gigantic hole between the Capitol and the Supreme Court and the Library of Congress, one sadly reminiscent of the great chasm in New York City where the twin towers of the World Trade Center had stood just months before.

Of course, every American experienced some aspects of this new environment, especially at airports, but by and large there was little comparison between the constant tension and anxiety in Washington and the atmosphere in the rest of the country, with perhaps the exception of New York

City itself. Somehow it seemed as if the action had shifted to the political and military capital of the country. This mood was heightened by occasional seat-of-the-pants responses to the threats. A few days after the anthrax attack on October 15, the Hart and Dirksen buildings were closed for what would turn out to be nearly four months; nevertheless, somebody decided to let people back into the buildings the day after the attack, for a while anyway. Evacuation plans seemed to change on an almost daily basis. Offices were assigned an outdoor meeting place to ensure that all could be accounted for in the event of another emergency, but because it kept shifting it was hard to remember where to go to be accounted for. And, as hard as it is to imagine ten years later, at this point people didn't have BlackBerrys or the multifunctional smartphones we now rely on, so it was no easy task for people in the various offices to find each other in these situations.

The fear was even more intense for some of my staff members, three of whom were among the twenty-eight people who initially tested positive for anthrax, out of the thousands of Senate workers. Steve Driscoll, a young staffer from Platteville, Wisconsin, was with the entire staff when they were told to see the doctor individually because they would all need to take Cipro. Cipro was commonly prescribed for other infections for no more than fourteen days, but the anthrax regimen was to be for a long 120 days. Driscoll was told, without any explanation, that he would have to take it for even longer. Mary Irvine reasonably assumed that Steve had been told in his private consultation with the doctor that he had tested positive, and she sought to reassure him, saying, "Just so you know, I know." But as Steve tells it, "I didn't figure it out until I went home and I was watching CNN and Judy Woodruff was announcing *x* number of people in Tom Daschle's office and two people in Senator Feingold's office have tested positive. I'm like, 'Oh my God. That's why I need to be on Cipro longer.'"

The cramped, makeshift offices in the US Capitol made life even stranger for the staff and senators who had to work in them. As Rea Holmes, my scheduler and driver, explained it, "We were out of our office, we were in tiny offices in the Capitol, which frankly we didn't want to be in because a) it's too small and b), 'when is the next plane going to crash in?'" One Capitol Police officer did not improve Rea's view of the situation when he said to her matter-of-factly, "Actually, the best place for the plane to hit is the dome." This was not the kind of conversation this young woman from Minnesota expected to be having when she went to work in DC as soon as she had graduated.

Once they got past the machine guns and the sniffing dogs, my staff met in their new quarters in the bowels of the Capitol. They kept their complaints to a minimum, but they also had to work in very close quarters, which added to the tension and the feeling of being besieged. We had my old small hideaway office as well as the one next door that Senator Chuck Robb had left after his defeat in Virginia. Steve Driscoll recalls that each of these rooms was "about the size of four phone booths. People would eat in there. It stunk to high heaven." And some people simply weren't meant to be in such proximity for such an extended period. Steve Driscoll and my deputy press secretary, Trevor Miller, exemplified this. As Steve tells it, "There was one time I was there and for some reason it was just me and Trevor and Trevor was chewing tobacco and I was like, 'Really? This room is gross in so many ways and now you're chewing tobacco in it?' "

Obviously it was worse for others—for our armed forces in Afghanistan and our first responders, for example. But confining policymakers and their staff in this way for an extended period, while critical decisions were being made, had an impact. The combination of fear and skittishness, difficult working conditions, and not knowing what would come next created the ideal environment for claims to be believed or accepted that would have been challenged and questioned under different circumstances. We had, of course, been attacked and had a right to respond, but the Congress was experiencing an atmosphere that was ripe for opportunism and hyped claims. This could allow those willing to exploit the situation to lead us in a very mistaken direction.

As 2001 waned and 2002 began, I began to see that there was a growing discrepancy between how this new 9/11 era was experienced by people at home in Wisconsin and by those who worked and lived in Washington. Back home, nothing much changed: you still drove out of your driveway and went to the grocery store without passing through any roadblocks.

There was no constant flicker of red and blue police lights. You might see a dead deer strapped to the top of a vehicle in November, but there were no machine guns in sight. What did change, obviously, was that there were more military vehicles on the highway and more men and women in uniform at the airports, many of them heading to Afghanistan (but this was nothing, compared to the way it seemed after the Iraq invasion in 2003). Most Americans appeared to support this military intervention then, in the belief that it would make short work of bin Laden and Al Qaeda, and then life could return to normal. In Wisconsin there was no feeling of constantly being on edge, or being tightly confined, or of imminent danger, although of course every American knew that Al Qaeda could attack suddenly, and anywhere.

My staff back in Wisconsin had a pretty good sense of this difference not only because their interactions with the DC staff were more difficult and tense but because they were affected by the anthrax, too. People were told to send their letters to our Wisconsin offices, if possible, while the letters going to Washington, DC, were now routed through some undisclosed location in Ohio, to be cooked to destroy any possible anthrax-type bacteria. So we would receive lightly charred letters that looked as though they had spent a couple of minutes on a Weber grill. This process did not let the state staff off the hook completely, however, as they shared the task of opening the mail that came to Wisconsin. It came with very precise instructions, including the requirement of wearing gloves and face masks. As my executive assistant Nancy Mitchell described it:

> We had to shut the doors. We would take the mail into the conference room, open it in there with shut doors so if anything would fly out, the person opening the mail would be the only one that would be affected supposedly. That happened for quite some time after and we wouldn't let interns open mail anymore, which was typically an intern task. This was like a couple of years later, we got this huge hooded machine and when you would open a piece of mail you would open it

underneath the hood of this thing. It looked like the front of
a car. It was giant but it had a suction system in it so if there
was anything in there it would suck it up into the hood of the
thing.

Without a doubt, my staff in the state were just as willing to perform their
role in these tough times as were the Washington folks. But the prospect
of opening the mail this way did make some of the staff a little nervous.
Jay Robaidek, the then assistant to my state director, and the son of a dairy
farmer from northeastern Wisconsin, was usually the ultimate calming influence in my organization. In this case, however, he got a bit exasperated,
saying, "Just give me the goddam mail and I'm not wearing gloves and a
face mask."

Most of us realized that the possibility of terrorism visiting Wisconsin
itself was not entirely out of the question, especially after the anthrax attack
in DC. One of my friends in Washington, a lawyer from Green Bay, told me
a story that was for her both very funny and very embarrassing. Her mother
was alone at home not long after the idea of being anthraxed had entered
our collective consciousness. When she spotted a white powdery substance
on her kitchen counter, she became concerned and phoned her husband at
a local university, as well as several of her children. Ultimately they advised
mom to call the authorities just to be on the safe side. Apparently it was a
spectacle that this quiet Wisconsin neighborhood had never seen before—a
huge truck arrived, out of which emerged several people in full hazmat rega-
lia. They gingerly searched the house, only to determine that the substance
had something to do with candy and nothing to do with Osama bin Laden.
This was a hilarious story in Green Bay, as Wisconsinites are particularly
good at poking fun at themselves. For people in Washington at the time,
however, seeing a bunch of people in hazmat gear going into a building was
not only not funny but almost normal.

At the listening sessions following the anthrax attack, there was some
discussion and evident concern about this new phenomenon. When I
greeted Gerald Bauer, the mayor of Durand, Wisconsin, prior to the town

meeting in Pepin County just days later, he jokingly but a little nervously asked me if I was "going to give him anthrax." He did not mention it in his introductory remarks, which included a sensible plea for bipartisanship at this time in our history. Marie King, an old friend from the area who actually remembered me from my high school debating days, listened to what I had to say about the anthrax attacks and commented, "I'm glad to hear that things are not as bad as they seem. In fact, a young man that was here [and] grew up farming said that actually in some respects farmers deal with that [anthrax] every day." In December in Chippewa Falls, Jan Morrow, one of the most vocal advocates for family farmers in Wisconsin, identified food security and the possibility of food contamination as an important national security issue. References to this or other possible threats to people's lives were, however, very few and far between as 2001 ended. I, for one, couldn't wait to escape Washington's suffocatingly fearful environment to get home for the holidays. As I now piece all this together I realize that the measured sense of common purpose between Washington and Wisconsin about going to war with Al Qaeda was real, but that at a gut level people back home did not feel particularly threatened about their own and their families' personal security. Those in Washington, however, did. This made a big psychological difference as the events of 2002 transpired.

As the gap widened between perceptions of fear or danger in Washington and in much of the rest of the country, I believe it had a significant influence on why representatives reacted to terrorism concerns in a way that was fundamentally different from most of their constituents. That's not to say that people back home didn't think they needed their fair share of homeland security antiterror funds. I personally fought for Wisconsin's National Guard to get a high-risk unit, which so many states already had. This had to do partly with terrorism; other potential problems such as natural disasters were also a consideration, especially at a time when so many of our ten thousand or so Guard members were being deployed overseas. Smaller states fought for antiterror funds and criticism came from what were understood to be more targeted states. While 60 percent of the funds of the Homeland Security Grant Program was distributed on the basis of a state's population, it was revealed that the other 40 percent was distributed evenly, but mind-lessly, across all recipients in a state, regardless of the population. So in 2004 Wyoming ended up getting $45.22 per citizen, four times more than New Yorkers or Californians received per capita. Joe Moore, Wyoming's director of homeland security, told the *New York Daily News,* "Every square inch of Wyoming is as vulnerable as every inch of New York. If you say there are no terrorists in Wyoming, that's just where they'll strike." Now, who am I to question Wyoming's judgment on this, but I did once say on the Senate floor that Texas may have the most oil and Alaska may have the most area, but Wisconsin has the most common sense. We fought for our fair share of the homeland security funds and won them, but there was some chuckling and some eye-rolling among the small-town mayors and village presidents who were receiving new state-of-the-art bomb-squad units. They knew the cost of providing all of this for all possible scenarios would be astronomical and they didn't really feel it would ever be used.

For those in Washington, DC, and New York, though, there was no eye-rolling. In fact there was a feeling of relief as the months went by after 9/11 and it seemed that the federal government was getting its act together and learning how to use proper antiterror equipment and procedures. This even extended to the ever-changing and often irritating procedures for airline security. Later, in August 2004, there were howls when it was reported that Senator Ted Kennedy showed up on the antiterror no-fly list when he tried to get on the shuttle to Boston for the billionth time. But those of us who experienced this type of security on a weekly basis and were involved in re-viewing the work of the agencies charged with these responsibilities could see firsthand the difficulty of balancing serious security concerns with common sense. Back home, though, it too often seemed like overkill, and not very smart overkill at that. About six months after 9/11, one Alia Kate, a sixteen-year-old high school student in Milwaukee, wanted to go to Washington, DC, to demonstrate against US aid to Colombia. Her ticket was for a 6:55

p.m. flight on what was then our own Midwest Express airlines, a source of state pride because of the superior accommodation on the planes (including freshly baked chocolate chip cookies). She got to the airport two hours ahead of time but was not allowed on the flight. In fact, twenty of the thirty-seven members of Milwaukee's Peace Action group, including a priest and a nun, were detained and questioned by Milwaukee County sheriff's deputies for so long that they missed the flight. Sergeant Chuck Coughlin of the Milwaukee Sheriff's Department defended his staff's actions: "The names of people in that group came up in a watch list that is provided through the federal government and is provided for everyone who flies. The computer checks for exact matches, similar spellings and aliases. In this particular case, there were similar spellings." As Matt Rothschild of Madison's *Progressive Magazine* reported, there was indeed a similar spelling, a very similar spelling, as one potential passenger, a University of Wisconsin–Milwaukee undergraduate, was menacingly named Jacob Laden. Not bin Laden, but Laden, the German word for "shop" or "store." It was the name of a young man in what has long been the most German city in America.

To say that my constituents became detached from the issues of Al Qaeda and international terrorism heading into 2002 would be inaccurate. The lack of any subsequent major attacks on the United States and the minimum number of terror alerts in the heartland, however, led most Americans to refocus on their own lives and their principal domestic concerns. The Afghanistan invasion was sold as a success, because the Taliban government seemed to be out of action; people seemed much less exercised about (or even aware of) the fact that we had allowed Osama bin Laden to get away at Tora Bora and that the head of the Taliban, Mullah Omar, had escaped on a bicycle. At least Al Qaeda seemed on the run and most people would have been awfully surprised to learn that it would take almost ten years to kill bin Laden. To the extent people focused on international issues at all in Wisconsin, they were just as likely to think about Iran, the Arab-Israeli conflict, North Korea, competition with China, and even changing events in Russia, while assuming that the "war on terror" was being won. Accordingly, when the first talk of a possible invasion of Iraq began in Washington in

2002, I doubt many people really thought we would do it at all. They certainly did not assume that it was a logical and necessary step to address the terror that was inflicted on America on September 11, 2001.

Those working in Washington, however, were predisposed to feel differently. Because of the constant alarms and intense security arrangements, the ongoing reality of the possibility of terrorist attacks was obvious and inescapable. Legislators and staff continued to receive briefings in which we were informed of possible plots. This added some texture to the color alert system that was mocked not only by late-night comics, but also by people I'd see at the store back home: "Hey, Russ, what color is it today, purple?" Those who studied the modus operandi of Al Qaeda were chillingly reminded that this organization was patient, willing to spend many years planning spectacular attacks, such as those they had mounted in Africa, Yemen, and the United States. While the absence of new attacks might have calmed the mood back home, this did not give lawmakers and their staffs the same sense of security. Rather, all of this underlying tension seemed to have the effect of priming members of Congress to accept administration claims of a connection between Iraq and Al Qaeda. Given the horror of 9/11, the last thing anyone wanted was to give Saddam Hussein a pass and then find out after another major attack that he was in cahoots with Al Qaeda after all.

Getting Congress to the point where it could accept the Bush administration's Iraq claims was not easy. But the administration's game of flimflam to justify the invasion was conducted in an environment of fear that was tailor-made for such a scam. Members of Congress began to realize in the fall of 2002 that the administration would try to force votes on invading Iraq so they would be taken prior to the November election. Meanwhile, another bizarre series of events added to the fearful environment in a way that truly terrorized anyone living in the DC area, even if they were finally getting used to the alerts and security roadblocks.

Beginning on October 2 and ending on October 24, 2002, terror came not in the form of a white powder but rather in the form of a white van. The DC sniper turned out to be two people. Their rampage had begun earlier in the year, including robberies and murders in Louisiana and Alabama. Nothing about their activity to that point suggested a link to international terrorism. In the cauldron of tension that the Washington metropolitan area became in the months following 9/11, however, it had a very different impact.

The DC sniper attacks occurred over a three-week period in Washington, DC, Maryland, and Virginia. Ten people were shot to death and three others were critically injured. A number of the attacks occurred at gas stations, and I recall hearing several staff members discussing the strategies they were using to outfox the sniper and refill their gas tanks. One was to furtively look around while pumping gas to see if any white vans or trucks were driving by, since it had been (inaccurately) reported that the sniper was using such a vehicle (the real one turned out to be a blue 1990 Chevrolet Caprice sedan). One radio station advised people to walk in a zigzag manner after paying for their gas and returning to their car. The attacks became even scarier when a pattern—a single bullet fired from a distance—was established in early October. The inevitable thoughts began. Was this a new Al Qaeda tactic to send the nation's capital into an even more confusing series of machinations to deal with yet another type of terrorist threat? Would a dirty bomb follow?

Of course, it did not help the situation when it was revealed that one of the sniper's names was John Allen Muhammad. In a nation that was still grappling with its first real encounter with Islam and the lack of knowledge about it, this was like pouring gasoline on a roaring fire. James Martin, a fifty-five-year-old program analyst, was shot and killed in a parking lot at a Shoppers Food Warehouse grocery store on October 2. On October 3, four different people were shot at four different times at four different locations, but all in the same morning and all in the same way. This had the feel of carefully orchestrated terrorism even though at any other time it might have been more easily seen as a lunatic on a rampage, which, in the end, it turned out to be. It seemed to be the next attack that we had all been wondering about on September 11, 2001.

All the communities in the area were panicked. Parents would either not allow their kids to go to school at all, or might pick them up early. Some schools just kept students inside all day. Gas stations put up awnings or tarps over their fuel pumps to make it a little harder to put a bullet in the head of someone who was filling up their tank. When Muhammad and his accomplice, John Lee Malvo, a minor, were finally captured at a rest stop off Interstate 70 in Maryland on October 24, it quickly became apparent that these two individuals were not Islamic terrorists trained in some camp in South Asia. During his later imprisonment, Malvo apparently went on some erratic tirades and used the term *jihad*. And at Muhammad's trial, Malvo testified that the killing spree was to kidnap children for the purpose of extorting money from the government and to set up a camp "to train children how to terrorize cities." Their ultimate goal, he said, was to "shut things down" across the United States. These motives, if even remotely true, were not known or reported at the time of the suspects' capture, and once the rampage was over, no one seemed to believe that this was part of an Al Qaeda operation or even a legitimate copycat version. But Malvo's stated goal of "shutting things down" had nearly come to pass in the nation's capital, where things had already been incredibly tense for over a year. And where the United States Senate voted on October 11 to go to war in Iraq.

The Iraq Deception

Senator, I'm ready to die for my country, but it doesn't add up.

Richard Nixon was the bête noire in our home in Janesville, Wisconsin. On the other hand, Adlai Stevenson and Hubert Humphrey were heroes. So was Franklin Roosevelt, whose portrait hung in the hallway over this inscription: "No man in American history has ever been more warmly loved or so outspokenly hated. There is no greater measure of a mighty man than that." But in our household, the mention of Nixon was the moral equivalent of saying Haman's name during the Jewish holiday of Purim. My father constantly railed about Nixon throughout my childhood, but when the Watergate scandal was in full bloom his contempt for this man entered virtually every conversation. My mother didn't disagree with him but wanted a little variety and finally said "Leon, you remind me of Cato in the Roman Senate repeating over and over again, 'Carthage must be destroyed.'" Then she said it in Latin, "Carthago delenda est," modestly showing off her linguistic skills. "What was that again, Sylvia?" my dad said with a grin. He then proceeded to find a way to work that Latin phrase into conversation after conversation at family gatherings for months until August 8, 1974.

That day I was in my undergraduate apartment on Dayton Street in Madison, Wisconsin, when the phone rang. I picked it up, not expecting to hear my father's voice, since my parents were at an American Bar Association convention in Hawaii. "Russ, your mother went with everyone else for a flower tour, I'm having some Cinzano, and Carthage has been destroyed: Carthago delenda est!" my dad giggled. I shared his delight and walked out to join one of the most raucous celebrations I had ever seen in Madison, including students dancing on State Street and bonfires in the middle of a sunny summer afternoon. If you had told me that nineteen years later this very same man, Richard Nixon, would prove to have given me the key to deciding how I would vote on the war in Iraq, I would have been stunned.

In 1993, shortly after Bill Clinton was sworn in as president and I began my first term in the US Senate, Clinton invited the disgraced Nixon to meet with him at the White House. So the former president, who was also a former senator and president of the Senate (as vice president), paid a visit to the Capitol. A notice went around inviting any interested senators to a private meeting with Nixon in the magnificent offices of Senator Robert C. Byrd, the chairman of the Appropriations Committee. Given how strongly we had all felt about Nixon for decades, I hesitated, but then I couldn't resist the opportunity to listen to one of the most interesting, controversial, and historical figures of our time. As I entered the ornate Appropriations Committee meeting room, with its huge conference table and sweeping murals, I saw a frail-looking Nixon chatting with a few of my new colleagues. When I met him I tried a friendly approach, saying that I had to apologize for campaigning against him in 1960 at the Rock County 4-H Fair in Janesville, Wisconsin, at age seven. He didn't bite, didn't seem amused, and stiffly replied, "So are you enjoying things here?" We then took our seats to hear him speak.

Instead of sitting himself, this rather sad-looking, battered man remained standing. After a brief introduction, Nixon spoke in a strong voice for nearly an hour, without notes or a break. I could hardly believe I was actually hearing him in person after all these years. He said, "I want to talk with you about Yeltsin" (who had just become president of Russia after the collapse of the Soviet Union). The former president introduced the topic of Boris Yeltsin with this admonition: The most important thing in foreign policy is to understand the psychology of world leaders so you can understand what they are likely to do. "You have to know the man; you have to understand the man." He then launched into a brilliant description of Yeltsin's background and motivations that made me realize why, years later, when a group of us asked Senator Daniel Patrick Moynihan of New York who was the smartest president he had served under or with, he unhesitatingly said, "Oh, Nixon." And it was Nixon's advice to look into the psychology or mindset of the leader in question that helped me analyze—and begin to doubt—the claim that somehow Saddam Hussein was in cahoots with Osama bin Laden and Al Qaeda.

What may surprise some people who associate me with intense opposition to entry into the Iraq War and with the subsequent demand for the withdrawal from Iraq is that my decision to oppose the war was not a snap judgment. That decision was not a "slam dunk," in the infamous phrase attributed to George Tenet, the director of the CIA at the time. When the possibility of an invasion of Iraq was beginning to be rumored in early 2002, so soon after the Afghanistan invasion, I was surprised and skeptical, of course, but by no means certain to oppose it. If a connection to Al Qaeda could be adequately demonstrated, and if it could be shown that removing Saddam Hussein was necessary to destroy the terrorist network that had been based in Afghanistan, then I could at least imagine seeing it as a proper next step.

The notion that there could be a full-scale invasion of Iraq only a year and a half after 9/11 and the Afghanistan invasion was, however, the furthest thing from my mind when I took my seat in the House chamber to hear President Bush's first formal State of the Union address on January 29, 2002. I was still fairly comfortable with the tone of the administration in conducting the Afghanistan invasion and with its approach to the broader international community. The president's reference in his September speeches to the existence of more than forty-five countries (although sometimes there were references to more than sixty) where terrorists were present both reassured and intrigued me. I was wary of any effort gratuitously to include groups just because we or our hard-line buddies didn't like them—for example, the political opposition in Colombia or Egypt. At the same time I felt as strongly as the president did that we had to destroy Al Qaeda. The actual means to this end were debatable, but not the determination to go after those who would help or harbor the 9/11 murderers. I was startled when the president shifted in his speech from this broader categorization of terrorist "nests" to home in on just three countries—North Korea, Iran, and Iraq. Not only had he broadened the list by adding Iraq but he had expanded the rationale for inclusion from those states supporting terrorists to any country believed to be developing weapons of mass destruction (WMD). This second criterion was broad indeed. It could easily include some of our best allies, since many nations have weapons of mass destruction. In what would have seemed an odd combination of countries even before 9/11, he lumped these three nations into what he called the "axis of evil," declaring that "states like these, and their terrorist allies, constitute an axis of evil to threaten the peace of the world."

A collective "What?" could almost be heard in the chamber. Why these three countries? Why now? Why North Korea? It didn't seem the kind of regime that would be terribly interested in an Islamic caliphate stretching from Indonesia to Spain. Iran? Dominated by a very hostile regime that likes to get involved in anti-American activity all over the world, yes—but why would the leading Shia regime assist a Sunni fundamentalist movement, given the prevalence of intrafaith conflict throughout the Middle East? And Iraq? It was led by a megalomaniac who was exactly the kind of Arab leader that Al Qaeda despised and sought to topple to further its grand goals for the region. It reminded me a bit of that first draft of the Authorization for the Use of Military Force (AUMF), before the Democratic Senate Caucus more carefully focused the resolution on 9/11 and Al Qaeda. That, however, was just a naked and generic attempted power grab at a time of crisis. This had a different feel to it. It was clearly an attempt to enunciate the still-new administration's foreign and military policy doctrine well beyond the issue of Al Qaeda. And, incredibly, it felt like a commitment to take specific and perhaps imminent action to further it.

There was surprise and some alarm, not only in Washington and in many places across America—Bush's "axis of evil" speech went over like a lead balloon in Europe. The French Foreign Ministry complained that it was a simplistic description of the situation, with Alain Frachon, the editor in chief of the French newspaper *Le Monde,* saying, "That kind of language is very . . . sounds very odd for us, very bizarre, and it does not cross well the ocean." Of course, there was negative reaction from many foreign countries and especially those in Europe, which provoked Secretary of Defense Don Rumsfeld's dismissive description of those concerned countries as "old Europe." But it was France that became the symbol of our sudden isolation after the international unity that had characterized the lead-up to the Afghanistan invasion. It led to the House of Representatives tetchily renaming its French fries "freedom fries." That is why Senator John Kerry was called the "French candidate," in one of the many attempts to denigrate him during the 2004 presidential election. This too was the beginning of an international perception that President Bush was not only poorly qualified to be president but was somewhat unhinged. It was bad enough that it came out during the 2000 election that he had very rarely been overseas. Now he seemed aggressively eager to mount some kind of an American effort to root out "evil" from the world regardless of the dangers and the costs not only to America but to many other countries.

I was disturbed by the "axis of evil" speech, but not because the French didn't like it. I was aware of how vigorous France (and Britain for that matter) was in protecting its economic ties to its former colonies. This made up a big part of France's policy toward African countries, so much so that French candidates for president felt compelled to campaign in West African countries to appeal to domestic voters back in France itself. For both France and England, traditional relationships with various Middle Eastern countries and especially Iraq were extremely important and not lightly sacrificed to some half-baked Bush version of an American Manifest Destiny. I took seriously the international and especially the European reaction, but with a grain of salt. I was still principally focused on 9/11, Al Qaeda, and Osama bin Laden. The president's remarks disappointed me, because it seemed as though he had lost focus in favor of a grander but unrealistic vision.

Since assertions had been made that Mohamed Atta, generally regarded as the leader of the 9/11 hijackers, had met with Iraqi officials in the Czech Republic, I needed to know more. After all, none of us had expected Al Qaeda to do what it did on 9/11 and I certainly didn't want to dismiss the possibility that Saddam, given his hatred for the United States, was forming some kind of marriage of convenience with Al Qaeda. I doubted that, but my job was to give a fair hearing and not rule out aggressive action against him if it were proven that he was involved with the terrorist network. Therefore, ruling out an invasion of Iraq or the removal of Saddam Hussein was not a "slam dunk" for me.

Second only to the photographs and video clips of Osama bin Laden, the simple photograph of 9/11 hijacker Mohamed Atta became the ultimate "face of terror" for most Americans. Bin Laden had a smug, mocking demeanor that was easy to hate, but there was something about the sheer intensity and coldness of Atta's expression that made him stand out in the gallery of hijackers. This guy wasn't the one who planned for suicide missions while hiding in Afghanistan; who had no intention of ever doing anything like that himself; who promised his operatives a variety of delicious rewards in the afterlife. That would be bin Laden who seemed almost cowardly, hiding behind the robes of the true jihadists, as it were. Atta was the leader of the September attacks. I for one was as interested in knowing how many more there were like him as I was in the upper echelons of Al Qaeda, populated as they were by jihadists who probably had no plans to join suicide missions.

It was Mohamed Atta's visage that became the shaky foundation of the case for invading Iraq that the administration began to build in early 2002. There's something about seeing the expression on the face of an actual mass murderer—whether it be Jeffrey Dahmer or John Wayne Gacy or Mohamed Atta—that is particularly frightening. It is not easy to pinpoint when the claims about Atta and Iraqi officials began, but not long after the attacks a story came out saying that Atta had been in Prague in the Czech Republic in the first half of 2000 and had met with an Iraqi agent, Ahmed Khalil Ibrahim Samir al-Ani. At the same time as this claim was made, the ruthlessly cold face of Mohamed Atta appeared on newscast after newscast and in newspaper after newspaper. The idea planted in people's minds was that there could have been collusion between Al Qaeda and Iraq over 9/11. And this included those who would have to decide whether to authorize an invasion of Iraq. Perhaps more such attacks on America were being planned.

But even before the administration began to beat the drum for the Iraq War in a public way, this story about Atta was discredited. By May 1, 2002, almost a full six months before the Senate vote authorizing the Iraq War, US officials admitted there was nothing to the report. The Czechs had already acknowledged that they may have been mistaken about this and now a US official admitted that "neither we nor the Czechs nor anybody else has any information he [Atta] was coming or going [to Prague] at the time." In fact, Atta had been in the United States, in Virginia Beach and Florida, at the time he had allegedly met with Ani in Prague. The BBC reported at the time of the admission about the nonexistent meeting that this "was a blow to US attempts to build a case against Iraq as a terrorist threat." Yet, according to Bob Woodward's account of a key White House meeting on January 25, 2003, Vice President Dick Cheney's top aide, I. Lewis "Scooter" Libby, was still including this type of material in a long presentation about Iraq to the president and other top officials right up until the invasion in 2003. Libby's claims were, according to Woodward, enraging to Deputy Secretary of State Richard Armitage, who saw them as "overreaching and hyperbole . . . drawing only the worst conclusions from fragments and silky threads." And, yes, even after pressuring a far too pliant Democratic-led US Senate to approve an invasion just prior to a major election, Libby was still telling the president that Saddam Hussein's ties to Al Qaeda "were numerous and strong." His "silky threads" included the claim that Atta had met with Iraqi officials on at least four occasions. The president, in his key speech in September 2002 justifying the eventual Iraq invasion, had not revived this old chestnut, but relied instead on even flimsier and less impressive claims about other links between Iraq and Al Qaeda. The damage had been done, though. Senators and congressmen working in the shadows of fear and worry had it in the backs of their minds that Saddam and Osama bin Laden had been plotting together. Indeed, as 2002 wore on and the administration danced its famous dance of "shifting justifications" for invading Iraq—from weapons of mass destruction to violation of UN resolutions—the notion that somehow Iraq was related to 9/11 became the psychological foundation for members of Congress who were afraid to vote against the president. Atta was influencing America's response to 9/11 from beyond his fiery grave.

It is often forgotten how unlikely an invasion of Iraq actually seemed in the first few months of 2002. The mood on the Hill early that year was one of mystification, even incredulity that somehow the next step in the war against Al Qaeda was the pursuit of Saddam Hussein. Years later, in 2006, I was returning from a congressional delegation trip to Iraq led by John McCain. The small plane was packed with senators, congressmen, and governors handpicked by John to check on a mission that he avidly supported. On the way over to Kuwait, Iraq, and Jordan, the group that McCain had assembled didn't congregate and exchange views easily (politicians who don't know one another being a wary lot). But after a few days in Baghdad's American-controlled Green Zone and other Iraqi garden spots, things had loosened up. We were freely conversing about everything from how we felt about our colleagues to the next presidential election, where the obvious unspoken assumption was that John McCain would be the frontrunner on the Republican side trying to succeed a Republican president who had dragged us into the Iraq War. I listened as the various Republican officeholders, including Senator John Thune of South Dakota, Governor Tim Pawlenty of Minnesota, and Governor Jon Huntsman of Utah, asked John his impressions of the entry into the war and its current status. I was quiet until I finally had to say in a mild tone, "John, you know darn well if you were president at the time, there's no way you would have chosen that moment to invade Iraq." John is not exactly a wallflower when he disagrees with your characterization of his views. This time, though, he simply looked down for a moment, said nothing, and changed the topic.

Indeed, I can't recall any member of Congress in the latter part of 2001 or the first few months of 2002 calling for an invasion of Iraq. This venture was driven almost entirely by the administration, for reasons that I have long been trying to fathom. But, as we subsequently learned, it was not without serious dissent from within its own ranks. As late as May 1, 2002, less than a year before the actual invasion of Iraq, Jules Witcover, one of the most distinguished reporters in the country, began a lead story in the *Baltimore Sun* this way:

> The White House wasted no time the other day shooting down a front-page story in the *New York Times* saying the Bush administration is focusing on "a major air and ground invasion" of Iraq, probably "early next year," using 70,000 to 250,000 American troops to drive Saddam Hussein from power. That the cautious Gray Lady played the story on page one caused considerable consternation among congressional figures who fear President Bush may undertake, without further congressional authority, the task he has often indicated he will carry out—removing the Iraqi threat of using weapons of mass destruction.

Just as the Mohamed Atta connection ruse was dissolving into thin air, the administration was apparently both denying and planning an invasion at the same time. As Witcover also reported, I was concerned enough that I used my position as chairman of the Judiciary Committee's Subcommittee on the Constitution to hold a hearing to establish at least some legal benchmarks. The testimony showed that the president could not simply invade Iraq without regard to Congress's war powers both under Article I of the Constitution and the War Powers Act, enacted in the 1970s, nor could he claim that he was free to do this under the AUMF of September 2001, which related specifically to Al Qaeda and its allies.

At this point I could not believe that Bush would actually follow through with his hidden agenda, but my uncertainty about this was growing. I wanted the hearing to establish ground rules, so that if the administration went too far off track from the Al Qaeda issue we could create a scenario where Congress could do the job the Founders of the country intended it to do—that is, use its war powers or "stop war powers" to curtail executive misadventures. This is a central principle of our system of government and the genius of separation of powers. It had worked effectively in the frenzied days just after 9/11, when the Senate put the brakes on the open-ended AUMF the administration had originally proposed.

I was the only senator to attend the hearing. This was unusual because the Republicans typically fielded a committee member who could respond on record to my opinion on the topic of the day, whether it be the administration of the federal death penalty or the growing concerns about racial profiling. On this occasion, everyone just stayed away from the hearing, including the ranking member of the subcommittee at the time, Senator Strom Thurmond. At this point Thurmond was, to put it gently, not functioning well, only occasionally reading statements at hearings in his distinct South Carolina accent. But he was still an old warhorse for the right, even in absentia, and he submitted for the record one dissent from my claims about congressional prerogatives in this area—a statement by Deputy Attorney General John Yoo. It insisted that the president was not bound by the War Powers Act, because of his powers as commander in chief under Article II of the Constitution. In time, Yoo's would become the name most often associated with the most extreme extraconstitutional doctrines about presidential powers in our nation's history, from war to torture to warrantless wiretapping.

Perhaps naïvely, I hoped that this Iraq issue would be handled rationally and in the same spirit of unity that had characterized the move to war in Afghanistan. I had to concede that it was possible that "the consultative process and debate may demonstrate that it may be necessary to take military action to limit Iraqi weapons of mass destruction." It also seemed important to remind ourselves, post-9/11, that whatever the outcome of the inquiry, "it is also clear that the United States must act from a strong unified position. The Constitution and the American people demand as much." Fearing, however, that the Bush administration might use the discredited Atta-Hussein connection as the justification for invasion under the AUMF, I laid down what became my primary marker: that "absent a clear finding that Iraq participated in, aided or otherwise provided support for" the attackers, "the President is constitutionally required to seek additional authority to embark on a new major military undertaking in Iraq."

Throughout the spring of 2002, the administration seemed reluctant to say that it would go forward with plans to invade Iraq. Given the feeling in Washington and around the country that we already had our hands full in dealing with an Afghanistan that was unquestionably connected to Al Qaeda, I believed that the administration might heed our warnings about proper consultation and so avoid a reckless course of action. When it came to actual discussions with Congress, Ari Fleischer, the president's press secretary, was evasive, saying only that the Pentagon had "multiple contingency plans" for dealing with Iraq, but that President Bush "had no plan on his desk" to implement military action. I'm confident that, as the summer of 2002 began, virtually no members of Congress imagined that we would be debating and voting on a resolution to invade Iraq even before the upcoming November elections and that we would actually invade Iraq within just five months of those elections.

As rumors of a possible Iraq invasion sometime in the future gradually increased in late spring and early summer of 2002, the chairman of the Senate Foreign Relations Committee, Joe Biden, began to warn us that "these guys are serious." Joe, of course, was legendary for the length of his presentations in caucus but he had such a command of previous interventions as well as the current situation in Iraq that it was worth paying close attention to him. Biden finally announced in midsummer that he would be holding an extensive battery of hearings in late July and early August on the wisdom and possible implications of an invasion. This was a bold and important move that signaled, even in this tense post-9/11 environment, that the Senate would not just passively accept whatever intervention the administration proposed. Joe, of course, was more hawkish than I most of the time and I was worried that the wrong set of witnesses could prejudice the hearings in favor of the administration's plans if Joe had decided that was a good idea or if the leadership of the caucus had predetermined that we had no choice but to go along for political reasons. Fortunately, this was not the way the hearings turned out, even though the witnesses generally suggested that they were in favor of military action against Saddam Hussein.

The usual practice in the Senate, especially after a senator has attained a fair amount of seniority, is not to attend entire hearings "gavel to gavel." This is in part because there are often several hearings of your different committees at the same time and the art is to run from one hearing room to another so you don't miss your turn to ask questions. Frankly, that also meant that you don't have to sit through the often tedious presentations (usually by senators and sometimes by witnesses) as they read the statements their staffs have prepared for them, ready-made for press releases regardless of what is really being discussed at the hearing (I was guilty of this, too). One of the early anecdotes from Senator Barack Obama's tenure in the Senate and on the Foreign Relations Committee was that, after he had been waiting for a couple of hours to ask his questions (he was way down on the seniority list), he sent a little note to his staff that simply said, "Just shoot me." Obama solved this problem by taking another job, but I was patiently working my way up the list and by 2002 could get my questions in fairly early.

My staff, well aware that sitting still is not my greatest strength, often deferred to my desire not to sit through overly long, repetitive hearings. When it came to the upcoming Biden hearings on Iraq, however, my top staffer for foreign policy came straight to the point. Michelle Gavin, one of the best people in Washington on US policy toward Africa and now our ambassador to Botswana, was then the principal person advising me on our post-9/11 foreign policy. She came into my office and said, without apology, "Russ, these five hearings are going to be back to back over two days and it will be very long but I need you to attend all of them in their entirety." Michelle is one of the most talented and dedicated people who ever worked for me but she was also sensitive to my workload in general and to my political situation. This request, as unusual and unprecedented as it was, really impressed upon me the gravity of the Iraq rumors. By asking me to do this, Michelle was telling me that she thought an invasion could well happen and that she knew it was not going to be a straightforward decision for me to oppose it.

The Biden hearings on Iraq were among the most substantive and helpful sessions I attended as a member of the Senate Foreign Relations Committee. Yet they were very different from the famous hearings on the Vietnam War chaired by J. William Fulbright of Arkansas; those hearings raised serious questions about an increasingly unpopular war that had been grinding away for years. This series of hearings was merely in anticipation of a possible executive decision to try to invade another Middle Eastern country within only a year or so of 9/11. Senator Biden began the proceedings on July 31, 2002, by welcoming everyone to "the beginning . . . of a national dialogue" on the wisdom and possible consequences of an invasion of Iraq. He did refer to the events of 9/11, but in so doing he quickly managed to broaden the issue of where and when to intervene well beyond Al Qaeda and its associates: "The attacks of 9/11 have forever transformed how Americans see the world. Through tragedy and pain, we have learned that we cannot be complacent about events abroad. We cannot be complacent about those who espouse hatred for us. We must confront clear danger with a new sense of urgency and resolve." These were not the words of President Bush or Vice President Cheney. They did not include such inflammatory phrases as "axis of evil" and they certainly were not necessarily a recommendation for imminent military intervention in Iraq. Rather, this was the same chairman who had played such an instrumental role in ensuring that the AUMF would not be open-ended but instead tailored to the Al Qaeda threat. Yet Biden continued without any pretense of linking Saddam Hussein and bin Laden: "Saddam Hussein's pursuit of weapons of mass destruction, in my view, is one of those clear dangers. Even if the right response to his pursuit is not so crystal clear, one thing is clear. These weapons must be dislodged from Saddam Hussein, or Saddam Hussein must be dislodged from power."

At that moment I realized for the first time that this invasion of Iraq really could happen—and happen soon—even though it did not seem to fit in with our post-9/11 priorities. The bright lights in the hearing room, the multiple flashing cameras, and the tense looks on the faces of many members of the committee confirmed for me that this plan had real momentum and would be very difficult to stop.

As disappointed as I ultimately was with the decision to go to war, and with Joe Biden's support for it, his skill in conducting the hearings as well as the quality of the witnesses he called made a big difference. These hearings gave the nation notice that this would not be the cakewalk Don Rumsfeld had suggested with his famous notion that grateful Iraqis would greet our troops with garlands of flowers. The questions raised by both the senators and the witnesses focused less on the question of whether Saddam was a threat and should be removed and more on the issue of whether it made much sense to invade at that time. It was questionable whether an invasion could be top priority in the period right after 9/11, and then we would eventually have to deal with the aftermath of war in Iraq. Biden at least began to put this issue back into a post-9/11 context when he said, "We want to explore Saddam's track record in acquiring, making, and using weapons of mass destruction and the likelihood . . . that he would share them with terrorists." And I was particularly pleased to hear Biden finally speak about what was most important to America at a time when the tendency was to consider this issue in isolation (what I later came to call our "Iraq-centric" view of foreign policy). Biden continued in his inimitable style: "My father has an expression, God love him. He says, 'If everything's equally important to you, Joe, nothing is important.' How do we prioritize? What is the relative value? What are the costs?"

What followed were two days of testimony from witnesses who seemed to support the invasion, but raised so many tough questions and such a "parade of horribles" (many of which came true) that it was hard to believe that anyone who had paid any attention could conclude that such extreme action was a good idea at this time. For me, as well as for those like Senator Lincoln Chafee, who was to be the only Republican to vote against the war, this was a somewhat reassuring development. This was also true for two Republican senators who later voted for the war but tried to use the hearings to vent legitimate concerns in the face of the Bush administration's hell-bent effort to get this war off the ground. Richard Lugar of Indiana and Chuck Hagel of Nebraska did their jobs. Lugar, referencing his long view of our policies in the region and in particular our previous war with Iraq, cautioned, "Ten years ago, the United States had done the military

and diplomatic spade work in the region. We had developed a war plan."
And Hagel sharply and presciently warned, "I can think of no historical
case where the United States succeeded in an enterprise of such gravity and
complexity as regime change in Iraq without the support of a regional and
international coalition."

The witnesses' testimony helped me define the issues I would need to
consider in deciding whether to support this war. In response to one of
my questions about our chances of getting other countries to support an
invasion of Iraq, President Clinton's former national security adviser Sandy
Berger made the important distinction that, in his words, "the fight against
terrorists and the threat of Saddam Hussein, while they are related, are not
identical." And he made the point that a war against Saddam could weaken
the support we need "in terms of the fight—the clearest and present terrorist threat—that is, the Al Qaeda, the Islamic Jihadist militants." He warned
that the costs in terms of other countries' cooperation could be great, making a "phase where military action [against Iraq] is only one dimension, and
may be a dimension of diminishing returns." When I asked the former Iraqi
nuclear engineer Khidir Hamza whether there was reason to believe that
"we now face an imminent attack on the United States" by Iraq, he ducked
the question but honestly reflected the Bush administration's alarming new
preemption doctrine: "Surely what we are talking about here really is a pre-
emptive strike for a possible future danger which is much larger than what
we have right now." The former chief of UN weapons inspections for Iraq,
Richard Butler, was more direct in response to the same question of whether
we faced any danger of an imminent attack from Saddam Hussein. He said,
"Look, Senator, my simple answer is no, we do not."

The hearings did not definitively resolve for me the question of how
I would vote on an Iraq War if it actually came to that. This was despite
the many concerns raised during the five Biden hearings—ranging from
humanitarian issues, civilian casualties, and what happens if the weapons of
mass destruction are dispersed all over Iraq, to what could we do to secure
the WMD as the invasion began—and despite my reluctance to support any
distraction from our main goal of destroying Al Qaeda. My usual instincts
about war did make me skeptical. This feeling was even more pronounced

now that I had supported the war on Al Qaeda in Afghanistan, a war in which we were now fully engaged. Yet I had decided that we should try to remove Saddam Hussein if either of the following were true: (1) his regime could be shown to have been in actual collusion with Al Qaeda in terrorist attacks on the United States or on Americans, or (2) that independent of any Al Qaeda connection, Saddam actually had dangerous weapons of mass destruction, was able to deliver them to attack us, and, most important, was inclined to do so.

This is where the advice from Richard Nixon back in 1993 helped. The critical thing was to "know the man, understand the man." Given what we knew about Saddam Hussein (and we knew quite a lot), the important question was whether it made any sense for him to coordinate with the likes of Osama bin Laden or to guarantee his own destruction by launching an independent WMD attack on the United States. These were sincere questions to which I wanted sincere answers from the administration. Instead what we got from August until the vote in October and then right up until the invasion of Iraq in March 2003 was a deliberate attempt to manufacture the notion of a Hussein–bin Laden connection and a reckless distortion of the likelihood of a direct WMD attack by Iraq. Actually, what helped persuade me to doubt Saddam's WMD capabilities and intentions was the obvious fabrication behind the efforts to pretend that Iraq had anything at all to do with 9/11. In the end, it was this dishonesty that turned me from a merely likely opponent of this war into the most vocal critic of the invasion and our continuing presence in Iraq long after Saddam was toppled. As false as the claims about WMD proved to be, it was the scam of the connection between Saddam and Al Qaeda that outraged me the most. Without that ploy, played out in an environment of fear, both literal and political, the invasion of Iraq would never have been authorized by the Senate.

Richard Nixon's advice to "understand the man" puts a high premium on the role that the characteristics of an individual leader, and in particular his psychology and goals, can play in the course of events. I certainly would not use this approach in isolation in trying to evaluate Vladimir Putin and Russia or Hugo Chavez and Venezuela. Given the oversize roles that the personalities of Saddam Hussein and Osama bin Laden played in their respective spheres, however, this kind of analysis came in handy in making a decision about what to do about George Bush's designs on Iraq. Obviously it was critical in trying to decide if Iraq and Al Qaeda had coordinated in the past or were likely to do so in the future. A bit more surprising, however, is that Nixon's advice was also extremely helpful in deciding the other big question: If Saddam Hussein had never had contact with Al Qaeda and even despised the organization, would he be likely to use weapons of mass destruction against us in the foreseeable future, if in fact he had them?

In the weeks after the Biden hearings, I focused on the WMD question. So did virtually all the other senators, since by now the notion of an Al Qaeda–Iraq connection had been largely undermined. The Biden hearings hardly touched on the terrorist connection issue, although the minority leader at the time, Senator Trent Lott of Mississippi, declared the issue settled. As I pointed out in my opening statement, Lott actually thought that "congressional debate [on an Iraq invasion] would not be necessary, citing, apparently, his belief that al Qaeda is operating in Iraq." Most senators were not so sure; even I conceded "that may well be true" but added, "I have not seen the evidence." However, there might be more evidence, as technical, convoluted, and shrouded as it was, for the claim that Saddam Hussein had up to three kinds of weapons of mass destruction: chemical, biological, and nuclear. And there was no question that he had already used biological and chemical weapons in genocidal attacks on Iraqi Kurdistan in 1988. Accordingly, as we returned from the August recess that had followed just after the Biden hearings, the Senate became consumed by this aspect of the justification for war.

As I looked further into the issue, I realized that the only serious basis for an invasion was a positive answer to three different questions; otherwise it made no sense to shift our focus and resources and to spill American blood in an Iraqi war. First, did Saddam possess these types of weapons of mass destruction, and in particular, did he really have nuclear weapons? Second, even if he had them could he deliver them effectively to attack

America or our allies? And third, and most important for me, à la Nixon, even if he had these capacities, was Saddam the sort of person who would take this action knowing with virtual certainty that it would seal his own personal fate? Although there were many speeches on the floor and intermittent news leaks and interviews touching on these crucial questions, the real action was behind closed doors. I was not yet a member of the Senate Select Committee on Intelligence, so I had rarely been in the secured room in the Hart Building reserved for its classified briefings. That changed years later, when I spent the better part of two or three afternoons a week in this cramped little chamber with no pictures on the wall and about twenty-five chairs beneath the raised dais that was reserved for Intelligence Committee members. At the briefings or executive sessions I attended after I joined the committee, there might be only a handful of staff from the intelligence, military, or law enforcement agencies in the chairs behind the witnesses. Occasionally the room would be packed with highly sophisticated operatives of our national security apparatus.

In the fall of 2002, on the two occasions when the Senate Foreign Relations Committee was invited there to be briefed on Iraq, the room was overflowing with unidentified staff who sat staring at this bunch of senators who were not part of the regular intelligence "club" they had grown used to dealing with. Since we had spent quite a bit of time listening to arguments about the moral justification for war in Iraq expounded by the likes of President Bush, Vice President Cheney, Secretary of Defense Don Rumsfeld, National Security Adviser Condoleezza Rice, and even, in his famous appearance at the United Nations, Secretary of State Colin Powell, I expected this secret hearing to be quick to affirm the administration's position on Saddam Hussein and WMD. I heard nothing of the kind. The experience had an enormous impact on my assessment of the WMD issue and of the administration's credibility, in regard both to its claims about Iraq and, frankly, to its entire post-9/11 military and related decision making. I began to realize that once the administration decided to do something, it would say or distort virtually anything to get its way.

On most occasions, the mood of hearings or briefings in the Intelligence Committee room was quiet, dispassionate, even dull, despite the serious topics covered. These are very professional government employees who work in an area where hiding unnecessary emotion and a "just the facts, please" demeanor were expected by members of the committee. As I listened to the case being made for the invasion I took into account that the intelligence community's job was not to sell this idea to the Senate. Nonetheless, as the briefings wore on, I perceived a bit of a dead affect and even a touch of embarrassment in the voices of the witnesses and on the faces of the staffers who would occasionally whisper something in the ear of a witness or pass them a note.

When the first issue of whether Saddam had WMD came up, there was some confidence that he had chemical weapons and modest confidence about his having biological weapons. But when the discussion turned to "nukes" the response was tepid at best. If true, this would be the real threat when it came to our country and Saddam, but no one could have come out of that room believing that Saddam had attack-ready nuclear weapons. Then, when it came to the question of effective delivery of any WMD, one senator asserted that he had heard that Saddam had unmanned aerial vehicles (UAVs) that could easily fly over the east coast of the United States. This surprised me and I waited to hear what the witnesses had to say. They looked at one another and shifted uncomfortably in their seats. The senator's claim was not confirmed and one witness turned the discussion to the generalities of Saddam's capacity to deliver WMD. Finally, I had the chance to ask the panel what I thought was the ultimate question. Even if Saddam had some or all of these weapons and the ability to deliver them, was he really the kind of guy who would be likely to mount such an attack on the United States at any time in the near future? The witnesses' heads went down and one answered by speaking about the nature of megalomaniacs like Saddam Hussein, whose ideology was based on ego rather than on some grander vision or even a perverted religious conviction, as in the case of Al Qaeda. When I asked if that meant Saddam was likely to mount such an attack, the equivalent of signing his own death warrant, the witness said with some firmness, "No, sir."

I came out of the second of these briefings shaking my head. When I got back to my office three floors above, I called in my top staff members. I said to them, "It sure sounded like a different story in there." Nonetheless, as October came, the administration mounted a full-scale campaign to get a congressional resolution of approval for the war. Perhaps the key moment was President Bush's sweeping defense of the idea in his speech in Cincinnati on October 7. He seemed slightly tentative at first, when he spoke only of Saddam "seeking nuclear weapons," not already possessing them. Shifting to more alarmist language, however, he argued that "Iraq is unique" because its regime was headed (as we all agreed) by a "homicidal dictator." But he added that this particular dictator was "addicted to weapons of mass destruction." To be fair, Bush used more moderate language for the claims relating to WMD, a moderation that was often absent in the calls for war led by the likes of Dick Cheney and Condoleezza Rice, laced as they were with references to rising mushroom clouds. Yet the tone and the overall message was the same: It was urgent and essential that we strike Saddam before he strikes us. After my careful review of this justification for war, I was not persuaded, and I was doubtful of the administration's candor on the intelligence concerning WMD. I became even more suspicious, however, when in mid-speech Bush proceeded recklessly to use whatever he could to draw Al Qaeda into the picture.

Bush attempted to bring together a potpourri of unrelated facts and Muslim-sounding names to make it sound as though Saddam had permitted Al Qaeda to organize in Iraq or, even worse, had encouraged it. Perhaps he hoped to evoke the image of Mohamed Atta, even though that connection had been discredited. He talked about Iraq providing safe haven for "terrorists" such as Abu Nidal—founder of Fatah, not part of Al Qaeda; or Abu Abbas, who had killed an American on the cruise ship *Achille Lauro* in 1985—but had nothing to do with Al Qaeda. He then constructed a dubious connection to Al Qaeda, saying "we know that Iraq and the Al Qaeda terrorist network share a common enemy—the United States of America" and "we know that Iraq and Al Qaeda have had high-level contacts that go back a decade." Not that I knew of. He then mentioned an Al Qaeda leader who had received medical treatment in Baghdad, hardly a justification for going to war. Not only was the president playing a game of shifting justifications, but he was shamelessly exploiting the still-nervous state of the

American public and in particular the personal and political fears of the 535 people who would vote on whether to go to war. This was a far cry from the man who gave that wonderful speech in September 2001, the man who I had come to believe could guide America on a straight and unified course when it came to the 9/11 crisis.

Two days after the president's Cincinnati speech, I was the first to go to the Senate floor to respond. In pointing out that I did not feel the president and the administration had adequately answered the questions critical to prove that we needed to invade Iraq at that time, I concluded:

> Both in terms of justifications for an invasion and in terms of the mission and the plan for the invasion, the administration's arguments do not add up. They do not add up to a coherent basis for a new major war in the middle of our current challenging fight against the terrorism of Al Qaeda and related organizations. Therefore, I cannot support the resolution for the use of force before the Senate.

The decision to vote "No" was my own but the phrase "do not add up" and its variants were not. I had heard it from my staff, particularly from Michelle Gavin, who had conferred with me several times a day on this question for months. I heard it walking through the Milwaukee airport when I ran into one of the prominent lawyers from my former law firm, Foley & Lardner. Nancy Sennett, a member of the management committee of Wisconsin's largest firm, pulled me aside and said quietly, "Russ, I'm not very political, but this thing doesn't add up." The most compelling moment for me, though, came months later, after the authorization had passed the Senate and the invasion was imminent. I had just finished a listening session in Dodge County at the pavilion of the Horicon Marsh, an enormous refuge for wild geese and other waterfowl. I had noticed a young man in an army uniform at the back of the room. Not surprisingly, he did not speak during the meeting, but as I was approaching my van in the parking lot afterward, he walked up to me, shook my hand, and said, "Senator, I'm ready to die for my country, but it doesn't add up."

This was the central sentiment of my speech on the floor and vote against the resolution for the use of force in Iraq. I believe this was what was bothering most Americans who were not caught up in the day-to-day tension and pressure of post-9/11 Washington and who may even have been part of the majority of Americans who, according to the polls, favored the invasion. It seemed almost unpatriotic to oppose our president's judgment so soon after the brutal attack on our nation. Yet many Americans found the case for war confusing and not terribly persuasive because of the inconsistency and dishonesty of the arguments being made for it. I tried to convey this in my floor speech:

> I am increasingly troubled by the seemingly shifting justifications for an invasion at this time. . . . I am not suggesting there has to be only one justification for such a dramatic action, but when the administration moves back and forth from one argument to another, it undercuts the credibility of the case and the belief in its urgency. I believe this practice of shifting justifications has much to do with the troubling phenomenon of many Americans questioning the administration's motives in insisting on action at this time. What am I talking about? I am talking about the spectacle of the President and his senior officials citing a reported connection to Al Qaeda one day, weapons of mass destruction the next day, Saddam Hussein's treatment of his own people on another day, and then on some days the issue of Kuwaiti prisoners of war.

What particularly drew my ire was the president's attempt to exploit the fear and emotion of 9/11 that seemed to hang over members of the Congress, in the expectation that memories of Mohamed Atta and the burning towers would override common sense. I thought that the president had "to do better than the shoddy piecing together of flimsy evidence that contradicts the very briefings we have received by various agencies. I am not hearing the same things at the briefings I am hearing from the President's top officials."

Despite my objections and those raised in speeches on the floor, as well as those murmured in private conversations at the back of the chamber or more vigorously advanced in the Democratic cloakroom, the Senate Democratic majority agreed to give in to the administration and let it have a vote early in October, just before the midterm elections. This was a terrible time for a vote on the most sober of issues, the decision whether to send American troops into battle in a foreign land. The Democratic caucuses that were hurriedly held, not in the Lyndon Johnson Room but in the even more crowded Room S-219 near the majority leader's office, were among the saddest spectacles I witnessed in eighteen years in the Senate.

Senator after Democratic senator, even those with very hawkish reputations, spoke of their reservations. No one seemed to think the invasion was a good idea at the time, yet people clearly understood and frequently referred to the brutal political reality that the slenderest Senate majority in history would soon be on the line. People who would later (and not much later) be candidates for president and compete for the anti–Iraq War mantle voiced substantive objections to the war then. But when it came time for the vote, Hillary Clinton, John Edwards, and John Kerry all rose from their seats and said "Aye" to George Bush's "war of choice." Sadly, not just a majority of the Democratic-controlled Senate voted for it, but a clear majority of the Democratic Caucus itself voted for the Iraq War. Only twenty-two of us opposed it.

One senator who did vote "No" does stick out in my mind, of course. Paul Wellstone of Minnesota was in a tough reelection race against Republican Norm Coleman. Even though he had voted for the Afghanistan invasion, Paul was under siege for allegedly being a classic, Vietnam-era antiwar professor type who didn't "get it" post-9/11. He gave several impassioned talks at those caucuses just prior to the vote, where he alternately poked holes in arguments for the war and then seemed almost to writhe about just how difficult this vote could be for him in the final stretch to reelection. He seemed to be saying to the rest of us, If I can vote against this, so can you. And vote against it he did. Just a few days after the final vote for war, we almost literally ran into each other (we both were smaller and moved more quickly than the stereotypical dignified senator) as he was leaving the chamber and I was entering. I had seen a new poll out of Minnesota showing that Paul had pulled out of a dead heat with Coleman and was now ahead by a comfortable nine points. I said, "Hey, I saw the poll." He kept a straight face and said, "I don't know," shaking his head and then, "Our numbers just shot up when I voted against it." I said, "Yeah, and you know you're going to win." He couldn't keep his game face anymore; he looked up at me, broke out in a huge grin, and said "Yeah." Those were the last words I ever exchanged with my colleague from Minnesota. We lost him just a few days later.

4

A Game of Risk

Iraq was yesterday's war, Afghanistan is today's war; if we don't
act preemptively, Yemen will be tomorrow's war.

Risk is one of those board games that nearly everyone in my generation
knew and played. Originally designed by the French film director and pacifist Albert Lamorisse, it was first published in 1957 by Miro as La Conquête
du Monde (The Conquest of the World). Two years later, Parker Brothers
published it as Risk. The board was a big colorful one representing a map
of the world with six continents, each "composed of several territories of the
same basic color." So, for example, South America, colored turquoise, was
made up of the territories of Venezuela, Peru, Brazil, and Argentina. We
found it exotic because it included place-names that none of us had ever
heard of, such as Irkutsk and Kamchatka (colored green), and we went after
the territories with unusual names with particular vigor. The primary object
of the game is "to occupy every territory on the board and, in so doing,
eliminate all other players," or, in other words, global domination.

In the years after the invasion of Iraq, I was struck by the similari-
ties between the Bush administration's post-9/11 strategy and that of the
game of Risk. This was not because of any world domination objective, but

because of its single-country-by-single-country approach to dealing with Al Qaeda and its affiliates. In Risk, when a player wants to take over a whole region of countries during the round, he or she does so by a series of battles determined by the roll of dice. After each successful battle, the attacker has to leave one army in the conquered country before continuing with the remaining attacking armies into the next country. The rule is "No territory may ever be left unoccupied at any time during the game." As America invaded Afghanistan, then sent troops to Iraq, and now seemed poised to do the same in Iran, I was mystified that top officials ignored obvious threats in places like Yemen and Somalia and even North Africa. Since groups actually associated with Al Qaeda were known to be operating in these regions, they required not an invasion, but some serious attention.

Perhaps the best example of the consequences of this linear way of thinking about how to counter Al Qaeda came years later. After almost eight years of strategic decisions about where best to deploy our resources in our war against the organization, the world got a shock on Christmas Day 2009. That day there was an attempt to blow up a Detroit-bound international flight by the so-called underpants bomber. Fortunately the attempt failed. But when the would-be suicide bomber was apprehended and investigated, his description didn't fit very well with the administration's narrative about America's terrorist enemies. The young man in question, Umar Farouk Abdulmutallab, was a Nigerian living in London who was apparently a devotee of the radical Muslim Anwar al-Awlaki. Awlaki was born in New Mexico to Yemeni parents and spent his teenage years in Yemen before returning to the United States to take degrees in civil engineering and education. After a year or so preaching in the United Kingdom, he had returned to Yemen in 2004, where he was propagandizing and plotting against the country in which he was born and educated. My friend and former colleague Senator Joe Lieberman expressed alarm: "Iraq was yesterday's war, Afghanistan is today's war; if we don't act preemptively, Yemen will be tomorrow's war."

The issue should have been where Al Qaeda was consistently operating. It wasn't Iraq in the first place and it wasn't Afghanistan anymore. In some respects it had been Yemen all along, at least all the way back to the attack

on the USS *Cole* in the harbor of Aden in 2000. For almost a decade I had
been warning that Yemen, Osama bin Laden's ancestral home, was fertile
ground for Al Qaeda's international network. Yet discussions in Washington
almost never considered the broad Al Qaeda landscape. They focused instead on wherever we had sent our infantry. They concentrated on the places
that we had already occupied, as if it were the game of Risk. Only this game
was played with real blood and treasure.

Moreover, this confused way of looking at the threats posed by Al Qaeda
was not just the result of some Cold War mentality, a lack of knowledge, or
even an honest misunderstanding. It developed in part as a post hoc justification for the bizarre decision to invade Iraq in 2003—as if that were the
correct next move in the fight against Al Qaeda and its affiliates. The falla-
cious foundations for the Iraq invasion have been discussed in the previous
chapter and documented in great detail elsewhere. What is less discussed is
the way the tortured logic for intervening in Iraq became a template for an
inefficient and illogical approach to containing and destroying the organization that attacked us on 9/11. Al Qaeda is an international syndicate with
franchises or copycat supporters located all the way from Indonesia to Mali
to Yemen. The Risk approach, however, seems designed to convince the
American public that the way to stamp out the organization is to invade
individual countries where Al Qaeda may or may not be present, or may
once have been present, or to which it may return.

The advantage of this approach is that it provides an easy, uncompli-
cated argument for military action. Effective and targeted operations against
Al Qaeda are harder to explain, since a more subtle and better-informed
approach would have to consider Al Qaeda's complex nature and a presence
in places that very few Americans can relate to or even find on a map, such
as Chad, Malaysia, or Djibouti. Having decided to invade Iraq, where there
were no WMDs, let alone Al Qaeda operatives, the Bush administration
employed a simple-minded argument that was easier to sell to the public,
because it could be justified as a straightforward war against "the bad guys."
Any full-scale war, whether against Afghanistan or Iraq or perhaps someday
against North Korea, leads to extensive public discussion and sometimes a
vote by Congress. This can lead to the equation of supporting the war with

supporting the troops, where any dissent becomes disloyalty. This promotes emotional but simplistic public debate and undermines any objective arguments about whether starting or continuing an invasion of another country is the best approach to solving a problem.

The irrationality of this country-by-country approach was highlighted on the occasion of President Bush's famous "mission accomplished" declaration. On May 1, 2003, about two months into the Iraq invasion, the president delivered a speech on the USS *Abraham Lincoln,* off the coast of California, declaring that the job was over and done in Iraq, thus intimating that this was a milestone in the "war on terror," as he would usually call it. A few weeks before this, I had noticed a very lightly reported development in Yemen. Ten Yemeni prisoners, who were being held because of their alleged involvement in the attack on the USS *Cole* in 2000, had all escaped from a military detention center in Aden just as our mission in Iraq was "accomplished." I went to the floor of the Senate to note the president's pledge on the aircraft carrier "that the terrorists who attacked America would not escape the patient justice of the United States." Not only had these Al Qaeda operatives who had killed seventeen American sailors not faced justice, but they had just plain escaped. What about our ability to focus on those responsible for direct attacks on America? Wondering why members of Congress and the media were so nonchalant about this development, I asked:

> How many people noticed when . . . ten men escaped from a prison in Yemen . . . ten men who apparently were being held on charges of involvement in the terrorist attack on the USS *Cole* that killed seventeen American sailors, including one from my home state of Wisconsin? . . . This escape occurred, apparently, just as our brave troops were entering Baghdad—at least in part in the name of stopping the threat of terrorism. But no one seems to be discussing at all this potentially dangerous lapse in Yemen.

What better demonstration that the Iraq invasion, which seems to have come almost out of the blue, was off-track or that it "didn't add up"?

I took to including in just about every speech or comment I made about Iraq and the 9/11 attacks a reiteration of Bush's own oft-repeated statement that Al Qaeda was operating in at least forty-five countries. I would hold up the list from the State Department's website and explain that the list had some obvious countries and some that were more surprising, "Now it's got Uzbekistan, Afghanistan, it's got Ireland, it's got the United States but it does not even have Iraq. . . ." As to the Yemeni escapees, I would say, "It'd be like an Osama bin Laden guy escaping . . . I mean think about the disconnect between what really happened to us and what we're doing in Iraq." Then, holding up another document, I would note the bait-and-switch approach the administration used when it became too uncomfortable to try to connect the Iraq invasion with Al Qaeda. The White House document was titled "Victory in Iraq" and I asked why he "doesn't put out a document called Victory over Terrorism or 9/11 Attackers or Al Qaeda. . . . How did a place that wasn't even on a list of forty-five countries become the central focus, as the President calls it, in the fight against terrorism? He says, 'Well Osama bin Laden says it's the central focus . . . so we better listen to him.'"

How did it get to this? This was the same president who had said over and over again that "we will fight the terrorists at a time and place of our choosing," but it sure sounded to me as though the president was saying that bin Laden had chosen Iraq for us now and we needed to join the battle he sought. I implored my audience and whoever would listen: "Al Qaeda likes it that we are stuck in Iraq. It plays into their hands. . . . We spend way too much of our time talking about Iraq. We can carve it up, should we do this, should we do that? Just think about what a mistake that is when we're dealing with a threat that exists in over eighty countries in the world."

While diverting the nation's military and intelligence resources from the continuing war in Afghanistan at a critical time, the Bush administration showed that it could play this game in reverse whenever it suited their purposes. When I visited Afghanistan in 2005 with John McCain, Hillary Clinton, and others, it was evident that that conflict had become the forgotten stepchild. The administration was consumed with justifying the enormous commitment it had made in trying to resolve the chaos in Iraq. Off the record, military as well as State Department officials in Afghanistan confided to me that they felt they had been abandoned. Despite the fact that the 9/11 attacks had been launched from that country, one could have sworn from the rhetoric that the attacks had originated instead in Baghdad. In one famous exchange before the House Armed Services Committee, Admiral Mike Mullen, chairman of the Joint Chiefs of Staff, admitted, "In Afghanistan, we do what we can. In Iraq, we do what we must." The administration showed some defensiveness on this point: Whenever anyone pointed out that no weapons of mass destruction had been found in Iraq and that it had not been part of the 9/11 attacks, they would play the "war on terror" game in reverse.

This was particularly jarring when the administration issued an executive order creating a special new award called the Global War on Terrorism Expeditionary Medal. Although the Afghanistan and Iraq wars had proceeded under different authorizations and had different names (Operation Enduring Freedom and Operation Iraqi Freedom, respectively), the administration insisted that bravery in both invasions be lumped together under one medal for fighting the "War on Terror." There was to be no separate "War against Saddam's WMD" medal. Due to the leadership of Senator Jeff Bingaman of New Mexico, however, an amendment forced the administration eventually to differentiate between these conflicts. The attempt to oversimplify the real nature of the fight against Al Qaeda was constantly reinforced by the conservative wordsmiths (especially at Fox News), who would sprinkle interview questions and commentary with emotive catchphrases, like "cut and run" or "the bad guys." This was just one instance of the intentional conflation of Iraq and Afghanistan when it suited the administration's purposes, while it in fact relegated the Afghanistan intervention as unimportant. If Afghanistan and Iraq were linked in the fight against terrorism, then anyone who questioned the Iraq intervention was also somehow questioning the pursuit of Osama bin Laden, which of course no one was doing. It then followed, of course, that if you did not support every military venture of the Bush administration you did not really support the troops and your patriotism was doubtful.

When it came to making an effort to understand the complex nature of Al Qaeda and its international affiliates, the administration and its allies didn't seem to be bothered. "Don't bore me with the facts" is a good way to sum up the prevailing attitude. The administration wanted everyone to believe that "victory in Iraq" was the key, and that the defeat of Al Qaeda would flow from that. Symbolism trumped candor. This could not be further from the approach taken by President Franklin Roosevelt after the last great attack on our nation. While Roosevelt provided reassuring "fireside chats" that carefully informed the American people about the war; this administration hunkered down in an almost entirely "Iraq-centric" mode— trying to force the square peg of Saddam's brutal regime into the round hole of Al Qaeda's international treachery.

For those who really wanted to find out more about where Al Qaeda came from, where it was present, and where it was going, there was much to be learned in places all over the globe. The prisoners who were brought to Guantánamo under suspicion of being involved with Al Qaeda represented a striking range of national and ethnic backgrounds. It was like a United Nations of suspicious characters from such disparate places as Yemen, Somalia, Tunisia, Malaysia, the Philippines, and Algeria. Algeria's Al Qaeda influence is a particularly interesting case that I had a chance to examine in detail when I traveled to Algeria on a foreign relations trip in January 2005. Reverting to the Risk game analogy, Algeria was not a place where we were interested in sending our troops. Yet as I traveled with John McCain in 2005 and 2006 to places where we were present on the Risk board, he would say from time to time, "The movie you have to watch to understand all of this is *The Battle of Algiers.*" His point had particularly to do with the nature of insurgency and counterinsurgency in Islamic countries, but the setting of the movie was of course Algeria. Algeria's fight for independence in the 1960s against its French rulers was one of the bloodiest in history; it was enormously traumatic for France and deadly for the Algerian people. When France withdrew from Vietnam, we chose to become deeply involved there, because of a fear that Russian and Chinese communism would spread into all of Southeast Asia—the so-called domino theory. On the other hand, we seemed happy to ignore the situation in Algeria.

A great deal had happened in Algeria between independence and my visit in 2005. In the course of several days in Algiers I learned that in the 1990s this nation had faced a form of Islamic extremism that rivaled or surpassed anything we or anyone else had experienced. When what was evidently a free election was held in 1990, an Islamic-based party, the Islamic Salvation Front, actually won the election against the party that had ruled Algeria since the successful revolution. The regime, however, did not accept the election results and canceled the next round of elections, which had been scheduled for 1992. That attracted the attention of violent activists. The Salafist Group for Preaching and Combat (GSPC) grew out of this situation. The GSPC were Algerians, but they had previously traveled beyond Algeria's borders to aid those resisting the Russians in Afghanistan. In other words, they went to Afghanistan to make common cause with Osama bin Laden and therefore with the United States as well; both were united in supporting the mujahideen in their battle to remove the Russians. Some three thousand strong, according to estimates, the Algerian fighters then returned home and enflamed the Islamic fundamentalist fervor there. They inflicted their brutal tactics not only on the government—with which the Islamists had a legitimate beef—but also on anyone else who resisted them. On the trip I heard horrifying accounts about their tactics, not only from officials of the regime but also from citizens who had joined us for dinner one night at the residence of the American ambassador in Algiers. Apparently the GSPC would arrive at a village in the vast southern region of Algeria to demand support and shelter. If the village refused, the operatives would slaughter every single person in town and then move on to the next place. It didn't take long for these Afghanistan-trained terrorists to find refuge from the regime's efforts to stamp them out, as villagers learned to choose the alternative to massacres.

By all accounts the regime's response was also extreme, not only to the GSPC but to any dissenters. This led to a period of violence and instability that rivaled the enormous difficulties experienced during the fight for

Algeria's independence. As the regime cracked down more and more vio-
lently in the 1990s, Algerian youth became alienated from the "fathers of
the revolution" and Algiers became one of the most dangerous cities in the
world. It should have been no surprise, then, that the remnants of the brutal
GSPC, which was moving from southern Algeria to Mali to Chad, would
reconstitute itself as Al Qaeda in the Islamic Maghreb and swear fealty to
Osama bin Laden. As far as I could tell, virtually no one in the Bush administration was paying any serious attention to these developments.

As the administration persisted in designing its foreign policy around Iraq
into the mid-2000s, I tried time and again to point out that we were failing
to awaken to the complex, global nature of the enemy, Al Qaeda. Speaking
on the Senate floor in support of the National Intelligence Reform Act of
2004, I warned against "geographic stove-piping" of intelligence and counterterrorism efforts "that hamper better coordination and good policy." I
pointed out that the problem was not just the willingness of the Bush administration to manipulate facts or half-truths to justify the Iraq invasion.
This stove-piping was a more basic problem. It meant that our foreign policy
experts were capable in their own geographic areas, but too often "policymakers who specialize in these places don't necessarily work together," even
when it was obvious that activities in nearby areas were having a big impact
on their assigned region. This became especially evident as the failure to take
Yemen seriously became more and more absurd.

In February 2006 another escape occurred from Yemen's suspiciously
porous prisons. This time Jamal al-Badawi, the suspected mastermind behind the bombing of the USS *Cole*, escaped from a Sana'a prison with thirteen members of Al Qaeda. Noting that this was his second escape (he was
one of the 2003 escapees), I wrote to Secretary of State Condoleezza Rice to
ask about the administration's reliance on the Yemeni regime "as a capable
partner in fighting Al Qaeda." Did we do anything ourselves to monitor
detainees who had actually attacked us or did we just defer to the inept
and perhaps duplicitous Yemeni officials? Moreover, after surrendering to

the Yemeni authorities in October 2007, al-Badawi was simply freed under the Yemeni government's revolving-door policy of releasing terrorists if they promised to forgo violence. I again tried to focus attention on Yemen, asking the Bush administration to explain what it would do to bring al-Badawi to justice and calling on all candidates running for president in 2008 to "commit to refocusing our national security where it belongs, on combating al-Badawi and others in Al Qaeda and associated terrorist groups." This was not, however, a plea to shift our focus away from Afghanistan or Pakistan and to invade Yemen. It was instead a plea to consider Yemen not just in relation to nearby regions, but in a complex international Al Qaeda context. A country-by-country Risk approach simply cannot adequately deal with the threat we face.

Actually, another game (my mother's favorite) is a useful contrast to the Risk model for combating threats like Al Qaeda. Sylvia Feingold was very good at Scrabble, but the best player I ever encountered was a man who sublet a room in our college apartment in Madison one summer during the time of Nixon's Watergate woes. He was Ru-Dong Wei, an advanced biochemistry graduate student from Taiwan. Probably in his mid-thirties or early forties, he had no interest whatsoever in our undergraduate summer antics nor in the Watergate excitement. We were horrified by his cooking of whole fishes—heads still on—with incredibly pungent spices that filled the apartment with exotic smells for days at a time. I had not yet learned to eat spicy food, but now love it and regret to this day that I didn't try the elaborate concoctions he prepared. We did find one area of common ground, however: We both liked to play Scrabble. The problem for me is that it was like trying to play basketball with LeBron James. Ru-Dong would rack up huge scores, regularly using up all of his letters at once for the bonus that the seven-letter play was awarded in this classic game. I was, and still am, very competitive and became exasperated. "How the hell did you do that?" I would ask. As he picked up seven more letters to destroy me again, he would say, "You must always think in two direction." I have used this expression often (maybe too often) in many contexts over the last thirty-five years, from campaign strategy to parenting. When it comes to the way we need to think about the nature of the post-9/11 terrorist threats, however, it can be an important principle to follow. Let me use the relationships between Yemen in the Middle East, and Somalia and Kenya to illustrate.

The mistake may be the Risk-style one of thinking within separate geographical confines. Or it may be, if one is playing Scrabble poorly, "thinking only in one direction." We could not afford to do either after 9/11. But, frequently, that's exactly what we did and what we too often continue to do, possibly out of habit. As students we are taught to look at foreign areas in terms of different continents or traditional groupings of countries, such as Africa or the Middle East or Southeast Asia or even Europe. This narrow way of understanding boundaries is reinforced in institutions like the US State Department and the Senate Foreign Relations Committee, which are organized on the basis of these regions. Experts tend to be trained to know one or two particular areas but do not work regularly with their counterparts, the experts for nearby regions. So there is the undersecretary for Africa in the State Department and the chairman of the Sub-Saharan Africa Subcommittee in the Senate, as I was on several occasions. What gradually dawned on me after 9/11 was how flawed and archaic many of these distinctions are when formulating modern foreign policy in general, and antiterrorist strategies in particular. The need to reach out to Muslim leaders and communities became painfully evident after 9/11. I began focusing on African nations that had significant Muslim populations, starting special coffee groups with groups of African ambassadors to the United States whose countries had Muslim populations. When I traveled to their countries, I asked to meet with groups of Muslim leaders and citizens to hear their views of our post-9/11 approaches to the Islamic world. All of this was useful and interesting, but unless properly connected to other Islamic peoples and countries beyond Africa, it had limited application.

This became clear to me one day when I was in my office staring at a map of the area from Africa to the Pacific. I noticed how close the Arabian Peninsula was to the Horn of Africa. I admit that I should have thought about this before, since even in first grade at religious school I knew that

Moses had led the Jewish people from Egypt (Africa) to Canaan (the Promised Land) just to the north of the Arabian Peninsula (the parting of the Red Sea having made the passage between continents possible for a people who had no time to build boats). I called in a staff member, one of several who had to answer my occasional quirky question to which I had to have an answer right away. "Just how far is it from let's say Yemen to the east coast of Africa, including Somalia?" I wanted to know. After years of trying to draw attention to possible Al Qaeda connections in both places, I confess I had never really thought about just how much significance there was to the proximity of these two seemingly separate hotbeds of Islamic extremism. Were they five hundred miles or two hundred miles apart?—on the map it looks like there's almost no distance across the Strait of Mandab. The answer came back soon. At one point the distance between Africa and the Middle East is only about twenty miles. In theory, a strong swimmer could cross it, were it not for the presence of powerful currents and some pretty nasty sharks.

In late 2008 I had the opportunity to visit the tiny country of Djibouti, right on the Somali border. I had gone there to meet with leaders of the Transitional Federal Government (TFG) of Somalia, who were temporarily based in a hotel there. This was not long before their gutsy decision to return to Mogadishu to take on the violent and repressive Islamic Courts and subsequently Al Shabaab, an Al Qaeda–affiliated group. I also had the opportunity to meet separately with Sheikh Sharif Sheikh Ahmed, who not long thereafter became president of the TFG even though this was not anticipated at the time. When, however, I was actually meeting with the Djiboutian officials, including the president, Ismail Omar Guelleh, I heard talk about the possibility of building a long bridge to connect Yemen and Djibouti. The plan was to promote economic development, but after years of worrying about Al Qaeda operatives traveling from one region to another, I could not help but suggest to my staff, quietly, but perhaps a little insensitively, "Hmm, a bridge for terrorists." That same night we were chauffeured through the streets of Djibouti City under heavy guard to a restaurant that had been cleared of all other customers so we could eat there in safety. It was a fish restaurant run by Yemenis where you could select the fresh Red Sea catch you wanted and have it prepared Yemeni style, it being explained that native Djiboutians didn't really like to eat this kind of fish. I chose barracuda and asked that it be cooked in *zhug,* a Yemeni red pepper sauce. As we ate, my aides and I began to speculate. None of our briefings from our own or Djiboutian officials had really said anything about this, but how likely was it that those who sought to harm us in both Somalia and Yemen, not to mention Djibouti itself, were not coordinating in some way, if they were so close to each other and were from societies and cultures that have been interconnected from time immemorial?

Djibouti is on the tip of the huge, snake-shaped nation of Somalia, one of the most ungoverned places in the world. Remember Somalia? After the "Black Hawk Down" disaster in the early 1990s, we had not only abandoned our military presence in Somalia but we had dropped out completely in almost the same way that we had abandoned interest in Afghanistan after the fall of the Soviet Union. As of September 11, 2001, we had had virtually no coherent policy toward Somalia for years. Amazingly enough, that continued for just as many years after 9/11, even though Somalia is just across the sea from Yemen, the scene of the attack of the USS *Cole* and an original home to the family of Osama bin Laden. For years the Somalis had been dominated by harsh extremist regimes exploiting their versions of Islamic fundamentalism to terrorize the population with mayhem, violence (especially against women), and even the prohibition of dancing and movies. Whether in the form of Al Ittihad or the Islamic Courts, these regimes were primed to be used by international, anti-American terrorists for plotting and for safe haven. In fact, several of the suspects in the Al Qaeda attacks on our embassies in 1998 in Nairobi and Dar es Salaam had been harbored by these regimes. As senator after senator made multiple trips to Iraq, where Al Qaeda had not been operating before 9/11, essentially no one from the Congress ever went looking for the likes of Al Qaeda in this region or investigated the interconnectedness of these hot spots. Especially because of the effort to justify the Iraq error, but also because of our outdated way of looking at these parts of the world, we seemed not to notice where the operatives who were conducting attacks for Al Qaeda around the world hailed from. Sure, there were some native Afghans and a couple of Iraqis and, of course, some Saudis. More often, though, when suspects were rounded up after terrorist attacks in places like Madrid after 9/11, they usually turned out to have come from places across the great swath of land from the west coast of Africa to the west coast of the Arabian Peninsula, from Morocco to Algeria to Tunisia to Libya to Somalia to Yemen.

It's insufficient, though, to concentrate on dominantly Islamic African countries adjacent to the Middle East while ignoring much of sub-Saharan Africa. Only rarely do we engage in a serious way with any of the nations of that region. When we do, it is because of Cold War concerns (as with Angola and the Democratic Republic of Congo) or, more honorably, to tackle the scourge of HIV/AIDS. In terms of our diplomatic resources and of a long-term vision for America's security and place in the world, however, sub-Saharan Africa has too often been treated as a backwater, at best. An illustration of this was my experience of getting to know someone I and many others regard as one of the best American diplomats of the last fifty years—Richard C. Holbrooke.

Just before Richard's untimely death in late 2010, he invited me to have breakfast with him at the Four Seasons in Georgetown, my first visit to this very posh power breakfast scene. I got there a little early and was already seated when Holbrooke burst into the room. He had journalists, political commentators, and officeholders accosting him not just as friends but also as people who wanted to know how his difficult assignment as special representative for Afghanistan and Pakistan (SRAP) was going. He wasn't there to see them, though: He was there to help a friend—me, a recently defeated US senator looking for a little advice about my future. As Holbrooke finally lumbered toward our table, he smiled warmly at me and reported that he had just gotten back from Pakistan at 2 a.m. And even though Holbrooke had always seemed to have a ridiculous amount of energy, this time he looked horrible. His eyes, underlined with dark circles, seemed to droop with fatigue; clearly this assignment was exhausting him—these special envoy jobs often do. I remember commenting to my aide Jeremy Tollefson as I got back into the car, "He looked like hell and he ordered eggs Benedict loaded with hollandaise sauce."

As Holbrooke devoured his meal he took the time to give me a few pointers on the relative merits of various positions the Obama administration might offer me, as well as on the other options I had. But we talked about his assignment in Pakistan and Afghanistan, too, a topic we had discussed many times before. As he gradually perked up I could see just how much Holbrooke wanted a breakthrough in this region, just as he had shown the same passion for resolving conflicts over ten years earlier when we traveled together to ten African nations.

In 1998, when his appointment as ambassador to the United Nations was being considered, Holbrooke and I discussed the possibility of a trip to Africa. What surprised me most was his admission that he had never been to Africa. Here was one of the great experts on Southeast Asia (going back to his years in Vietnam), a central player on Europe and former ambassador to Germany, one of our top-notch people on the former Soviet Union and Russia, and, of course, the architect of the famous Dayton Peace Accords to end the conflict in the Balkans. This was a classically worldly man, but even after decades of work on almost every kind of conflict imaginable he had never set foot in Africa until we made what may have been the first ever joint executive/congressional foreign relations trip. In December 1999, over twelve packed days, we managed to visit ten African nations, from Mali to Namibia to Uganda and Niger, and many places in between. We met heroic African leaders like Nelson Mandela in his own home, as well as the worst of the worst, including a tense Robert Mugabe, who was about to plunge Zimbabwe into more than a decade of disaster, and the buffoonish dictator of the Democratic Republic of Congo, Laurent Kabila, who was assassinated at his desk by one of his own guards not long after we visited him in Kinshasa.

The main purpose of our trip was to try to persuade all the African leaders we met to agree on one facilitator for the implementation of the so-called Lusaka Accords, which were aimed at stopping the African war that had engulfed Kabila's Congo. This conflict had become a pretext for the exploitation of the rich natural resources of this long-suffering nation that composes much of the heart of Africa. Holbrooke was simply brilliant in cajoling each leader, including Kabila, to accept Quett Masire, a former president of Botswana, as the facilitator. No one was a quicker study and no one knew how to turn discussions into ideas and action faster and more aggressively than Holbrooke did.

I mention this because I couldn't help but wonder why, given this man's enormous talents at conflict resolution, he had never visited Africa before. I'm glad Richard got there and that Africa benefited enormously from his involvement in its issues, especially in the fight against HIV/AIDS. But this huge continent had remained outside the range of his diplomatic vision for decades. When our little plane was hovering over the ever-twisting Congo River as we began to descend toward Kinshasa for the first time, all we could see was the huge river and endless thick forest. Holbrooke smiled, not like the seasoned diplomat that he was, but more like a little kid seeing Disneyland for the first time. All he said was, "The horror, the horror."*

Understanding the enemy is a prerequisite to successfully confronting

---

* An echo of Mr. Kurtz in Joseph Conrad's *Heart of Darkness.*

it. When it comes to Al Qaeda, anything less is a failure to do our best to protect the American people from a group of fanatics who have left no doubt that they would like to kill each and every one of us. This is why coming to grips with intricate connections between the Middle East, the Horn of Africa, northern Africa, and sub-Saharan Africa is so important. A country-by-country model impairs our ability to see the tentacles of Al Qaeda and its allies.

My favorite illustration of this is what I call the "lobster boat" story, which I frequently used to illustrate my concern about the Risk approach. In fact, I used it so often that my staff would sometimes roll their eyes when I'd begin to tell it. Nevertheless it is a straightforward example of the real nature and techniques of the terrorist network.

On Thanksgiving Day in 2002, we learned that terrorists had blown up the Paradise Hotel, an Israeli-owned resort in Kenya, because it was frequented by Israelis who had long enjoyed the location for vacations. Thirteen, including nine Kenyans, died and eighty more were injured. Al Qaeda boasted of its success: "Al Qaeda announces officially it's behind the two attacks in Mombasa. This statement comes as a challenge to the American enemy and to let it know it's capable of reaching anyplace in the world." On that same day in Kenya, an attempt to blow up an Israeli plane in mid-flight with two shoulder-launched surface-to-air missiles just barely missed its mark. One of the most prominent and influential of all sub-Saharan African nations, Kenya is bordered in part by Tanzania, Sudan, Uganda, and Ethiopia as well as by the Indian Ocean. Our approach to these nations has typically been to ignore them, unless there was an immediate crisis that threatened the stability of the region. While Kenya, Sudan, and Uganda had all been involved in such crises since 9/11, none had been considered in terms of Al Qaeda and the way it exploits instability. One other country shares a border with Kenya, however—Somalia. Since our quick military departure from there in the early 1990s, our policy concerning this critical region had been virtually nonexistent. In recent years, more of our policymakers, our military, and our intelligence community were becoming increasingly aware of the role of Somalia regarding Al Qaeda and its Somali affiliate, Al Shabaab. Still, we should resist the tendency to see

Somalia in isolation, for Somalia, Kenya, and Yemen have porous borders, as much on the water as on the land. This is where the lobster boat comes in.

After the attacks on the Israelis in northeastern Kenya, it was discovered that the armaments the terrorists used had taken a sea route from the Arabian Peninsula to Somalia and then down to Kenya by means of a fishing boat. The mortars, apparently shipped over the Strait of Mandab, made their way from Yemen to Somalia, where they were stored on fishing boats that then made their way to Kenya. In the meantime, one of the Al Qaeda operatives had joined fishermen in the ancient harbor city of Mombasa. Dominantly Islamic, this part of Kenya is very close to the southern border of Somalia. The fisherman-terrorist apparently worked for six weeks or so with other fishermen who shared the same basic religious and ethnic background. In other words, he could prepare for the attacks without raising suspicion, and when the time was ripe to kill Israelis, he could float the mortars under his lobster boat to those who actually carried out the attacks in the Mombasa region.

This example should not suggest that we suddenly change direction, bomb all the lobster fishermen in Mombasa harbor, and turn our full attention to Kenya. Rather it's about understanding the potential relevance of a multitude of countries to the war on terror and having the curiosity to discover the interconnections. The lobster-boat episode is not an isolated example from sub-Saharan Africa. When Al Qaeda actually blew up our embassies in Kenya and Tanzania in 1998 and attempted to do so in Uganda, the perpetrators were not from Iraq or Afghanistan; they did not flee to safe havens in the Middle East and South Asia. Instead they fled to Islamic communities not only in Somalia but as far south in sub-Saharan Africa as possible—South Africa.

Sometimes I am pessimistic about our ability to adjust to the post-9/11 world, simply because of the ease with which Al Qaeda and its sympathizers can operate from hundreds if not thousands of locations, worldwide. Developing sufficient knowledge of the scores of Islamic countries, let alone the many other countries with significant Islamic populations, is daunting. My generation grew up in a simpler world where the number of countries and independent forces was smaller and somehow more comprehensible. It reminds me of how few professional baseball or basketball teams there were in those days. Even a casual fan knew the teams and could pretty easily follow them. And so it seemed with the major powers in the world. Due to the independence of so many nations in a little over half a century, globalization, the information explosion, and many other factors, it is asking a lot for anyone even among our top policymakers to have a sense of the whole and to be able to anticipate every place where threats may arise. Even so, there are some aspects of our extreme tunnel vision that make no sense. Indonesia is Exhibit A.

Since 9/11, one of the most critical regions in the world in the fight against Al Qaeda is Indonesia and nearby nations. Given the enormous sacrifices this country made in the ill-fated effort to prevent the unification of Vietnam under communist rule in the 1960s and '70s, it would seem reasonable to continue our engagement with the region, and in some regards (economically and militarily) we have done so. But otherwise our involvement there has been minimal. (Perhaps having a president now who spent part of his youth in that country may improve the situation.) After 9/11, though, our attention to this nation was very limited compared to Iraq, where Al Qaeda hadn't even been active. When I finally had the chance to make the long trip to Indonesia in early 2006, our hardworking ambassador, B. Lynn Pascoe, seemed excited to see me. He told me that I was only the second US senator to have visited the country in the previous three years. My Republican colleague from Missouri, Kit Bond, who had a longstanding interest in the region, had visited there. But while some senators boasted that they had been to Iraq during the 2000s as many as seventeen times, no one besides Bond had visited Indonesia even once.

Why should this be a big deal? Well, Indonesia is the fourth-largest country in the world in terms of population. It is composed of 17,508 islands, some six thousand of which are inhabited. It is not just overwhelmingly Islamic; it has the largest Islamic population of any country in the world with approximately 86 percent of its some 245 million people calling themselves Muslims. It doesn't take much to argue that this place deserves our attention regardless of its religious and ethnic composition, but after 9/11 how can we justify taking it for granted? What makes this attitude even more absurd is that one of the most potent affiliates of Al Qaeda, Jemaah Islamiyah, was based there and pulled off some of the most spectacular and deadly attacks anywhere in the world. It was this organization that mounted the grisly bombing at the nightclub in Bali on October 12, 2002, killing 202 people, including eighty-eight Australian partygoers. They also blew up a hotel in Jakarta on August 5, 2003, killing twelve and injuring well over a hundred. On our trip in 2006 we first visited Thailand, then Indonesia, followed by a brief stop in Kuala Lumpur, Malaysia. At each place and in many briefings we heard about the problem of Jemaah Islamiyah (JI) and its efforts to further the goals of Al Qaeda throughout Islamic Southeast Asia and beyond. The prevalence of the discussion about JI in the region was in sharp contrast to the almost complete absence of it in the halls of Congress and in the American media. Naturally, those Americans in the region would be more focused on JI, but as the Bush administration desperately tried to link Saddam Hussein to Al Qaeda, we heard little or nothing at home about this organization that touted its ties to Al Qaeda and demonstrated a potency for killing that rivaled its parent organization.

Despite the shortcomings of our general policy toward Indonesia, there are individual examples of the effectiveness of some of our efforts to counter JI in this region. In fairness, these successes were facilitated by those working for the Bush administration, many of whom had been confirmed by the US Senate. And of course much of the activity that led to the weakening and containment of JI had to be done covertly. I came away from that trip believing that at least some of the work we were doing in cooperation with the nations in that region was an exception to our general tendency to think only country by country. At least some of those who were charged with confronting our enemy in this part of Southeast Asia did not suffer from tunnel vision, seeing not a Risk board but a more intricately interrelated region.

When I was in Jakarta, I found someone who, contrary to my expectations, seemed highly skilled at "thinking in two directions." When I was checking out the facilities at the Four Seasons hotel where we were staying,

I was most interested in the swimming pool. It was dusk and I noticed an attractive, regal-looking couple walking around the grounds near the pool. Since I was scheduled for a pre-trip briefing from him a few minutes later, I realized that the husband had to be Admiral William Fallon—no one more looked the part in navy whites than this tall, tough-looking person.

Fallon was the commander of the United States Pacific Command (USPACOM), one of the most important positions in the US military, covering an enormous part of the world from India to China to Japan to Australia. This was the position that John McCain's father, Admiral "Jack" McCain, had held during much of the Vietnam War. The home of the USPACOM commander is, according to John McCain, gorgeous, with beautiful vistas of Pearl Harbor in Hawaii. (John never got to spend much time there, though; as he had reminded me, without actually saying so, he had been otherwise occupied—imprisoned and tortured at the so-called Hanoi Hilton.) It was while the McCain family was residing there that both John and Jack refused the North Vietnamese offer to release John earlier than other prisoners of war. Given the vastness of the role of the USPACOM commander in any era, it's clear that Jack McCain didn't get to spend much time in Hawaii, either. And so the case certainly appeared to be for Bill Fallon, too.

As I walked into the hotel conference room, it appeared to me that this could be a pretty grim twenty-four hours with the admiral. I wondered how he felt about having to squire a politician throughout the region the next day. Maybe he was wary of me; after all, I had become a very strong, even strident critic of the administration's overall post-9/11 strategy, including overmilitarization. In any event, the conversation began slowly, but the admiral seemed to appreciate my genuine interest in understanding even the smallest details about JI and other possible threats in the region. My aides, Evan Gottesman and Grey Frandsen, had done a good job of teaching me enough about the region so I could generally keep up with the admiral. Fallon launched into a thoughtful analysis of the terrorist threat in the entire region, in language that was not obscured with military jargon or simplistic descriptions of bad guys in Indonesia. He gave me an excellent description of the lay of the land (or the lay of the land and sea). He spoke of the Sulawesi Sea and its relationship to JI. Through the joint efforts of the United States and other nations in the region, many of JI's key leaders had already been killed or arrested, whether in Indonesia or Thailand or somewhere else in the world. It was one of the few real success stories in the pursuit of Al Qaeda since the Afghanistan invasion. But JI was not done. The admiral explained that JI's operatives were hiding, converging, and plotting in the very remote regions surrounding and in the Sulawesi Sea. The Sulawesi is bordered by three different countries—Indonesia, Malaysia, and the Philippines—all of which have had difficulties with terrorism sponsored by exploiters of Islamic extremism.

The next day we started early. The admiral had offered to take us from Jakarta to the Aceh region in northwest Indonesia, and then on to Kuala Lumpur, Malaysia, at the end of a long day. As we pulled up to the admiral's plane, his staff members (also dressed in their whites) made room for the commander. We followed and I found that, instead of being seated in the main cabin with my staff, the admiral had arranged a comfortable spot for me directly across from him in his own cabin. His wife sat just across the aisle from us. Instead of getting on the phone or meeting with his aides or reading background materials for the day, he picked up our conversation where it had left off the night before. And this is where I learned that the admiral was one of those who could think in more than one direction. He talked about everything from war games with the Chinese to the bizarre regime in Myanmar (Burma) to the upheavals in Nepal. In so doing, he never minimized the Al Qaeda–JI threat but interwove it with the numerous currents and seemingly unrelated issues throughout the vast region he covered. He then briefed me on our trip to Medan and then to the Aceh region.

Our plane landed in the largest city in this part of Indonesia, Medan, where the United States had a modest diplomatic presence in a residential-type home rather than an embassy or formal consulate. The admiral had assembled a group of Indonesian and American military, diplomatic, governmental, and law enforcement officials for a full discussion both of JI in the region and of the separatist movement known as the Free Aceh Movement (Gerakan Aceh Merdeka, or GAM), which had led to serious conflict in that region. Aceh had been the scene of some very questionable crackdowns by the Indonesian government, obsessed as it always is with maintaining its territorial integrity in the vast regions from Papua to East Timor (previously part of Indonesia) to Aceh itself. The problem with these tactics was that they seemed to fuel rather than quell the separatist movement, possibly driving it closer to groups associated with violent extremists and perhaps JI. Given the region's proximity to dominantly Islamic Malaysia as well as Thailand, whose southern provinces were also dominantly Islamic and experiencing violence, this was another area that deserved transborder attention. At the meeting there was some optimism that the negotiations with the GAM were going surprisingly well, for both sides were now united—at least temporarily—in common cause. The reason for that was a tragic one.

At the tip of Aceh, where the admiral flew us next, is Banda Aceh, one of the areas most affected by the deadly tsunami of 2004. In minutes tens of thousands had been killed, from residents of the expensive resorts in Phuket, Thailand, to the remote fishing villages on the west coast of Aceh in Indonesia. We drove for a while across placid fields of rice where farmers and water buffalo were hard at work. It was hot but the sky was perfectly blue as we approached a village on the shore and could see the tower of what was once a church. The trip had been long and we were getting a little loopy in our conversations as our vehicle followed the admiral's. We were brought up short by our embassy assignee, though, when he explained that twenty thousand people had drowned in minutes with only one warning—provided by their animals racing for the hills. It was one of the most chilling things I had ever tried to imagine.

But we could see that progress was being made to restore the village through international aid, especially from the United States. Some had already noted that our abysmal popularity ratings in Indonesia, among the worst in the world, had greatly improved with the outpouring of help for the tsunami victims. Something similar occurred later, albeit very temporarily, in Pakistani Kashmir in 2005, when we provided significant aid after devastating earthquakes there. But Admiral Fallon understood that goodwill on its own would have only an ephemeral effect. So he and other officials seized the moment to promote an accommodation between Indonesia and the GAM.

While in Aceh, the admiral hosted a luncheon under a tent for members of the community. I was seated with him and a group of separatist leaders. Their lives had been equally devastated by the tsunami and they seemed as ready as the Indonesian officials to make this tragedy a catalyst for fairness and appropriate autonomy without separation from the nation. So often the United States leads with a military face in negotiations of this sort and ends up appearing like a conqueror, but in this case Fallon, a military man, calmly seized the moment to make nonmilitary progress. At the same time he never lost focus on the pursuit of JI itself. Later on, Fallon was wisely tabbed to run the United States Central Command (USCENTCOM), the next huge military command, one over from USPACOM. USCENTCOM included such garden spots as Iraq, Afghanistan, and Pakistan. But before long he was unwisely removed from that command when he dared to speak the truth about the distorted priorities of the Bush administration's post-9/11 policies and the possibility of yet another invasion, only this time of Iran.

On June 10, 2011, as I finished writing about Indonesia and Admiral Fallon, I got up from my computer, took a look at what was going on outside at the bird feeder, and turned on the television. I saw that quite a bit of attention was being devoted to one international situation. The coverage could not, of course, compare to our twin "Anthony" national obsessions of the moment—the Casey Anthony trial and the continuing woes of Congressman Anthony Weiner of New York. (And this is in the America that had experienced, just over a month before, the dramatic story of the killing of Osama bin Laden almost a full ten years after 9/11.) Now the international coverage was about Yemen. It was reported that the United States was intensifying a series of air strikes aimed at Al Qaeda operatives in Yemen who were said to be exploiting the growing chaos in that country to plan and mount attacks against the West. Just a few days before, President

Ali Abdullah Saleh, the longtime strongman ruler of Yemen, had been injured in an attack on the Presidential Palace, just as the pressure on him to resign had reached fever-pitch intensity. He left for Saudi Arabia to be treated for what were eventually acknowledged to be serious burns. On the streets of Sana'a the demands began for the United States and the international community to prevent his return to Yemen and to absolute power. The *New York Times* had reported the day before that

> Al Qaeda's affiliate in Yemen is believed by the C.I.A. to pose the greatest immediate threat to the United States, more so than even Qaeda's senior leadership believed to be hiding in Pakistan. The Yemen group has been linked to the attempt to blow up a transatlantic jetliner on Christmas Day 2009 and last year's plot to blow up cargo planes with bombs hidden inside printer cartridges.

Yes, and what about the USS *Cole* in 2000, and the killing of a soldier outside a military recruiting station in Little Rock, Arkansas, in June 2009, and the Fort Hood massacre in Texas in November of that same year? All of these had some relationship to Al Qaeda activists in Yemen. So maybe Joe Lieberman was right when he said that "Yemen will be tomorrow's war." The previous focus on Iraq, the emphasis of the last couple of years on the president's Afghan surge, and the rhetoric about Pakistan (now that bin Laden is gone) as the real ball game are waning. Now we are told to shift our thoughts to Yemen. In his live appearance on Fox News in late 2009, Lieberman enunciated the need to act preemptively in Yemen because of the Christmas Day attempt: Yemen now "becomes one of the centers of that fight. I was in Yemen in August. And we have a growing presence there, and we have to, of Special Operations, Green Berets, intelligence. We're working well with the government of President Saleh there." But, throughout the summer of 2011, President Saleh wasn't even in the country. For now it's Yemen 24/7 for the media and our government's spokesmen. And yet we should have been paying attention to Yemen since at least 2000.

This has the same old feel of our past errors. We're focused on Al Qaeda in the Arabian Peninsula in the false belief that Al Qaeda's potency is now concentrated there. Yes, the Arabian Peninsula does require our intense attention and it has for many years. But as we finally give Yemen the attention it must receive, we need to figure out a way to think in at least two directions.

If you turn to the immediate west from Yemen, just across that narrow Strait of Mandab to Africa, you will find a very active Al Qaeda affiliate, Al Qaeda in the Horn of Africa. It is supported by affiliates in the region including especially the Al Shabaab organization in Somalia. And, just as the media began confidently to report that Al Qaeda was now principally working in Yemen, a lot was happening in the Horn of Africa. On July 10, only a day after I wrote the previous section, it was reported that the interior minister of Somalia, Abdi Shakur Sheikh Hassan, had been killed by a suicide bomber (reportedly his niece, an Al Shabaab recruit) at his house in Mogadishu. So on June 11, just two days after printing the comments about the CIA's view about the new centrality of Yemen in the "war on terror," the *New York Times* reported that "it was the second suicide attack in Mogadishu in two days: bombers struck the port on Thursday, killing one person and wounding four others. The Shabab, one of the most feared of the country's insurgent groups, said it was responsible for that attack."

There was also good news from Somalia later in this same weekend as Secretary of State Hillary Clinton announced that Somali security forces, despite the difficulties of the Transitional Federal Government (TFG), had managed to identify and kill Fazul Abdullah Mohammed, one of the Al Qaeda operatives who had engineered the bombings of our embassies in Africa in 1998. This manhunt had obviously gone on for some time and should be seen as another major achievement of the Obama administration in tracking down significant Al Qaeda figures. This is a sign that this administration, compared to the last one, is more interested in and capable of addressing the terrorist organization in an effective way and better understands its complexities. Yet I still worry that our strategy will too often dwindle into a country-of-the-day (or month) approach.

Somalia certainly had our attention a little over a year ago when pirates started attacking more ships and pleasure boats off its shores. When it became clear that these attacks, although not apparently related to Al Qaeda, were a direct result of the ever-growing anarchy of Somalia, there were congressional hearings and temporary wall-to-wall coverage of the situation. Once the attacks appeared to subside, Somalia fell off our radar screen again. Maybe no nation nor even the world can keep track of so many threat locations at the same time. The great danger for us and the great strength of a group like Al Qaeda is that they understand this; it is part and parcel not only of their elusiveness but of their ability to terrorize psychologically as well as physically. To meet this challenge we must get beyond our game-board way of thinking.

5

In for a Penny, in for a Pound

*Your Excellency, Senator Feingold here is a member of the
Communist Party.*

My first visit to Pakistan was a quick overnight in Islamabad. The only
reason we were in Pakistan was that the 2005 McCain Codel (congressional
delegation) wanted to visit both major post-9/11 theaters of war—Iraq and
Afghanistan—on the same trip. The most direct route would have been to
fly over Iran. But of course, given our relationship with Iran, such a flyover
would not be permitted for five US senators and their military escort, so we
chose a longer route via Pakistan. On arrival, we (Senators McCain, Hillary
Clinton, Susan Collins, Lindsey Graham, and I) were whisked from the
airport under heavy security to Rawalpindi, site of the army compound near
Islamabad where President Pervez Musharraf ran Pakistan and often met
with dignitaries. Along the route, the several past attempts on Musharraf's
life were discussed in some detail, and, as we passed them, two grungy gas
stations were pointed out. Apparently an attempt had been made in the
past at this very spot to blow up gas tankers on each side of the road as the
president's motorcade passed. While we were waiting at the compound for
the president to appear, we met a dashing younger foreign minister, about

whom Hillary Clinton teased her aide, Huma Abedin, who was of Pakistani origin and then single. When we finally met with Musharraf, we found him interesting and cordial; after all, this guy was on our side. On the surface at least, we were among friends.

After the meeting we were taken to our hotel, the Serena, for a little time before dinner and a brief night's sleep before rushing to get another military flight over the lower Himalayas to Afghanistan. According to materials I had been given, the Serena was one of only two hotels in the capital city of Pakistan that were considered safe for Americans. I stayed at the other one, the Marriott, in late May 2008 on my own Codel to India and Pakistan. The Marriott didn't seem nearly as nice but it was hard to be sure, because every time I left the lobby our security officers surrounded me and told me to keep my head down as I went the few yards between the hotel and our vehicles. And it turned out that the Marriott was not at all safe for Westerners. A few months after my visit it was blown to bits by a suicide bomber driving a "jingle" truck, a vehicle traditionally decorated with hundreds of little ringing bells, bangles, and sparkly designs. More than fifty people were killed and more than two hundred injured. But that was 2008. By that time we had a growing understanding that Pakistan was the headquarters for the top leadership of Al Qaeda. We were told on that 2008 trip that most people believed that Osama bin Laden himself was hiding in Pakistan. It was believed that he was probably in a cave in Waziristan, the virtually ungovernable tribal region a couple of hours west by plane, on the border with Afghanistan.

That first visit to Pakistan in 2005, however, had a somewhat different feel to it. The Serena is a grand, older hotel with sumptuous rooms and tasteful decorations in the lobby. I have found that swimming can be really energizing, especially after hours of sitting on a plane or in a car, so checking out the hotel pool was one of my first priorities. There I was, a Jewish US senator, striding through the Serena's elegant lobby in a bathrobe heading for a beautiful pool overlooking the city. But there was no one at the desk at the pool and no one in the pool. It was pretty chilly—and a bit *chilling* to look out over Islamabad with its monuments and mosques, where this group of US senators had been told it would be unwise to go to a restaurant, other than the one at the hotel itself. As I swam I knew how lucky I was to be able to see such a place at all, let alone have the opportunity given me by the people of Wisconsin to work on our policy for this region. I was fascinated to be in Islamabad as the call to prayer emanated from a nearby mosque and the capital city began to wind down after a busy day.

Dinner in the hotel was delicious, including a wide variety of Pakistani and other regional foods. The conversation was substantive and lasted more than two hours. Our host was our ambassador to Pakistan, Ryan Crocker, whose mild-mannered skills have been subsequently employed in our embassies in both Iraq and Afghanistan. He was deluged with questions by all of us, but especially by the two heavyweights in the group, McCain and Clinton. Very little of the conversation was about Al Qaeda itself. The discussion ranged from the wars in Iraq and Afghanistan, to Pakistan's relationship with China, to Pakistan and its military and nuclear capacity, including the risk from A. Q. Khan, a dangerous arms dealer in the region.

Then suddenly Hillary Clinton held up her hands and said, "Okay, that's enough. Lindsey, I want to hear some Strom Thurmond stories." This was the same woman who had thoroughly impressed me earlier in the day when we were given a little downtime at the embassy to do some souvenir shopping there, at its own shop. Hillary and I used most of the time to talk about Pakistan and its domestic challenges. I could see that she not only had long known most of the key players in the country, but also had a detailed understanding of its culture and history. That was the moment when I realized that this former first lady was ready to be president. But right now, after a very long day, she wanted to be entertained and was not disappointed. Lindsey Graham told hair-raising stories of Strom's amorous adventures in South Carolina. Susan Collins chimed in after a while to explain how female senators still had to fend off the daily Thurmond clench on the arm, despite his being in his nineties. (He still lifted weights.) As the one-upmanship on Thurmond stories accelerated, we exploded in laughter, and no one laughed more heartily and naturally than Senator Clinton. Then it was time for all of us to get to bed; McCain's usual early morning instruction to our group to "march or die" was only a few hours away. Before going to sleep, though,

I looked out the window at the splendor of the lights of Islamabad and the looming Margalla Hills. As eerie as the place seemed, I did not even remotely consider the possibility that Osama bin Laden would finally be killed almost six years later—not in Afghanistan, not in Waziristan, not in Iraq, but in a Pakistani city just thirty minutes away.

Wherever he was at the time, Osama bin Laden weighed in with his opinions just before the 2004 presidential election in the United States. There are those who believe, and John Kerry is one of them, that bin Laden's menacing speech tipped the close balance of the election just enough in George Bush's direction to ensure his reelection. The video of bin Laden's speech has to be one of the most instructive guides to the traps into which Al Qaeda has led us. The strategies and tactics are openly conveyed, but if you are not awake enough to listen carefully to the enemy or are hell-bent on a different agenda, then you miss what is right in front of your nose. And you are liable to repeat the same mistakes over and over again. After praising Allah and thanking him for permitting "the wronged one to retaliate against the oppressor in kind," bin Laden begins his October 30, 2004 speech by addressing the American public. "People of America this talk of mine is for you and concerns the ideal way to prevent another Manhattan." He says that America has been ignoring his message, presented in various interviews he had done from *Time* magazine to CNN. And then, threateningly, "You can observe it practically, if you wish, in Kenya and Tanzania and in Aden." After justifying the terrorist attacks and accusing Bush of having imported "expertise in election fraud" from the Middle East to Florida, he got to what I regard as the critical section:

> All that we have mentioned has made it easy for us to provoke
> and bait this administration. All that we have to do is to send
> two mujahidin to the furthest point east to raise a piece of cloth
> on which is written al-Qaeda, in order to make the generals

race there to cause America to suffer human, economic, and
political losses without their achieving for it anything of note
other than some benefits for their private companies.

This is in addition to our having experience in using gue-
rilla warfare and the war of attrition to fight tyrannical superpowers, as we, alongside the mujahidin, bled Russia for ten
years, until it went bankrupt and was forced to withdraw in
defeat. All praise is due to Allah. So we are continuing this
policy in bleeding America to the point of bankruptcy. Allah
willing, and nothing is too great for Allah.

Taunting America and especially President Bush for having become en-
snared in Iraq but blaming the intervention on American corporate greed,
bin Laden gloats:

The darkness of the black gold blurred his vision and insight,
and he gave priority to private interests over the public interests of America. So the war went ahead, the death toll rose, the
American economy bled, and Bush became embroiled in the
swamps of Iraq that threaten his future. He fits the saying "like
the naughty she-goat who used her hoof to dig up a knife from
under the earth."

Somehow George Bush was reelected on November 2, 2004, and this
time it did not require the Supreme Court to decide the outcome. He also
got an even greater majority in the US Senate, the Republicans having
barely regained control after the vote to authorize the Iraq War in October
2002. In retrospect, these Bush victories seem a bit difficult to account for
in light of his position on bin Laden and Al Qaeda. It was now clear that
his Iraq War had not been related to Al Qaeda from the outset and was pre-
mised on phony claims about Iraqi weapons of mass destruction. The Iraq
War had proven to be anything but a "mission accomplished." It was more
reminiscent of the quagmire-like quality of the Vietnam War (or, as the Pete
Seeger rendition of the song described it at the time, "knee deep in the big

muddy") that undid President Johnson and led to Nixon's victory in 1968. Iraq had become deadly for the ever-increasing number of American troops sent there. Jihadists from around the world had heeded bin Laden's call and headed for Iraq to join the attack on the "American occupiers." Somehow the Afghanistan war limped along at the same time, but without any clear sense of purpose or serious belief that bin Laden and his principals were still in that country. It was well on its way to becoming the longest-running conflict in American history. And the ultimate bad guy was still at large, able to mock the president and the presidential election of a proud nation that had vowed to bring him to justice.

Bush's victory in 2004 can be explained in a number of ways, from the mobilization of the conservative right, to the famous "guns, God, and gays" slogan, to the ruthless distortions of John Kerry's superb war record. However, as someone who stood for reelection that same night, I believe that Bush won because of an intentional and successful appeal to American pride in our ability to win wars. Of course, this obscured a relative inability to cut our losses when a mistake is made. Somehow American military intervention in recent decades has followed a long-term all-or-nothing policy, in contrast to our behavior when we ultimately recognized that our undertakings in Vietnam and Somalia had gone well beyond the point of diminishing returns. Much of this has to do with our elected officials' overwhelming fear of being accused of betraying our troops in the field. They did not want to be labeled as unpatriotically wanting to "cut and run" or waving the white flag of surrender. It even got to the point where operatives like Dick Cheney would accuse those who advocated limiting an intervention of being content to wait till the enemy meets us on the streets of New York, or Los Angeles, or Cleveland. Somehow this rhetoric worked, even though people generally understood that Al Qaeda was no longer operating out of Afghanistan and that Iraq had been a mistake. In the end, many Americans seemed willing to suspend common sense, because they believe that once you're committed to doing something, whether building a house or occupying a country, you have to finish the job no matter what. The new post-9/11 principle for military action seems to be "In for a penny, in for a pound."

On my February 2005 visit to Iraq and Afghanistan, I found that high-ranking Americans displayed different degrees of urgency. In both places, though, I found incredibly talented and upbeat members of all our armed services—regular troops, sailors, marines, National Guard members, reservists. They were men and women, blacks, Latinos, and kids from farm families in rural America; some were just past high school age and others middle-aged officers who had left spouses and growing families to serve their country. They made up a collage of devoted Americans who found themselves in different locales, from Fallujah, Iraq, to Kabul, Afghanistan, places that couldn't be farther removed from their hometowns. And, of course, quite a few of them were Badgers, that is, Wisconsin natives. Their posts were an awful long way away from the Polish Club in Superior, or Hansen's Ice Cream in Green Bay. But Wisconsinites tend to have a friendly, open manner wherever they go. I never appreciated that more than when I visited these foreboding places.

Most of my encounters with Wisconsinites in both countries were brief. After traveling by transport planes, helicopters, and bulletproof SUVs, we would arrive somewhere like Baghdad or Kirkuk wearing flak jackets and helmets. We would be greeted by professional military personnel who made sure we were quickly stuffed into the next vehicle. I liked to tell audiences back home that when we would get off a plane on the McCain Codel in 2005, all the enlisted men would rush up to McCain for photos, and all the enlisted women, augmented by local women, would surround Hillary Clinton for snapshots. I also liked to claim that I "was left holding the suitcases" while this happened, although it is true that I did find myself holding clumps of cameras as the celebrity senators kindly obliged. But upon arriving in Baghdad the first time in 2005, I remember how much I appreciated being recognized by one of our Wisconsin troops. When I met the Wisconsinite, I said to him, "Look, I brought a box full of beef jerky from Jack Links in Minong. Will you promise to eat all of it yourself"—it was a hundred dollars' worth—"or give it to other Badgers?" With a big smile he said, "Yes, sir," and, as I jammed the box into his arms, he jammed me into the waiting truck. I also remember the pride the 440th Airlift Wing, then based in Milwaukee, took in being in charge of the C-130 Hercules that took us back from northern Iraq to Kuwait at the end of our trip. It was dark and the Wisconsin crew invited me to join them in the cockpit, handing me night-vision goggles that allowed me to see Baghdad, in great detail and in bright green lines. As much as I had opposed the war in Iraq, I felt proud of my fellow Wisconsinites and deeply patriotic about our country with its military populated by people of this caliber.

The military personnel I encountered on those trips had a different profile from those I had come to know when I was growing up in Janesville and throughout my career until 9/11. I was raised among family friends, teachers, and community leaders who were World War I, World War II, and Korean War veterans. Closer to my own generation were the Vietnam veterans. As a state and then United States senator I got to know the veterans of that conflict well, as we fought together to improve their health and other conditions. Some had gone voluntarily to Vietnam, but many had been drafted. The combination of conscription, an ill-conceived and futile mission, and the embarrassing loss of the war helped make these Americans, who were in fact part of a great generation, feel more like a lost generation. Every bit as brave as their predecessors, they had not been properly welcomed home when they returned. Yet no one has shown more care and affection for our more recent veterans and active military than these Vietnam veterans. At a reunion of Vietnam veterans called LZ Lambeau at Packer stadium in 2010, one man said to me, "When I went to Vietnam I was alone, when I came back from Vietnam I was alone. Today for the first time I'm not alone." He and most other Vietnam veterans I have encountered have made it their mission to provide a different scenario for soldiers and sailors returning from the variety of post-9/11 conflicts in which we are engaged.

The Wisconsin men and women I met in Iraq and Afghanistan, as well as in Kuwait, Djibouti, and Germany, had a different experience in the military. With the advent of the all-volunteer army, many had of course volunteered all their time to the standing armed forces. Another group, the National Guard, constituted a large number of Wisconsin's servicemen and -women in these theaters. They were volunteers, too, but no one could have predicted the scope of US military engagements in the first decade of the new millennium. Their expectations about the commitment they had made to the military were dwarfed by reality, as Afghanistan and Iraq required resources that could not adequately be met by the standing forces. The integration of standing army with National Guard was so seamless that when I met with them, I could not immediately tell the difference.

On the trips with McCain in 2005 and 2006, the procedure allowed each senator on the Codel an opportunity to spend an hour or so in a private room with the troops from his or her own state, with no supervision by anyone from the military or the State Department. I cherished these meetings. In each encounter there was initial shyness and hesitance on the part of the Wisconsinites in uniform. I'm not sure the troops knew what to expect, and wonder if they found it a bit odd to meet this political guy they had heard about but did not know personally. Some seemed slightly aware of the role I increasingly played as one of the leading critics of our post-9/11 military strategy. I would begin the sessions by asking each one to tell me their hometown. I tried to put them at ease by mentioning a park, restaurant, or even a bar I knew there. (In the course of nearly one thousand listening sessions, I had been to almost every one of their hometowns.) Then I would simply ask if anyone had any questions or comments.

The Wisconsin volunteers were pretty slow to talk. When they did, the first question was usually "Is Favre coming back next season?" And they weren't kidding around. A passion for the Green Bay Packers is common ground for any group of Wisconsinites, and that was the news from home that they really wanted to hear. The Packer season was something these brave men and women could look forward to as their tough assignments dragged on. This, of course, was all about Brett Favre when he was still the most beloved person in the state of Wisconsin and the gift of a number "4" green and gold jersey was as common at Christmas as a decorated tree. This preceded his jump to the New York Jets a few years later, the annual Hamlet-like performances about possible retirement at the end of each season, and finally his betrayal when he joined the much-despised Minnesota Vikings. "I sure hope so" was the best I could say in response to that frequent question. I would then prompt further discussion by asking, "How's the food?" and was pleased to hear them say that it was good, with a lot of healthy options. This is not to say some good Wisconsin bratwurst and especially some Point Beer from Stevens Point would not have been a lot more welcome than some politician.

I probed a bit more at a meeting in Fallujah in Iraq and did hear a cautious but troubling account of the inadequate number of night-vision goggles for those going out on patrol in what was then the epicenter of our difficulties, Al Anbar province. None of these meetings ever turned into a complaint session, but they did provide me with information about how we could better protect and facilitate the work of our fighting men and women. What I especially remember, though, was that at meetings like this in both 2005 and 2006, the same question was asked—without prompting—near the end of each session. More than one of these volunteers, many of whom had been forced to go well beyond their understanding of their original commitment, simply and politely looked me straight in the eye and said, "Senator, when are we going home?"

The meetings with our servicemen and -women were the high points of the 2005 trip. Each of us came back from our separate sessions inspired by the volunteers from the big cities and tiny towns in our states who were willing to put their lives on the line for all of us. But much of the rest of the trip featured low points, particularly in Iraq. We met with General George W. Casey Jr. in an office in one of Saddam Hussein's former palaces, decorated with intricate mosaics and a gigantic chandelier. Casey was in charge of our Iraq Command, and he did his best to put a positive face on the situation. John McCain seemed impatient, even grumpy with the four-star army general as he sought information about the training of Iraqi troops. When I got the chance to ask a question, I followed up on Casey's statement that the number of bombings in the country and especially Baghdad had been reduced. I said, "Well, how many is 'reduced'? How many are there now?" He replied, sheepishly, "Oh, fifty or sixty a day." Lindsey Graham and Susan Collins gasped and Hillary Clinton shook her head.

We were required to remain exclusively in the Green Zone while in Baghdad on this trip and we all traveled from one location to another within the zone in an armored SUV. Susan Collins remembered that, on her previous visit to Baghdad, daily activity seemed to be fairly normal and they had been able to walk freely in many parts of the city. Not now. One of the most ardent supporters of the war, Lindsey Graham commented sardonically as all five of us were crowded into one SUV after the Casey meeting, "If things get any better, we're going to have to be in a tank next time." Nearly two years after the president's "mission accomplished" speech, we were in the middle of a real quagmire. No one could have emerged from that visit feeling encouraged.

Nonetheless, when it came to public comment during the trip, the other four senators quickly closed ranks in support of the administration. In one of the most interesting moments of my career, the five of us held a press conference in the Green Zone on February 19, 2005. From their remarks, all four of my colleagues (each of whom I admire and like to this day) seemed to have witnessed a completely different reality than I had. In my comments, I pointed out the oddity that "our CIA director the other day said that Iraq has now become, instead of Afghanistan, the leading place of training for international terrorists," and then wondered "what implications that has for Iraq and our own safety and what we can do together with the officials here and in other parts of the world to make sure what we're doing here not only ensures that the people of Iraq have a democracy, but that it is consistent with the number-one issue in America, which is making sure we deter the people that attacked us on September 11." McCain, on the other hand, expressed what I would call very cautious optimism: "We believe, hope, and pray that the dynamic has changed from the Iraqi insurgents versus the US and our troops, to Iraqi insurgents versus the Iraqi government. Under the second scenario, if it applies, then I think we have an opportunity to succeed." John's words were a little more reserved than I would have expected, but Hillary Clinton's remarks confounded me. We were all on a riser facing the reporters and cameras, and I remember turning to look at her as she seemed to give unnecessary credence to the unbelievable claims of the administration that the "insurgency was in its last throes." Clinton was asked a question about the fact that we hadn't been able to leave the Green Zone while in Baghdad, and said in reply, "So, while yes it is somewhat disheartening that there is so much security, that we ourselves are subjected to. On the other hand, I think that the election and the desperation of this so-called insurgency is becoming clearer by the day."

After numerous briefings, from Fallujah to Baghdad to Kirkuk, I had formed a completely different impression. Perhaps my colleagues thought they might discourage our fighting men and women by painting a more accurate but bleaker picture. That was a sentiment I fully understood. But I could not imagine hiding from the people of Wisconsin the fact that they were being snowed by their own government.

The next day John and Hillary, assumed to be the front-runners in their respective parties for the 2008 presidential nominations, made a fascinating joint remote appearance on NBC's *Meet the Press* in a makeshift studio in the embassy area of the Green Zone. To get there on time, they cut short a meeting with the top British military official in Iraq and left me in charge. Once upstairs, Hillary, asked by NBC's Tim Russert about the wisdom of a timeline for withdrawing our troops, told America that "we don't want to send a signal to the insurgents, to the terrorists that we are going to be out of here at some, you know, date certain. I think that would be like a green light to go ahead and just bide your time."

But that wasn't at all what I was hearing at the meeting McCain and Clinton had just left. In fact, I heard the opposite. They had left me to my own devices, so I decided to try a long-shot question, hoping that a British official, who was less tied to the Bush administration's official line, could be a little more candid. When I asked him what he would think of our announcing a flexible timetable to give an indication of when we would be likely to withdraw our troops from Iraq, the general seemed reluctant to reply at first. But then he said firmly, "Sir, nothing would better take the wind out of the sails of the insurgency." And nothing I heard overseas did more to strengthen my growing resolve to end this intervention than that one remark uttered in the heart of war-torn Baghdad.

In early 2003, after voting in the minority against the Iraq War, I still hoped there was a chance that the president would find a way to avoid this ill-advised invasion. As Saddam Hussein was given his final warnings in March 2003, however, the president showed he clearly meant business, and our military was fully mobilized. A year and a half earlier, when I was in

Door County, Wisconsin, watching the president announce the Afghanistan invasion, my emotions had been somewhat different. But my reaction to the decision to invade Iraq was fundamentally the same: I wanted us to succeed, now that our democracy had decided to go to war—as flawed and even fraudulent as the process to do so might have been. I hoped that we would at least depose and maybe capture Saddam and, if there really were weapons of mass destruction, that we would find and destroy them. Of course, my greatest hope was that our casualties would be minimal. I wanted our servicemen and -women to be able to return home or be posted to places that were actually more related to our legitimate national security needs. Accordingly, I did not feel that it was appropriate to criticize the war effort then. We had to present a united front, unless the invasion immediately proved to be a misadventure in its execution as well as its inception.

Back in Wisconsin, I continued my town meetings. My procedure was always the same during my eighteen years in the US Senate. There was no set topic. I would usually start the meeting with a news item or a brief report on an initiative of mine. I would then invite my constituents to speak about whatever they wanted, which is precisely what they did. Despite the events of 9/11 and two major wars later, health care was still the most discussed topic in 2003 and 2004, although the Iraq War combined with some other foreign policy issues came in second. It was not until 2005 and 2006 that foreign policy—principally issues pertaining to Iraq—came in first. Around the time of the invasion, there were several negative comments about the decision to go to war and its costs. Some wondered, "Where will these guys invade next?" At the Dodge County listening session in late February 2003, Donald Wendlandt of Randolph identified himself as a Korean War veteran and stated that "going to war with Iraq is ridiculous." Up in Menomonie, near the Twin Cities, Bill Edwards said he "didn't understand why we are in Iraq," adding, "We can back the troops, but that doesn't mean we have to back the president." He then asked me to visit his coffee group at the Silver Dollar, which I subsequently did, finding a like-minded group of older men, who told me that they got together there each day "to solve the world's problems." Others, like Henry Kerber in Eau Claire, not only did not believe there were any security implications for us in Iraq, but claimed that "Bush only went there for the oil." Another constituent, Greg McMahon of Baraboo, cheered the invasion on April 12: "I support the war . . . we also need regime change in North Korea, Iran, Syria, and Cuba." Even in the context of the relatively modest number of comments on Iraq in 2003, that sentiment was rarely evident. More common was the fear expressed by Joan Warga of Hancock just a few days after Mr. McMahon's call for more invasions. At the Waushara County town meeting she challenged me, "What are the Democrats going to do to stop the Bushies from spreading war to other Middle East countries?"

As 2003 wore on and the mission was obviously not so easily accomplished, a series of other concerns began to crop up. As early as April 21, Janette Mullenberg of Mauston, whose son was stationed at Camp Udairi, Kuwait, near Iraq, was concerned that "the needs of the troops are not being met. Ten thousand troops are living in camps established for six thousand." By late May, Suzanne Engebretson of Beloit, noting the fact that the Iraq War was going to be far more involved than the administration had anticipated, asked if we could "be reimbursed for the costs of the war in Iraq?" And by early August 2003, the strain of the war was beginning to show in some of the most rural areas of Wisconsin. The sheriff of Taylor County, Jack Kay, told me that the National Guard troop deployments were "creating problems with his staffing" and he asked if the "troops [were] coming back just for leaves or are they coming home for good?"

At no point during this time did Wisconsinites, in any significant numbers, come to my town meetings to express support for the war. On the other hand, strong opposition to the war was not initially overwhelming, either. Even though the death and casualty levels followed no consistent pattern from mid-2003 through 2006, people gradually became more concerned and then alarmed about the continuing deaths of American troops. Some months it was under fifty, but more often between fifty and one hundred, and occasionally even more than that. The attitude seemed to be that these casualty rates are to be expected when you invade a major country, and most people accepted them, with sadness. Still, the accumulation of American deaths and injuries began to take its toll. Senator John Glenn of Ohio used to refer to the Dover, Delaware test—how long could the American public watch brave young Americans return in coffins to the air force base at Dover before saying enough is enough. The Bush administration and the military actually went to great lengths to try to prevent the press from photographing the flag-draped coffins, especially when they arrived in large numbers.

What made the duration of the war even more trying for the administration and the public alike was the absurdity of finding no weapons of mass destruction, not a single one. Maybe we should have been relieved to learn this, but as the funerals and wakes became more and more frequent, especially in the small towns of Wisconsin, words like *embarrassed* and *ashamed* crept into comments at the town meetings. There are few things more depressing than watching a neighboring family mourn the untimely death of their son or daughter. What is even worse—and almost sickening—is to know that the basis for their sacrifice had been political at best and cynically manipulated at worst. Nevertheless, I wanted these families to look at this another way: No soldier or sailor can really die in vain in defense of this country. That hero did his or her patriotic job for this country after our democracy had made its decision to go to war, regardless of whether that decision was right or wrong. Their sacrifice is made in defense of our system of government, our Constitution, and our fellow Americans, and no one and no underlying defects or revelations can change that.

As the war in Iraq raged on, and the Afghanistan intervention continued in the distant background, it began to dawn on the public that neither of these operations was going as predicted. Compared to Iraq, we kept a relatively modest number of troops in Afghanistan, with the apparent purpose of preventing Al Qaeda and its Taliban sponsors from taking over the country again. Although there was precious little talk about it, presumably we were still hoping to get Osama bin Laden and his top lieutenants, if they were still there.

In Iraq we discovered no weapons of mass destruction. It was also evident that there had been no original connection to Al Qaeda. That, however, changed when our invasion of Iraq more or less invited Al Qaeda to support angry Iraqis, who now formed their own franchise: Al Qaeda in the Land of the Two Rivers or, conveniently for the administration, Al Qaeda in Iraq, led by the brutal Abu Musab Al-Zarqawi. When Americans faced these facts, they began to understand that they were being asked to man and fund two wars costing hundreds of billions of tax dollars, neither of which seemed related to its initial purpose. And there was no end in sight. Our government insisted that both wars had to be open-ended commitments in terms of time and resources. Politicians and the military, concerned about how it might look, were reluctant to limit the drain they were putting on our military and our economy. You're either in it to win it, or you're not, seemed to be the prevailing notion. This in turn played right into the hands of those who supported the vast commitment of our resources in places that had little to do with countering Al Qaeda. We had made certain choices and now it seemed we had to follow through regardless of their wisdom—the strategic thinking amounted to nothing more than the rationale that once you're in for a penny, you're in for a pound.

Those of us who not only voted in Washington but who listened regularly to our constituents at town meetings began to hear more and more people express a different attitude. The constant funerals and flags at half-staff began to resonate with the cable television announcements of the latest explosions and casualties. How many died? Was it Iraq or Afghanistan? How many were Americans? Okay, any from Wisconsin? In late spring of 2005, more than two years after the invasion, I reached the point where I felt I had to call for an end to the Iraq intervention. I proposed a bill that would ask the president as commander in chief to outline a flexible timetable for withdrawing our troops that would give us some sense of when this drain on America would end. Given my original opposition to the war, my proposal was not entirely unexpected. But, given the growing public opposition, what was a little unexpected was the fact that the twenty-two other senators who had voted against the war didn't seem even remotely interested in joining me to start the movement to end it. The biggest surprise, though, was a member of the House of Representatives who came up with essentially the same plan as I did at the same time.

Representative Walter Jones of North Carolina had as different a political profile from mine as possible. He isn't just a Republican, he's a very conservative one. He doesn't just have one of the largest military bases in America, Camp Lejeune, smack dab in the middle of his district. He was actually the guy who was so in favor of the Iraq War that he came up with the idea of renaming French fries in the House Dining Room "Freedom fries," presumably as a way to punish the French for demurring on the Iraq invasion. He was also identified with the evangelical wing of the Republican Party. I checked the report about his proposal for a timeline to get out of Iraq several times before deciding to give him a call. Walter couldn't have been nicer even though we had never met and were unlikely ever to work on anything together. He told me of his gradual realization that "these boys are dying for I don't know what" and that he had searched his soul and felt he could no longer support the war. This was a courageous act for a politician of his background and his district, and I told him so. He just said, "Well, God bless you, Senator," a statement that actually seemed a sincere expression of feelings rather than a mere salutation. It intensified my efforts to end this mistaken war.

During the summer of 2005, what I heard in Wisconsin on the subject of Iraq became increasingly different from what I heard in Washington. Senators at the Capitol acknowledged the growing opposition on the progressive side with hand-wringing or just changed the topic. My modest call for a resolution asking the president to present a nonbinding, flexible plan for our withdrawal of troops from Iraq was met with silence by the White House, while many leading Democrats treated it as a radical cry from the American left. There was national support for my efforts from left-leaning groups, especially in the emerging netroots, but what finally drove me to go beyond this to a proposal for a more formal timeline for withdrawal was what I was hearing at home.

I knew concern was growing in Wisconsin—even more in the conservative areas of Wisconsin than in the liberal ones—but I was not prepared for the outpouring of sentiment that I encountered during my listening sessions that summer of 2005. On June 25, in Iola, Waupaca County, one of the most conservative in the state, Jane Ricchio encapsulated the mood:

> My biggest question has been puzzling me . . . the insurgents in Iraq, aren't they surging against the US? And if we would leave, there might be some internal strife. They have a government now, they have a constitution. We could give them aid like we do to everybody else and which I believe in, but I think the insurgency and the terrible lives that these Iraqi people are living under because we are there, I just don't understand. Bush keeps saying we can't leave because the insurgents are in their last throes. . . . But if we left, wouldn't the insurgency die down?

I responded with some gratitude, poking a little fun at myself at the same time:

> I'll tell you something. One senator in the Democratic caucus this week said what you said, only you did it better. And they looked at me like I was nuts. This is a recruiting technique for the insurgency. "Come to Iraq and get the Americans." It's finally dawning on just about everybody including some very conservative Republicans that this is the very fuel of the international terrorist movement.

But the remarks of Daniel Naylor later in that same meeting were even more telling. Two of his children had already served in Iraq, but he wasn't speaking only for his own family when he reported:

> In April of this year the town of Farmington in Waupaca County passed a unanimous resolution to set a timetable for the withdrawal of our troops. . . . You are the only person who promised to follow through on that resolution. . . . It is clearly time for Congress to assert its responsibility regarding this war.

Naylor and the town of Farmington had clearly had it. Despite their original support for the war, its demand for open-ended commitment no longer comported with their common sense. Naylor concluded this very serious plea with a lighter comment: "I only facetiously suggest you support the institution of the draft starting at the beginning of the alphabet with Ashcroft, Bush, and Cheney."

In August we began our annual foray into the most remote parts of the state, often referred to as "up north." On August 3, 2005, a warm summer day, we drove over nine miles on a very bumpy dirt road to reach the Newald Community Center in Forest County. After passing through acres and acres of nothing but trees, we found a good little crowd waiting for us. One person asked me which road we came in on. "Double Bend," I replied, and the constituent responded, "Oh yeah. That's one of our better roads." I spoke briefly about the upcoming confirmation hearings for Judge John Roberts to the Supreme Court and then turned to another subject at the end. "The second thing I mention that gets me more emotional and I try not to be, you have to stay objective but I just got a report that fourteen marines were killed today." The crowd let out a gasp. I continued, remembering what the British general had told me in the Green Zone in February:

> The best way to take the wind out of the insurgents is if there is a clear public vision of when we're getting out of there. That's the worst thing for us, is that people think that we're never leaving. They consider that humiliation. I want people to start thinking about this. The president got up in front of the nation after a series of other tragedies and he said, "You know, unfortunately, people who criticize our policy in Iraq don't understand the lessons of 9/11." I say George Bush doesn't understand the lessons of 9/11.

To which one constituent yelled out, "You bet!" I was not leading, but following the lead of Wisconsinites when I prepared my next proposal.

A couple of weeks later I held a town meeting in Marquette, Wisconsin. I used the occasion to propose the first legislation for a set one-year time-

table for the withdrawal of our troops from Iraq. Though announced in a
small town hall, it drew immediate and fairly intense national attention as
a strong but probably extreme proposal. I appeared on *Meet the Press* a few
days later to discuss it. But for some back home this was weak tea. As Kate
Houston said to me in the Liberty Grove town hall discussion in Door
County, "I don't believe in a timeline. I would bring the troops home now."
What seemed radical, trail-blazing—even reckless—to many in Washington
and the national media already seemed too tame to many in Wisconsin.
People in Wisconsin can generally be characterized as mild-mannered and
relatively slow to anger. One minister, however, summarized the growing
mood in Wisconsin when he spoke at the Star Prairie Community Center
on August 26, 2005, my first listening session after I had proposed my one-
year timetable bill. Reverend Andrew Tetzlaff confessed:

> I have been angry sometimes, livid with anger, every day since
> March 19, 2003, when we moved against Iraq. . . . I have told
> the congregation I preach to how I feel about this. Some liked
> it and some didn't like it. There's no use in you telling me not
> to be angry. . . . And I can no longer look at the president. If
> I see his face, I turn away. And if I hear him speak, I hit the
> mute button.

Across the country, the emotion was building. You could find it all the
way from the liberal salons of New York and Los Angeles to the taverns of
rural Montana to the coffee shops of northern Wisconsin. Yet you wouldn't
have known it from conversations on foreign trips with elected officials
from these same places. Never was this more evident to me than in February
2006, when John McCain asked me to join him again on one of his frequent trips to Iraq. This time he assembled a more unusual combination
of public officials to observe the situation there. The group combined both
House and Senate members, as well as several governors of states from different regions of the country. I couldn't help but notice that Representative
(now Senator) Tom Udall and I were the only Democrats of the nine on the
trip. The Codel also included at least three relatively unknown but clearly

up-and-coming Republicans who were potential running mates, or at least potential good supporters for McCain in 2008: Senator John Thune of South Dakota, Governor Tim Pawlenty of Minnesota, and Governor Jon Huntsman of Utah. A couple of hours after we were wheels up from Andrews Air Force Base and on our way to Kuwait, Iraq, and Jordan, McCain convened all of us in the main cabin of the military plane to explain how he had been reading Brigadier General H. R. McMaster's manual—based on his experience in Vietnam—on how to clear and hold communities in an insurgency situation. I was intrigued that McCain did not hide his unhappiness with the progress of the war in Iraq. Given what was now my lead role in opposing the continuing intervention in Iraq, the Republican officeholders looked puzzled to see me right next to John as he held forth.

After a few basic questions from the governors who until then had not been particularly focused on Iraq, I interjected a few comments about the likely futility of continuing in Iraq. John, in good humor, allowed my dissent, but then added, "This is Russ Feingold. I bring him along because he is consistent, consistently wrong." The conversation continued until we arrived in Kuwait. We were there primarily to transfer to military transport planes to Iraq. First, however, we were scheduled to pay tribute at a lavish banquet to the emirs who ran this incredibly wealthy totalitarian nation. We were given a few hours to adjust to jet lag. Some of us went for a jog, or just relaxed; I, as usual, took a swim. This time it was in what had to be the most elaborate complex of pools and fountains I'd ever seen, at a fabulous Kuwait City hotel. Upon arriving at the palace for dinner we were greeted by a coterie of men identically dressed in dishdashas. Despite our excellent briefing materials, it was difficult to figure out who was who.

The leading Kuwaiti official present, Foreign Minister and Deputy Prime Minister Mohammed Sabah al-Salem al-Sabah, formally greeted us before dinner. He then turned the discussion over to Senator McCain, who thanked our hosts and briefly explained the purpose of our trip. He asked a question or two about the Kuwaiti view of the progress of the war, then, as protocol required, introduced the nine of us in order of seniority, beginning with me. In a matter-of-fact way, McCain told the foreign minister and the other cabinet ministers assembled with us, "Your Excellency, this is Senator Feingold. He is a member of the Communist Party." The emirs smiled at me uncomfortably and exchanged nervous glances. My face turned red and I laughed heartily (it was very funny), hoping to suggest to them that this was not my party affiliation. Nevertheless, I did not explicitly correct McCain, imagining a headline, "Feingold denies being member of Communist Party." What emerged was an almost unspoken fear on the part of the Kuwaitis that we would either suddenly exit from Iraq, leaving them with a huge new refugee problem, or that we would stay in Iraq forever, creating an impression that Kuwait was an American military base.

During the long dinner, which must have included fifteen courses, I tried to make conversation with the emirs seated near me, some of whom knew virtually no English. I thought of what I had been told by Muslims in America after 9/11. What they most resented in the Middle East was the relationship America had with regimes like this, who made a mockery of our values of democracy, human rights, and women's rights. These thoughts were reinforced the next morning, when we slowly made our way to the American base in a heavily armored motorcade. We snaked around a central square where hundreds of young men in tattered clothes and sunbaked skin were sprawled, waiting for work. Needless to say, they were not Kuwaitis, but discontented young Islamic men, most of them from impoverished Middle Eastern and South Asian nations. They looked just like the characters so well portrayed in George Clooney's *Syriana,* the desperately poor men sullenly watching this parade of their "masters"—Kuwaiti billionaires and the American military machine—on their way to review their occupation of a prominent part of the Islamic world. We had drifted far from our initial post-9/11 realization of how important it was to understand how others perceived the United States. Now allies like Kuwait had become essential to our investment in Iraq. We continued to throw good money and American lives into Iraq for no logical reason, apparently just because we were already there.

I returned to the Green Zone on that 2006 trip. We flew in an open military helicopter wearing flak jackets, helmets, and goggles, passing over palm trees and Saddam Hussein's swimming pools. Once safely on the ground, we were hustled into a cramped room for a meeting with General

David Petraeus, who was in charge of training the Iraqi troops. And just as he had done with Generals Casey and Petraeus one year before, McCain gave Petraeus the third degree about his numbers and the reliability of his time frame for the readiness of Iraqi troops. John seemed increasingly irritated as the meeting continued. I had a chance to ask some fairly tough questions, too. As all nine of us traipsed out of the meeting, I heard one of the Republican governors in our group, Bob Riley of Alabama, say to McCain, only slightly in jest, "John, I'm getting a little worried. Feingold is the only one who's making sense to me." McCain harrumphed. But soon all seven of the Republicans were singing out of the same hymnbook about the positive progress on the ground in Iraq. John Thune even suggested, as we traveled in a little bus for dinner with an Iraqi official, that "Feingold be put in a special lead vehicle," since roadside bombs were in abundance at the time. His gallows humor was welcome in this tough environment.

After Iraq, we stopped to see the king and queen of Jordan in their new palace. McCain, in commandant mode, explained that we had to change out of our casual Iraq clothing quickly, before we met the monarchs. So upon arrival at the airport we were all ushered into one room where Jordanian guards watched our flustered group change into suits and ties—a sight few would have wanted to witness. We drove some distance to the outskirts of Amman to a newer palace. Although it was not explicitly stated, it was clear that this palace had replaced the old one because of fear of unrest in Amman itself, a precursor to the Arab Spring, which erupted some four years later. During our meeting, the always smooth and reassuring young King Abdullah gave us reason to hope that the Palestinian-Israeli negotiations could finally go well. He, like our Kuwaiti hosts, sought to impress us with the cooperation his country was giving to our efforts in neighboring Iraq, despite the pressures that put on his own nation. But what the king really wanted to talk about was not Iraq and the US government's near obsession with it. He was more animated than I've ever seen him when he said, "Now what we most need to be concerned about is the Shia crescent." He drew a crescent shape with his hands as Queen Rania watched. He was speaking, of course, about Iran, but not only Iran. He referred to the Shia ascendancy in Iraq that our invasion had created. He then drew points on his arc representing Syria, Saudi Arabia, and various smaller oil-rich kingdoms. Although all of us and the US government felt good about our relationship with Jordan, King Abdullah had a far broader vision of events in the Middle East and the Islamic world as a whole than our administration had demonstrated. It's not that the administration wasn't aware of the consequences of its actions, but they were so focused on justifying the continuing overcommitment of our resources in Iraq that these more nuanced issues got short shrift.

When I returned to my Democratic colleagues in Washington, I discovered that their focus was similar. From mid-2005, I was the leading voice in the Democratic Caucus for a timeline for withdrawal. Many caucus members expressed concern about the growing opposition to our presence in Iraq. Our leader, Harry Reid, gave me little comfort but did not openly undermine my efforts. However, two senators (easily two of the nicest in the Senate) did drive me nuts as they thwarted any serious attempt to differentiate Democrats from the White House on the issue of Iraq. Our leaders on the Armed Services Committee, Carl Levin of Michigan and Jack Reed of Rhode Island, were deferred to on such matters by much of the caucus, so when these two sought to turn *timeline* into a dirty word, they slowed our progress.

But two things aided me and the many progressives across the country who were trying to get us out of this war. The first was a switch by Harry Reid himself. One thing you get used to around Harry is that sometimes he says the first thing that pops into his head—more like a Great Nile of consciousness rather than a stream of consciousness. He is very funny, but it's not always clear if he is being intentionally so. One time his filter clearly wasn't working when he called a caucus lunch to order on a Tuesday afternoon with these words: "My colleagues, I was standing next to Mel Martinez in the urinal this morning. . . ." Whatever Harry said next was drowned in calls of "Harry, no!" and "Stop right there." As the hubbub died down, California's Dianne Feinstein rose, having composed herself before the rest of us, and pleaded, "Harry, too much information." Wherever the Senator Martinez anecdote was going, the point was lost and we moved on immediately to a new topic.

But it was a very different Harry Reid who called me into his office in the Capitol early one morning in March 2007. Such a meeting, where I was given no clue of the topic, was rare, and I found Harry looking almost mournful when I arrived. Having thought carefully about what he was going to say this time, Harry got right down to business and said, "Russ, I've been over to Walter Reed [Army Medical Center] more times than I can remember and this morning I was out there again. Those men . . ." He paused and then described some of the severely wounded troops he had visited. "Russ, I can't take it anymore, I want to be a lead cosponsor of your Iraq timeline bill." I was never more pleased to gain a cosponsor on a bill. That a fairly centrist Democrat and the majority leader could offer such support did a lot to counter rhetoric against the proposal. My amendment demanding the orderly withdrawal of American troops within one year was known as the Feingold-Reid bill.

The other development was, of course, that as 2007 began, so did the race to succeed President George W. Bush, whose unpopularity had far more to do with Iraq than anything else. The possible candidates for the 2008 Democratic nomination who had voted for the Iraq War were beginning to lean toward a timeline strategy; so was a very junior senator from Illinois who had called the Iraq intervention a "dumb war." John Kerry, Hillary Clinton, John Edwards, and Barack Obama all carefully watched our maneuvers on the timeline proposal, not wanting to lose any opportunity to capture a portion of the potent antiwar vote in the Democratic primaries. John Kerry did not, in the end, seek the nomination, but he soon joined me in another version of the proposal, the Kerry-Feingold amendment. We took a vote on it on June 22, 2006. It garnered only thirteen votes. I'm sure that Senator Obama himself was tempted to be more aggressive in his support, but he was very carefully managed by high-powered advisers who correctly saw in him not only a political phenomenon but a future president, and that in the not-too-distant future. He and I had a number of cordial conversations on the Senate floor about his political future. He even asked me if I was planning to run, since there had been some speculation that my vote against the war would distinguish me from the obvious lineup of candidates. I told him I was unlikely to run. I asked Obama if he was serious about running. He was not definitive but did say that "it would be four hundred and thirty-one tough days and then it would be done." I thought to myself, "Not if you win," and concluded that he really was going to run.

Our subsequent conversations about the war, however, though always civil, involved me trying to get him to sign on to or vote for my latest attempt to establish an exit plan for the war. Whenever I was able to force a vote on another version of the amendment, he and Hillary Clinton would watch each other carefully to see who would vote first, and how. On May 16, 2007, I offered another amendment to begin the end of the Iraq War. Obama was standing just in front of me in the well as the roll call proceeded. When it was his turn, he said, "Aye." I was very pleased with his support for the cause, but I couldn't resist giving him a little dig. "Finally," I said, as I followed with my own "Aye." The future president turned around, gave me an "Okay, wise guy" sort of smile, put his arm over my shoulder, and said, "Russ, I'm always with you—just six months later."

As of this writing, it is not just six months, but more than four years later now and our troops are still in Iraq. Obama is president and has been for several years. I don't believe he would have won the nomination of the Democratic Party had he not been perceived as the most antiwar of the candidates. I voted for him in the Democratic primary in Wisconsin particularly because he had gone on record at the time of the invasion as saying it was a bad idea. Obama has lived up to his pledge to get us out of combat position in Iraq and I am hopeful that the full withdrawal he has promised will be implemented soon. It is now more than five years after the full withdrawal date I originally proposed in an old town hall in Marquette, Wisconsin, in August 2005. Late as it is, Obama deserves a lot of credit for this. But it is unfortunate that the president fell for the same "in for a penny, in for a pound" logic when he turned his attention to the Afghanistan intervention shortly after he assumed the presidency.

Like Barack Obama, I had often tried to highlight the mistaken basis for the Iraq intervention by trying to turn attention back to the region from where the attacks came on 9/11: Afghanistan and, more often now,

Pakistan. This was only part of my effort to get policymakers and the public to respond to the global threat Al Qaeda had become, and not just shift our focus from one country or region to another. Unfortunately, as campaign rhetoric and public opposition to the Iraq War grew, some came, absurdly, to refer to the Afghanistan intervention as "the good war." In my own race for reelection in 2004, all three of my potential Republican opponents questioned my commitment to the so-called war on terror, specifically criticizing my position on the Iraq War. I would speak of my initial support for the Afghan intervention and of the harm that the Iraq War did to our efforts there.

But as the 2008 election approached and two people I knew very well had been nominated to be the next president, I saw reports that the commanders in Afghanistan were going to seek a huge increase in troop numbers, as many as forty thousand more—despite the horrific strain that the Iraq War had already placed on our military. It was time to ask some hard questions about the wisdom of continuing that intervention, when it seemed almost certain that Osama bin Laden and his top lieutenants were no longer in Afghanistan. In September 2008, I asked my staff to arrange off-the-record phone calls with the top military people—from General Anthony Zinni to General John Abizaid—who had served in Afghanistan in recent years but had now left. I asked the same questions in each interview and was amazed by the total lack of consensus when they answered my question about why we would still have troops in Afghanistan or why more were needed. Some spoke of containing insurgents in certain key areas, a few spoke of training the military and others of training the police, while still others emphasized development or destroying the poppy crop. No one spoke with conviction about any connection to Al Qaeda and everyone seemed almost apologetic when they attempted to justify expanding our presence in what would soon become America's longest war. A few weeks before the election, I wrote a piece for the *Christian Science Monitor* titled "More US Troops in Afghanistan?" in the hope that the next president would at least pause before making a huge new troop commitment.

Barack Obama became president and did pause. Some say he paused too long and was too deliberate. I was pleased with the new president's caution; had my friend John McCain become president there would have been virtually no chance to refuse the military's request for tens of thousands of additional troops. I was also encouraged by well-confirmed reports that Vice President Joe Biden, with whom I had disagreed on Iraq, was forcefully leading the group that was advising Obama not to go deeper into this quagmire. Sadly, whether the military made a better case or whether the politics of withdrawal was just too scary for the president and his advisers so early in his term, they made the terrible decision to double down in Afghanistan. Once again we were there, we had to stay the course, any withdrawal had to be dictated by conditions on the ground—the Bush administration's aphoristic litany was simply recited again. There was little attempt to provide a rationale or even any serious connection to the international Al Qaeda network.

It hasn't always been so. Even in the turbulent Iraq- and Afghanistan-dominated years following 9/11, one American response to an international crisis might serve as a shining example of how to develop strategy, efficiently achieve a goal, and then leave. Maybe it was because President Bush had just visited sub-Saharan Africa. Or maybe it was because of our historical relationship with the nation in question. Maybe, unfortunately, it was because we tend not to take crises in Africa so seriously when it comes to our vision of our national security. Or maybe it was simply because the Bush administration felt safe to come out of a post-Iraq bunker mentality once they perceived that the situation did not obviously involve issues of Al Qaeda and Muslim populations. Whatever the reason or reasons, the Bush administration followed a quiet, deliberate, and effective strategy that led to an excellent result when it came to military action in Liberia. And this occurred just a couple of months after the Iraq invasion in 2003.

Americans have had a special relationship with the West African republic of Liberia ever since its founding by freed slaves from the United States in 1820. During the Cold War, the United States followed its usual blinkered approach when dealing with African nations, and readily supported

Samuel Doe when he seized control of Liberia in a bloody 1980 coup. Doe might have been the first indigenous president of Liberia, but we backed his regime primarily because of his anti-Soviet position. Ignoring the brutality of the regime and its outright theft of the 1985 elections, the United States contributed nearly $500 million in economic and military aid, effectively propping up Doe and his government. Not surprisingly, though, when the Cold War ended, the United States lost interest. Charles Taylor's rebellion ensued, and the nation descended into gruesome conflict. The United States simply evacuated American citizens and watched from the sidelines as the country tore itself apart. I witnessed this tragedy in person on my first visit to Africa, in May 1994, when I accompanied Senator Paul Simon of Illinois on a brief, harried visit to the nation's capital, Monrovia, and its ramshackle, battle-damaged presidential palace. After a few years of chaos, war-weary Liberians elected the even more brutal Charles Taylor as president in hopes of stopping the civil war. Taylor's criminality was not long confined to Liberia; he became the prime instigator of the conflict in Sierra Leone. He was the leading patron of the Revolutionary United Front (RUF) in Sierra Leone, a ruthless army that used thousands of children as slaves and soldiers. The RUF terrorized the people of Sierra Leone with their sadistic tactics, including their trademark: hacking off the limbs of men, women, children, and babies. This was the sad reality I had witnessed in refugee camps on a visit to Sierra Leone in 2001. The RUF supplied Taylor's regime with riches from Sierra Leone's diamond mines in exchange for military support and protection.

During my visit to Sierra Leone, I became the first American official to refer specifically to Charles Taylor as what he had become—a war criminal. I repeated this accusation on the floor of the Senate on my return home. Then, in early 2003, the Special Court for Sierra Leone, formed by the United Nations, unsealed an indictment formally charging him with war crimes. President Bush promptly called for Taylor to step down. But given the many headaches (self-inflicted and otherwise) that the administration was experiencing, there was little talk of military intervention to depose and arrest Taylor. On July 9, 2003, I urged taking action and said that "Taylor should have no veto over internationally backed US action. His days of dictating the destiny of the West African people are over." Using language that made it clear that I was eager to avoid another Iraq, I laid out my hopes about how that action might be taken:

> US action may involve sending American troops. But before making that decision, we need to answer several questions. I have not seen the scenarios or projections for any kind of action or intervention that have surely been worked up by the administration. I should see them. We should all see them. And we should see them sooner rather than later. And we need answers to the questions: Will United States' participation and leadership overstretch our resources? What are the costs? What commitments are we making? What is our exit strategy? And, what are our plans for the coordination of long-term stabilization efforts?

I concluded, voicing my fear that the action required here would end up as another overcommitment to military involvement:

> No one should understand my remarks today as some sort of "anything goes" endorsement of any and all proposals that may emerge. But I do believe that we must do something, and that we need to confront these questions quickly. . . . I urge the administration to begin undertaking consultations urgently so that we can move forward with an informed, effective, and timely response.

I assumed that my remarks would be ignored by the administration. Much to my surprise, not only did the administration pay attention to what I and others in Congress and the State Department had been saying, but it immediately began serious consultations, answering questions and genuinely seeking advice. Just one week after my statement on the floor, I and a few other members of Congress were asked to meet with President Bush in the Cabinet Room to discuss the situation. Given my opposition to the Iraq War and the Patriot Act, the invitation to a meeting in the White House surprised me. In addition to the president, those in attendance at this relatively small gathering included Vice President Cheney, Secretary of State Powell, Secretary of Defense Rumsfeld, and National Security Adviser Rice. What most impressed me was the president's demeanor—he was fully briefed on the situation in West Africa and spoke throughout the meeting without notes in a very engaged manner. When he finished his initial remarks he turned to me and said, "Russ, what should we do?"

I suggested a circumscribed military action that would involve repositioning parts of our naval fleet and ordering marines to enter Liberia on a limited basis to drive Taylor from his sanctuary. The discussion was cautious: The goal would be to drive Taylor from power, while ensuring that we didn't get caught in a long-term military commitment. Everyone had a chance to offer their views on this plan. This meeting exemplified how our system of government, with its built-in balance between the executive and legislative branches, really can work well in matters of war. What was even more important to me, though, was that the administration did act, commencing on July 25 with three navy ships full of marines repositioned off the Liberian coast. Taylor, who saw that he could not win, accepted an offer of safe haven from the government of nearby Nigeria and fled. A monster who had been terrorizing an entire region was gone from Liberia. In 2005, only a couple of years later, Liberia held clean elections and made Ellen Johnson Sirleaf its president, the first woman ever to lead an African country. And within just two months of her inauguration, Nigeria decided that Charles Taylor's time as a guest in their country was up and that his tenure as a prisoner in the dock at the International Criminal Court in The Hague should begin. And we had left Liberia without finding reasons to stick around with a continuing military presence.

Mission accomplished.

PART 2

MANIPULATING THE TRAUMA
OF 9/11

6

An Old Wish List of the FBI

Is there any senator in the chamber who desires to vote, or
who desires to change their vote? If not, the ayes are ninety-
six and the nays are one. The bill is passed.

The United States Senate chamber is a lot smaller than it looks on C-SPAN.
In fact it is almost cozy. That is something I immediately noticed the first
time I entered the floor in 1992, a newly elected senator. The walk from the
back of the floor to the well of the chamber is a very short one—you can do
it in a few steps or a leap or two. But on the evening of Thursday, October
11, 2001, as the final roll call began on the antiterrorism bill we had been
forced to finish that night, the walk to the well seemed long and slow. It felt
anything but cozy when the presiding officer asked for my vote on the bill
and I said, "No."

I always preferred to be seated in the back row on the Democratic side.
It was nearer to my staff, and Senator Ted Kennedy was often engaged in en-
tertaining banter a seat or two away. One of the best routines was Kennedy
tormenting Senator Jay Rockefeller for not contributing enough cash to
the Democrat candy drawer. Ted would hold up a fifty-dollar bill and say,
"Hey Jay!" as he dropped it in the box. I could see just about everyone in the

chamber from this perspective, whether I was giving a speech or just count-
ing votes in my head concerning an upcoming amendment. Sometimes
being in the back allowed me to avoid a colleague who was going to ask me
a question I didn't want to answer, since I could easily slip into one of the
ten old-fashioned phone booths in the adjoining Democratic cloakroom.
The full view of the chamber often made me think of the history that had
unfolded there. I enjoyed giving nighttime tours of the chamber and telling
visitors that the Senate had just moved into this very same room when the
nation was torn asunder by the Civil War. I would conclude those tours in
front of the desk of the senior senator from Mississippi. Today he is Thad
Cochran, but in April 1861 he was a man named Jefferson Davis. The desk
still bears the mark of a Union soldier's bayonet, made in a thrust of anger
after Davis had left the chamber with the other Southern senators who were
joining the Confederacy.

But when it came time to vote that October night, I left my desk and
walked down to the well to see for the first time in bold letters the con-
trived moniker this massive legislative freight train had been given: The
Uniting and Strengthening America (USA) by Providing Appropriate Tools
Required to Intercept and Obstruct Terrorism (PATRIOT) Act of 2001.
The congressional art form of giving controversial legislation titles that form
acronyms to make it that much harder to vote no had reached new heights.
I gulped and said, "No," without knowing if anyone would join me in pro-
testing this rush to judgment. I thought that perhaps Senator Dick Durbin
of Illinois, who was moving up the leadership ladder but had a great record
on civil liberties, might join me, especially after I had heard him voice some
concerns about the bill. In subsequent years Dick became one of my most
diligent and effective allies, as we tried each year to amend the Patriot Act.
In the end, no one else—not even those who had spoken for any of my
three amendments—voted no on the bill. Shortly after realizing this would
be the outcome and having returned to the back of the chamber, I heard
Senator Zell Miller of Georgia, the presiding officer, announce that "the
ayes are ninety-six and the nays are one. The bill is passed."

Several years later, I was interviewed by then comedian-celebrity and
now senator from Minnesota Al Franken on an Air America radio program.

Franken hyped my appearance just before I came on the air, saying I was a "hero" for having been the only senator to have voted no on the Patriot Act. As the introductory music faded, Franken said to me, "Boy, I bet you missed Paul Wellstone that day." I hesitated but knew that Franken's timing was off by a year, and then quietly said, "He was there." We then quickly moved on to a different topic.

For eighteen years I had the experience of walking out of my apartment building at 110 Maryland Avenue Northeast in Washington, DC, into reminders of major crises in American history. The land on which this building and the US Supreme Court Building across the street now stand was once used for a prison for some of the Lincoln assassination co-conspirators. It was also the site of the gallows on which Captain Wirz of the infamous Andersonville Prison was hanged. A few hundred feet away to the northeast is the seemingly out-of-place old redbrick Sewell-Belmont House, now a national women's history museum. During the War of 1812 it was the place where the American troops spent their last night in Washington before the British forces overwhelmed them. The next day, after subduing the Americans, the Redcoats marched to the US Capitol, just a couple of hundred yards away, and burned it down. Whenever I left or returned to my apartment, the elegantly rebuilt Capitol dome loomed, whether in brilliant sunshine or under a sky full of stars on a clear night.

Most of the time I thought of this neighborhood as simply the place where I went to work each day. But on September 12, 2001, I emerged from my apartment building knowing that the United States Senate was preparing to go back into session at that Capitol building, even though Al Qaeda had come extremely close to destroying it just twenty-four hours earlier. Senators had been told that we would each be afforded the opportunity to speak on the floor briefly to express our reactions to the previous day's events and to discuss a way forward. It seemed unlikely that many Americans would be focusing much attention on these speeches in the midst of all the fear and chaos that had engulfed the nation. Nevertheless, it seemed right to seize this first opportunity to set a tone that could serve us well in the coming weeks and months, as we began to adjust to an abrupt shift in our nation's priorities and reevaluate our relationship with the rest of the world.

Many senators spoke carefully and thoughtfully. The Senate on that day gave the appearance of a body that could take an entirely unexpected blow and respond with dignity, reason, and a certain measuredness. My own comments amounted to the equivalent of only a few paragraphs in the *Congressional Record,* but I wanted to make four points that had been uppermost in my thoughts as I joined so many Americans in spending a virtually sleepless night before. After expressing my condolences to all those who had suffered such great loss, and noting my visit to Pearl Harbor just three weeks earlier, I spoke of how irresistible it was to compare the events of September 11, 2001, to those of December 7, 1941. No one seemed to question the appropriateness of this comparison and I was moved by the historical connection to say, "Really, what it is about is an expression of gratitude and love across the generations but in different times in our history. Whether it be Pearl Harbor or yesterday's attack, the American people are asked to do extraordinary things—to defend our freedom."

In speaking of defending our freedom, I was trying to define several different ways in which we were being called upon to do so. By citing "two elements of resolve and two cautions," I was urging that a balance be struck between our determination to defeat those who were seeking to destroy our freedom by attacking us and the need to guard against undermining our own Constitution and freedoms as we responded to our enemies. We would need a "strong and aggressive military response when we were able to determine exactly whom we should be going after." And we should resolve not to make the mistake of allowing those who attacked us to drive a wedge between our nation and its allies in the world, including, in particular, the state of Israel. The cautions, on the other hand, included one that was echoed by many, that "this should not be an occasion for ill-treatment of Arab Americans, Muslim Americans, South Asians, or others in this country." The other caution was this: "As we look for answers and we look for solutions and we look for things we must do, domestically as well as externally, we must continue to respect our Constitution and our civil liberties in this country."

Noting my role as chairman of the Constitution Subcommittee of the Judiciary Committee, I recognized that "this is a different world with different technologies, different issues, and different threats." Yet I pleaded with my colleagues to examine every item proposed in response to these events, to be sure we were not rewarding "these terrorists by giving up our cherished freedoms that they do not believe in and that they would like to destroy."

At this point I did not consider my concerns to be beyond the obvious ones any member of Congress would have in a situation such as this. Within just a few weeks, however, it was only the last of these four points that seemed to be largely disregarded while so much care was given to "getting it right" on so many other matters. And, candidly, when it came to concerns about the US Constitution and civil liberties, I was not without my own doubts as I tried to imagine how the framers of our founding document would have reacted to these spectacular events. They were almost inconceivable even for us, and light-years away from the reality the framers lived in. Even in the latter hours of September 11, a phrase I had read in law school kept running through my mind: "The Constitution is not a suicide pact, the Constitution is not a suicide pact." To my chagrin, I could not remember what case it was from or even what it was about. So I asked my chief counsel on the Judiciary Committee, Robert Schiff, who just hours before was consumed with matters of campaign finance reform, to get me the case and reference as soon as possible. He returned quickly and I learned that the full context was even more relevant and pointed for those of us who had made much of our public careers about guarding against the undermining of civil liberties. "While the Constitution protects against invasions of individual right, it is not a suicide pact," the Court's opinion read. I took these words as a challenge to my concerns about civil liberties at such a momentous time in our history—that we must be careful not to take civil liberties so literally that we allow ourselves to be destroyed.

What really surprised and heartened me, though, upon reacquainting myself with this case, was its ruling or holding and the other language in the Court's opinion. In 1963, in *Kennedy v. Mendoza-Martinez,* a case concerning draft evasion, Justice Arthur Goldberg, in the United States Supreme Court's opinion, had made this famous "suicide pact" statement. But he did so in the course of ruling *in favor* of the civil liberties position. Justice Goldberg elaborated:

> It is fundamental that the great powers of Congress to conduct war and to regulate the Nation's foreign relations are subject to the constitutional requirements of due process. The imperative necessity for safeguarding those rights to procedural due process under the gravest of emergencies has existed throughout our constitutional history, for it is then, under the pressing exigencies of crisis, that there is the greatest temptation to dispense with fundamental constitutional guarantees which, it is feared, will inhibit government action. The Constitution of the United States is a law for rulers and people, equally in war and peace, and covers with the shield of its protection all classes of men, at all times, and under all circumstances. . . . In no other way can we transmit to posterity unimpaired the blessings of liberty, consecrated by the sacrifices of the Revolution.

As I read and reread these words in the days following September 11, 2001, I found them moving and even stirring, timely, reassuring, and ultimately useful as our government, with a Democratic majority in the Senate, disregarded these wise words and set itself on a path that led to the passage of the so-called USA Patriot Act.

Just as it was immediately obvious on September 11 itself that Congress would have to pass a resolution authorizing military and other actions to allow for the vigorous pursuit of Al Qaeda, it was not long until the need for new antiterrorism legislation became evident. From insufficient statute-of-limitation periods for certain terrorist crimes to ensuring that new kinds of terrorist crime such as bioterrorism were included in the criminal code, updating *was* needed. The complex set of new challenges that the attacks painfully highlighted meant that resources had to be beefed up for everything from the CIA to the FBI to the Immigration and Naturalization Service. Many stressed that legal barriers on information-sharing between the FBI and the CIA had to be revised, after embarrassing revelations about a "failure to connect the dots" when people were signing up at flight schools to learn how to fly a plane but not how to land it. Despite my watchful approach toward any unjustified broadening of the government's ability to intrude on the privacy of innocent Americans, I could not dispute, and did not want to dispute, the need to broaden the scope of certain existing wiretapping powers. For example, the current statute allowed wiretapping certain phone conversations under court supervision, but did not allow listening to voice-mail messages, because there were no voice mails when the law was first drafted. This was common sense, and frankly, most of the ideas that were being considered and that ultimately made it into the Patriot Act were exactly that—practical and measured responses to the reality of international terrorist threats in the earliest years of the twenty-first century. Just as I had enthusiastically supported the properly revised Authorization for the Use of Military Force passed just days after 9/11, I hoped to be able to help shape and then vote for a carefully crafted piece of antiterrorist legislation as well.

Then the Bush administration actually sent up a bill purporting to address these matters just a week after the 9/11 attacks. Both houses began their work on the bill. The House of Representatives moved more quickly, but also fairly thoughtfully. The House Judiciary Committee, still with a Republican majority, followed an open process of amendments and was able to incorporate some changes sensitive to the concerns that had been raised by the American Civil Liberties Union and others. This reflected the serious work of left-leaning Democrats such as Bobby Scott of Virginia and Jerry Nadler of New York, but also of the chairman of the committee, an erstwhile nemesis of mine in Wisconsin politics, Congressman F. James Sensenbrenner. I was relieved and pleased to see the improvements that the House committee had come up with and expected we could address even more concerns in an appropriately quick but genuine markup of the legislation in the Senate Judiciary Committee. This committee was chaired by Senator Patrick Leahy of Vermont, one of the Senate's most consistent voices for civil liberties. Unfortunately, the Democratic leadership caved in to pressure from the administration and we were never afforded the opportunity to take up the bill in committee. Instead it was simply rushed to the floor of the Senate.

Understanding the urgency of this legislation and its potential threat to civil liberties, and wanting to be ready for what I anticipated would be full committee consideration, I immediately held a hearing of my Constitution Subcommittee on October 3. Titled "Protecting Constitutional Freedoms in the Face of Terrorism," the hearing aired a carefully selected list of concerns. It was just after this, however, that the process deteriorated into closed-door negotiations between the administration and congressional leaders, with only a handful of members in a position to influence the direction of the legislation. As the bill was being rushed to the floor, I took the fairly unusual step of calling a former Senate colleague of mine and now attorney general, John Ashcroft, to raise some of my objections. Despite his well-earned reputation as a hard-line conservative, I had found Ashcroft to be a surprisingly affable and sometimes open-minded colleague during his tenure on the Senate Judiciary Committee. He had listened to my concerns about racial profiling in law enforcement, when he chaired the Constitution Subcommittee. My vote to confirm him as President Bush's attorney general was certainly one of the most difficult of my career, for it generated genuine rage and feelings of betrayal in thousands of my supporters in Wisconsin and around the country. Once again, however, John Ashcroft—although he later made some outrageous comments before the Judiciary Committee about people wrongly imagining "phantoms of lost liberty"—did not let me down. He wasn't just a polite listener. He knew I was sufficiently concerned about the shape this bill was taking that I might use certain procedural rights I had as senator to slow down the bill. We went over some of the provisions carefully and he agreed that some of my points were at least reasonable. "I hardly agree with you on anything, Russ, but I want you to be able to support this bill." He then told me he would seek some of these changes. I reported to the Democratic leadership staff in the Senate Democratic Cloakroom that Ashcroft had agreed to these changes. A young staffer just laughed at me and said, "That's not happening." As we later learned, not only did the White House block any further changes, including those endorsed by its chief law enforcement officer, but it was also increasingly apparent that the Senate majority Democratic leadership was part and parcel of this "deal." This helped set the tone for a process that questioned the patriotism and resolve of anyone who challenged any part of the bill, even before it was given its provocative name: the USA Patriot Act.

In the end, the process that led to the passage of the Patriot Act was as truncated and unprofessional as the process to pass the Authorization for the Use of Military Force was careful and historically sensitive. On the Patriot Act, the White House and the congressional leadership just decided to draft the bill on their own. Senator Leahy, as chair of the Judiciary Committee, tried valiantly to soften some of the more extreme proposals made by the administration, but he was outmatched in the secret negotiation process. The bill in its entirety was then presented to the Senate as a nonnegotiable document: It had completely bypassed the full Senate committee process. This was legislation on the fly, unlike anything I had ever seen in a career of some eighteen years of legislating. Not only was the process disturbing and one of the first indications of the mistakes that were to multiply in the years to come, but it was done with inappropriate speed, given the range of matters covered in the extensive legislation. Some urgency was certainly justified, but many members of the Senate have since admitted that they had never read or even gained a basic understanding of what was in the Patriot Act, partly because there was so little time to review it. Just as members started to hear concerns from groups and individuals who were trying to follow this piece of legislative greased lightning, the leadership in the Senate announced it would not only bring up the bill immediately, but also propose an agreement to have just a few hours of debate and a final vote, with absolutely no amendments allowed.

To pass this bill without considering even a single amendment to a document that exceeded two hundred pages of criminal, intelligence, and military-related provisions, when the bill had not been seriously reviewed by the Senate Judiciary Committee, seemed tantamount to abandoning any semblance of a real legislative process. Equally troubling to me was that there would be no opportunity to call public attention to the serious constitutional problems with the bill, including the unnecessary breadth and sheer sloppiness of some of the provisions proposed. As chairman of the Constitution Subcommittee and someone who had sought to become a US senator so I could work to protect the integrity of the Constitution, I felt I had no choice but to try to prevent this error. As important as much of this bill was to making sure we had all the tools necessary to fight Al Qaeda and other terrorist threats, I felt I had to let people know what was being slipped through the Congress. The only power I had left in order to keep my oath to uphold the Constitution was the right given to every senator on each piece of legislation: the power to object. So, on October 9, I filed an objection to the unanimous-consent request to vote on the bill in a few hours with no amendments.

With this objection, I found myself at odds with many colleagues I admired and with whom I had been working smoothly in the challenging post-9/11 weeks. It also brought about one of the most difficult exchanges I ever had with a colleague. Senator Tom Daschle of South Dakota had become majority leader in part because of his polite and unfailingly calm demeanor. We were not close (I had not supported him for leader on two occasions) but we often worked closely together, especially on issues related to campaign finance reform, where the support of the Democratic Caucus was critical to my bipartisan efforts with John McCain. When Daschle got wind of my objection to the unanimous consent agreement, he came flying across the hall from the majority leader's office to confront me on an essentially empty Senate floor. I was consulting with some of my staff members, who were on the red staff benches behind a wooden bar at the back of the Senate chamber. He did not ask to confer with me privately and spoke in a tone that one rarely hears from a colleague in this sometimes artificial but very polite body: "I just got Senator Byrd to sign off; now I have to deal with you." Daschle simply demanded that I drop my objection. I turned to my chief of staff, Mary Irvine, who said, "I'm not hearing an offer."

I tried to explain to him some of the amendments that addressed the specific concerns I had after having carefully read the bill. Daschle wouldn't hear it. He did make the legitimate point that opening up the bill to amendments could make it worse if any Democrats supported harsh Republican amendments. This would further intrude on the civil liberties of law-abiding

Americans. I suggested we could ask our Democratic colleagues to stick together on something like this, as we had done on the Authorization for the Use of Military Force. Clearly feeling the political heat and overall pressure from the constant demands on him in the weeks following 9/11, Daschle seemed uninterested in pursuing my ideas. In fact, he was obviously enraged with me and let our mutual staffers know it as he stalked out of the chamber. Later, in response to my concerns and objection, the majority leader stated that he wasn't just disappointed in his caucus member from the Judiciary Committee—he was "very disappointed." Our feelings were mutual.

Looking back at this incident now, I can think of no better example of the suffocating atmosphere in the Senate during the process that led to the passage of the USA Patriot Act than those angry moments with someone I considered a valued colleague. In the end, because I refused to drop my objection to unanimous consent, the leadership had to agree to let me offer a few amendments, but only if all of them were done together on the night of October 11 and under very short time agreements, as opposed to open debate. They didn't want even this but knew that if they had to overcome my unanimous-consent objection they would have to go through the much lengthier process of getting cloture on the bill. This not only meant getting sixty votes, a supermajority, but it would have also taken several days. For my part, I was not happy with the limited number of amendments, the short time agreements, and the rushed hour for the debate, but I realized it would provide the only opportunity publicly to raise concerns about this bill and force a few votes on it. It was never my intention to try to filibuster the bill; I wanted it fixed so I could support it. That is why Senator Daschle's dismissive attitude toward my amendments was a particularly black mark on the Democratic-controlled US Senate—by the time I offered them, there was a unanimous-consent agreement allowing only my amendments, so there was no longer a danger of any amendments that Daschle had postulated "could make it worse."

When the debate began, I set out my position on my first amendment, which concerned computer trespass issues, that is, making sure a terrorist who had hacked into a computer network could be identified and pursued. I sought to demonstrate that this provision was so broadly drafted as to include such innocent actions as online shopping for Christmas presents at work against an employer's rules. A reasonable debate ensued with the ranking member of the Senate Judiciary Committee, Senator Orrin Hatch, a Republican from Utah who opposed the amendment. Senator Arlen Specter of Pennsylvania, who was then also a Republican and one of the most respected minds on the Judiciary Committee, actually spoke in favor of my amendment. We were about to yield back a little time and get on to debating the next amendment when Senator Daschle sought recognition and repeated his notion that if we opened the bill to amendment it would only get worse in terms of protecting civil liberties. Again, this made no sense because the Senate had already limited the amendments only to those I had insisted on having the opportunity to offer, all of which were seeking to protect civil liberties.

Senator Daschle was even more blunt, and certainly more candid, when, in response to my first amendment, he decided to address all of my amendments in one fell swoop even before I had offered the rest of them. He conceded that his "argument is not substantive, it is procedural." He went on to say, in what we all liked to call the greatest deliberative body in the world, "I hope my colleagues will join me tonight in tabling this amendment and tabling every other amendment that is offered, should he choose to offer them tonight." My colleagues were not only being told to vote against my amendments; they were being told, despite bipartisan support for some of them, to do so for no substantive reason. The message could not have been more clear: Do not vote on the merits, just keep moving the bill, no matter what the cost to our Constitution. Needless to say, I was not pleased. Although no match for Daschle in his generally calm and sunny demeanor, I don't think I was perceived by my colleagues as quick to anger. But this time, I *was* angry and responded to my leader's request in what I hope was an appropriate expression of outrage.

> Madam President, on this bill there was not a single moment
> of markup or vote in the Judiciary Committee. I accepted that
> because of the crisis our nation faces. This is the first substan-

tive amendment in the Senate on this entire issue, one of the most important civil liberties bills of our time, and the majority leader has asked senators to not vote on the merits of the issue. I understand the difficult task he has, but I must object to the idea that not one single amendment on this issue will be voted on the merits on the floor of the Senate. What have we come to when we don't have either committee or Senate deliberation on amendments on an issue of this importance?

After this exchange, the Senate continued to work our way through my amendments as allowed under the time agreement. There was a brief debate on each, including one in which then Tennessee Senator Fred Thompson bucked the Republican Caucus and spoke in favor of one of my amendments. I was grateful for these acknowledgments that something was needed to prevent this bill from being jammed through without proper consideration. This was indeed an intimidating time, and I was particularly impressed when one of the most recent additions to the Democratic Caucus courageously delivered one of her first addresses as a senator in favor of some of my amendments. Senator Maria Cantwell of Washington had just been elected by a razor-thin margin in a race against a powerful Republican incumbent, Senator Slade Gorton, who certainly would have helped lead the charge for the Patriot Act and would have fought all amendments. After winning in a recount, Cantwell put us in a position to tie with the Republicans, and that enabled the subsequent party switch by Vermont Senator Jim Jeffords to give us the majority in April 2001. Yet we only picked up a handful of votes, including a Republican or two, on each of the amendments. Under the unanimous consent agreement, as soon as all the amendments were voted on and defeated, we had to vote immediately on final passage of the bill in the Senate. It would be sent straight to the House or to conference committee. Within only fourteen days it had passed both Houses in its final form and was sent to President Bush for his signature.

I will always marvel at the way in which ordinary people in Wisconsin and around the country intuited that something was fishy about the USA Patriot Act. One of the only communications I actually received from my constituents concerning the Patriot Act was a petition from well over one hundred students and other Amnesty International activists at the University of Wisconsin–Eau Claire asking that "any proposals that might curtail freedoms Americans have always cherished should be examined carefully." This was delivered to me in my office in Washington in a yellow envelope postmarked October 1. I was surprised to get it and even more surprised to see that the first name on the petition was Jessica Feingold, my older daughter.

Given the tremendous fear and confusion generated by the 9/11 attacks on our own soil, I assumed it would take a long time for people to figure out that parts of the Patriot Act had little or nothing to do with these particular terrorist attacks or even with terrorism in general. Some, who had a historical perspective on these matters, could tell that something unusual was going on. Conservative columnist Robert Novak pointed out that aspects of the legislation included an "old wish list of the FBI" that would never have passed prior to 9/11. But how could people throughout the country be familiar with the often arcane details of the provisions in the bill that unjustifiably threatened their privacy? Presumably most people did not actually read the bill. I had read it as carefully as possible as it was being rushed through Congress, but most of my colleagues had not, and certainly did not have time to absorb the intricacies of, for example, so-called pen register provisions and "national security letters." I had essentially no knowledge of these matters before seeing this proposal. Somehow, though, people seemed suspicious of the process employed to pass the bill and were open to discovering that the administration was overreaching in a supercharged, fearful environment. Interestingly, these suspicions preceded the Iraq credibility debacle that followed a year or so later.

The people were right. These general suspicions and instinctive desires not to give up constitutional freedoms unnecessarily were justified by a range of provisions that were included in the Patriot Act. But what was this talk of violations of civil liberties all about? Perhaps the provision of the act most cited to illustrate the abuses in the bill was Section 215, the "Business

Records" provision. The criticism gained popular recognition in part because Section 215 allowed broad authority to obtain the records of individuals, including their public library records; in other words what books they checked out and what they chose to read. This ignited the rage of a group of people it is best not to enrage—the librarians of America. Through the leadership of the American Library Association, which typically lobbies legislators for funding for libraries and reading programs, this provision was exposed for what it was—an unnecessarily sweeping authority not at all tied to terrorist suspects. Rather, it seemed an open-ended means to get anyone's records. John Ashcroft criticized the librarians for being "hysterical," which led to a proliferation of buttons with the motto "Another hysterical librarian for the Constitution."

While the Section 215 authority was supposed to be limited to terrorism investigations under the Foreign Intelligence Surveillance Act (FISA), it removed the previous requirement that the records sought had "to pertain to a foreign power or agent of a foreign power." This was a crucial limitation in a statute that authorizes secret investigations supervised by a secret court, the Foreign Intelligence Surveillance Court, which even now Chief Justice John Roberts admitted—in response to my question at his confirmation hearings— he was surprised to find existed. In other words, the new provision turned a carefully drafted 1970s statute into an invitation for fishing expeditions concerning anyone's private papers and records, just so long as the records are "sought for" a foreign intelligence or terrorism investigation. And the secret court established by the Foreign Intelligence Surveillance Act was given no discretion to deny these requests on any basis, whether the lack of relevance of the records to terrorists or even the absence of any suspicion about the person whose records were requested. Add to this the fact that the custodian of the records, for example a librarian, was prohibited from telling anyone—and specifically the person whose records were taken—anything about the investigation. One can obviously see why the librarians of the nation were in an uproar soon after the bill was passed.

Congress was right to update the law to allow business records to be subpoenaed under FISA. However, by eliminating the requirement that records actually pertain to the target of a legitimate investigation, the law was permanently open to abuse. Fearful that not only travel and hotel records but also the records of doctors, librarians, and booksellers who served completely innocent Americans could be obtained at the whim of the FBI, I offered an amendment during the brief Patriot Act debate to limit this. That failed, but we managed to keep language, known as a sunset, that put a time limit on Section 215. We tried year after year to rein in this dangerous authority. The administration prevailed every time, claiming that the new powers in Section 215 were a crucial tool in the fight against terrorism. Yet I noticed that none of the advocates for this measure blushed—even slightly—when it was revealed that this supposedly crucial provision had not been used even once between October 26, 2001, and September 18, 2003, two very critical years in the fight against global terrorism. But there it continues to sit in our laws, nothing more than a rubber stamp for invasive and unconstitutional FBI activity.

Let me turn now to an example where the overly broad provision, justified as necessary for terrorism cases, has been extensively used, but not for terrorism cases. The Fourth Amendment to the United States Constitution contains one of the most cherished freedoms in the entire Bill of Rights. It provides that no American can be subjected to "unreasonable searches and seizures" without proper notice. This was inspired by the Founders' bitter resentment of the British colonial authorities' practice of entering residences and businesses at will and without a search warrant under the pretext of criminal investigation. Throughout our history, the Fourth Amendment has protected the privacy of Americans' homes and property; if the police come to your door and want to have a look around, you have the right to say, "Do you have a search warrant?" Given the popularity of crime-related television shows and movies in our culture, this is familiar to virtually every American. Still, the practice arose in some jurisdictions in the decades before September 11, 2001, of allowing limited exceptions to this rule in various narrowly defined "emergency" situations.

Courts in some regions of the country doubted the constitutionality of these searches-without-notice, while others permitted a short period (usu-ally seven days) during which they could be conducted, and then only with court approval. If a necessity were shown, court-approved renewal of the permission for a "secret search" might be allowed for another tightly limited period. These surreptitious intrusions came to be known as "sneak and peek" searches and, simply put, they meant that the police or the FBI or some other authorized government authority could determine that you weren't home, enter your residence and business, search the premises, and not tell you they had been there at all. This exception to the clear mandates of the Fourth Amendment, an exception also known as "delayed notification," was allowed if a court was convinced that prior notification would have adverse results such as endangering the life or physical safety of an individual, or causing a flight from prosecution, destruction of or serious tampering with evidence, or the intimidation of potential witnesses. Before the passage of Section 213 of the Patriot Act there had been general agreement among the various circuit courts that sneak-and-peek searches could be permitted in certain circumstances, but the different circuits did not agree on one set of standards and rules for these presumably rare unnoticed searches.

The USA Patriot Act was used as a vehicle to fulfill the "wish list" of the FBI and other federal authorities to make the rules for sneak-and-peek searches not only uniform but also as permissive and open-ended as possible. It was only in the highly charged environment of the weeks following 9/11 that such sweeping and constitutionally dubious changes could so easily be codified in the federal statutes. As I read Section 213, I discovered that the administration had adopted the expansive standards of the Second Circuit (New York) cases. These included the justifications listed above, as well as an extremely broad, catch-all exception that allowed secret searches simply if *not* allowing the search would "seriously jeopardize an investigation or unduly delay a trial." How the plain language of the Bill of Rights could support such a vague and limitless grant of power to the authorities was beyond me. But what was particularly alarming was that there was a naked and successful effort to allow this broad authority for *any* investigations, not just terrorism cases. The only reason the entire bill was being considered was that we had been suddenly and brutally attacked by foreign-based terrorists.

Despite that, Section 213 blatantly failed to limit this significant government power to terrorism cases; there were no limitations to case type at all.

During the rush to pass the Patriot Act, I attempted to raise concerns
about these new sneak-and-peek provisions and sought unsuccessfully to
offer an amendment that would at least narrow Section 213. I was willing to
agree to some standardization of sneak-and-peek rules as they related to terrorism cases. While a threat to life, flight, or destruction of evidence seemed
understandable grounds for this codification, it seemed far too easy for the
government to justify its actions in *any* case, whether terrorist-related or
not, by asserting, for example, that a trial would be delayed or that somehow
an investigation would be jeopardized. In the years after the passage of the
Patriot Act, in some respects Section 213 caused more controversy than any
of its other provisions.

A bipartisan group of us tried to revise it by bringing it within justifiable
limits through the Reasonable Notice and Search Act and as a portion of
the so-called Safe Act. In the course of doing so, we learned that as of April
2003, more than one and a half years after 9/11, the administration had
reported obtaining these "delayed notification" warrants forty-seven times
and not a single one had been in connection with a terrorism investigation!

Moreover, it turned out that the government was routinely requesting
initial periods of ninety days for the delay of notice, rather than the previous normal grant of seven days. Apparently the courts weren't yet granting
such long delays, but the attempt further illustrates what an unrelated and
dramatic power grab the new sneak-and-peek provisions represented. In a
time of national crisis relating to largely external terrorism threats, the FBI
and other authorities were placing a high priority on expanding their powers
in general and exploiting those powers across the whole range of domestic
cases. This seemed to me to be a troubling bait-and-switch in a climate
that demanded caution and balance, not a "let's get all we can get now"
approach.

A third example of how extreme some of the provisions of the USA
Patriot Act were involves something we weren't able to flag and carefully
review before the legislation was passed in October 2001. A practice known
as issuing "national security letters" (NSL) was authorized by the legislation

and was later proven to have been aggressively and often recklessly used by FBI agents across the country. Prior to the Patriot Act, in a FISA investigation having to do with counterintelligence or international terrorism, the FBI had the power to obtain certain records from telephone companies and Internet providers simply on the written request of a senior FBI official, without a court order. Therefore, unlike the sneak-and-peek searches, which required a court order, agents could effectively act on their own. Before the Patriot Act, the FBI was also required to certify that the information sought in the requested records related to a suspected terrorist or spy.

Under Section 505, the USA Patriot Act expanded the National Security Letter Authority well beyond its previous limits by eliminating the so-called individualized suspicion requirement. Now all the FBI had to do was certify that the information sought in the NSL was "relevant to an authorized investigation to protect against international terrorism or clandestine intelligence activities." For the first time these non-court-approved orders from the FBI allowed access to records of both suspected terrorists and persons who had no connection to terrorism at all. So, while the authorities were limited only to terrorism cases, there could be a vast expansion of government fishing expeditions. This was possible so long as the government claimed, without any showing of evidence, that the records sought were related to an investigation, even if the targeted person was not connected to terrorism or had not been engaged in any wrongdoing at all. Moreover, under the NSL authority, a recipient of an NSL demand was forbidden from disclosing that he, she, or it had received such a letter, except possibly to a lawyer.

Indeed, this authority under Section 505 led to one of the most embarrassing moments for the government after 9/11. Apologists for anything the government wanted to do in this area constantly hounded critics of the Patriot Act with the mantra "show us one abuse, show us one abuse." Of course, this was extremely difficult to do given the combination of classified and secret investigations coupled with statutory gag orders on those who may have experienced an abuse. But the dam broke when the Justice Department had to face the carefully documented but damning report published in March 2007 by the inspector general of the department, Glenn Fine, titled "A Review of the Federal Bureau of Investigation's Use of National Security Letters." The report showed that FBI practice had run amok as the new NSL authorities were relentlessly and even sloppily used by unsupervised agents who sometimes didn't even photocopy them before issuing a demand on what was often an innocent American. I will never forget how sheepish but straightforward the director of the FBI, Robert Mueller, was when he called me the evening before the report was issued to tell me of its contents and to say I was right to have been worried about this inadequately checked authority. The fact that the director, whom I regard as one of the best and most honest public servants I've worked with, couldn't control his agents with such unsupervised power had less to do with a lack of leadership on his part and more to do with a legislative failure to write adequate safeguards into the statute in the first place.

For years the Bush administration had insisted there had been no abuses and that critics, like myself and the ACLU, were wrong. It mostly stopped doing that once the inspector general's report on abuses related to national security letters came out. Those abuses proved our point—the need for better checks on executive branch discretion and particularly judicial oversight. We subsequently proposed significant changes to the NSL authority in the SAFE Act and other bills that were never enacted despite the documented abuses. And as to the use of "sneak and peek" searches? That authority was used thousands of times post–Patriot Act. Were those abuses? It's hard to know given the classified or confidential nature of so much of this activity. In any event, time has shown that the amendments I originally offered were sensible, moderate, and consistent with the checks and balances of our governmental system and the protections of individual freedom that are so important in the Constitution. Just because no one knows about an abuse doesn't mean that there haven't been some or many or that it is unnecessary or wrong to protect against them. In fact, it is the job of elected representatives to do such oversight and demand such accountability.

A Pre-1776 Mindset

John, first of all, is there any way you guys could at least mention the Constitution?

Despite the Bush administration's apparent insensitivity to factual accuracy and disregard for the Constitution, not everyone on their team was always so reckless. I just mentioned FBI Director Robert Mueller, a former federal judge, who tried earnestly to answer my questions. He seemed to understand my responsibility to insist on legal compliance by agencies such as the FBI. I found the director helpful in several settings: public hearings of the Judiciary Committee, private briefings to the Intelligence Committee, and private meetings in my office. The latter included such delicate matters as the Somali population in the Twin Cities and the problem of young men from that community returning to Somalia to make jihad. While I didn't always agree with him, Mueller struck me as someone who was not in cahoots with the Bush-Cheney inner circle. He seemed to be one administration official who wanted to get it right in terms of dealing with terrorism. He was sensitive to how posterity would regard the *way* we went about that fundamental task.

This takes me to what we might call the Strange Case of John Ashcroft.

One of the first people to call me after I was defeated in 2010 was this Republican, the former state attorney general and governor of Missouri, US senator, and ultimately attorney general of the United States under George W. Bush. John had always seemed more approachable and affable than most of my colleagues. So I felt comfortable enough when he called me that November to say, "I'm sorry you lost," to respond, "John, that's okay, I mean you once got beat by a dead guy." (Ashcroft lost his Senate seat in 2000 to Governor Mel Carnahan of Missouri, who, unfortunately, had died in a plane crash a couple of weeks before.) While John and I conversed, I remembered watching him running up the US Senate steps at full speed, with sweating younger aides stumbling after him with their arms full of binders and books. I initially expected to have nothing in common with this guy, a member of the radical right that started descending on Washington in droves in 1994, the Contract with America year. We developed a good rapport, though, and one night John invited me over to his house after session for some ice cream (he doesn't drink alcohol, for religious reasons). The brief ride in his car to his place on Capitol Hill, where he and his wife lived when they were in Washington, was hair-raising. He was a terrible driver, and that comes from someone who could use improvement in this area as well. Once safely inside, we talked while we ate ice cream. I don't believe I've ever seen anyone consume that much ice cream in one sitting. I walked home that night wondering how someone who seemed so friendly could be such a hard-core right-winger. Whenever I spoke with John directly I sensed that he, like Mueller, sincerely wanted to get things right.

That perception of Ashcroft contributed to my controversial vote to let his nomination go through the Senate Judiciary Committee in early 2001. Many Democrats and progressives were still seething from what was, with some justification, viewed as Bush's theft of the White House. And now Feingold's going to help Bush make one of the biggest right-wingers in the country his attorney general? I would never have chosen Ashcroft for the post. And he, of course, would never have chosen me. But I believe in the principle that the president—any president—has the right to pick people of his own ideological orientation to be in his cabinet. As the events after 9/11 unfolded, I began to fear that Ashcroft was just part of the team, or worse. The envelope was pushed time and again well beyond what was necessary to pursue terrorists, much to the detriment of civil liberties. Indeed, his remarks about librarians fueling "baseless hysteria" and people seeing "phantoms of lost liberty" were among the most ill-chosen of the era. I found, however, that Ashcroft was willing to listen and try to understand my objections, not only when he agreed to help address some of my concerns with the Patriot Act, but also in the weeks and months after that. In January 2002 he invited me to meet with a pretty tough bunch at the Justice Department, including Solicitor General Ted Olson, whose wife, Barbara, had died on one of the hijacked 9/11 airplanes. After a meal in his elegant dining room there, Ashcroft let me set out at length my concerns about a lot of things the Justice Department had been doing. Then we all got down to a good, substantive, and polite discussion.

It was also unexpected when John asked me to have dinner with him to "just talk a little" about what had been going on since 9/11. I certainly wasn't receiving invitations like this from any other Bush administration officials. We agreed to have dinner at Full Kee, a wonderful, earthy restaurant in Chinatown that I had come to like and where Ashcroft regularly ate lunch. I took Mary Irvine along so she could let people know if I were shipped off to Guantánamo for my frequent criticism of the Patriot Act and other administration policies. When we got there, a huge Secret Service security guard was blocking the outer door of the restaurant. As we entered, we passed the unlucky Peking ducks hanging in the window and were escorted to the lower level, which had been cleared for us. After we ordered and made small talk, I watched Ashcroft match and then exceed my hard-earned reputation for eating a lot of food quickly—the victim being a massive helping of General Tso's chicken. Then as we sipped tea, John asked me what I thought they could be doing differently. What I had to say to the attorney general of the United States was this: "John, to begin with, is there any way you guys could at least mention the Constitution of the United States when you're doing some of these things?" It was a serious comment, but one delivered in a slightly flippant way. He took it in good humor and said "Yes," and then we discussed the importance of reassuring Americans that we did not intend to let Al Qaeda weaken our commitment to the basic principles of our country.

Years later it was revealed that John Ashcroft had stood up for the rule of law in one of the most difficult circumstances imaginable. In March 2004, he was in George Washington University Hospital after surgery to remove his gallbladder. While Ashcroft was still under the influence of the drugs used for the procedure, Alberto Gonzales, counsel to the president and later attorney general himself, tried to take advantage of the situation. He and his minions turned up at Ashcroft's hospital bed with the intention of getting him to sign off on reauthorization of some of the plainly illegal warrantless wiretapping methods that were later to explode in the face of the Bush administration. The ailing Ashcroft simply refused. This was a courageous act for a man of whom few would have expected such a response on such an issue. I have *many* reservations about the positions taken and decisions made by Ashcroft over the years. Yet there is something about the way he tried to conduct himself across party and ideological lines in this critical time in our history. It sometimes makes me wish we had more like him in Washington from both parties.

The passage of the USA Patriot Act was hurried and flawed and some of its provisions are dangerous. In the nearly ten years since the bill became law, they have not been properly narrowed or eliminated. However, this act was passed by Congress and signed into law by the president in public. The American people could find out what it said and at least inquire about how it was being implemented. Its provisions could be challenged in court, as long and difficult and often unsuccessful as that process might be. Several of us in the Senate and House tried on many occasions to debate those provisions and change them through legislation; some of the most objectionable provisions have been sunsetted, that is, they expire unless explicitly renewed by a date certain. And those efforts continue in both houses of the Congress after my departure from the Senate, due to the bold work of people like Senator Ron Wyden of Oregon and Senator Mark Udall of Colorado.

Both Ron and Mark are currently members of the Senate Select Committee on Intelligence, Mark having taken the spot on the committee I vacated in 2011. They went to the floor of the Senate in the first half of that year to warn the American people that certain aspects of the USA Patriot Act were being exploited. In Wyden's words, "When the American people find out how their government has secretly interpreted the Patriot Act, they are going to be stunned and they are going to be angry," and would be even more so if they had the classified information these senators had been exposed to as members of the committee. Unlike the provisions of the act itself, the classified details of the resulting practices could not be discussed publicly and I recognized the frustration these senators experienced as they tried elliptically to warn us that something was very wrong. But at least they, the duly elected representatives of people of the United States, know about these practices and can try to change them by legislation or by seeking declassification of the information to expose the problem. Neither approach is ever easy. But, again, at least they know what's going on. This, however, was not the case years earlier when I joined the Senate Intelligence Committee after an opening occurred with the departure of Senator Jon Corzine, who left the Senate to become governor of New Jersey.

I will always be grateful to Harry Reid for keeping his word that he would award me the next available slot on this committee. Frankly, I had never been interested in joining prior to 9/11. And choosing me was no easy matter because Senator Joe Biden, then the ranking member of the Foreign Relations Committee, had decided to ask for it. Harry stuck with me even though many assumed I wanted to join the committee to raise hell about post-9/11 civil liberty concerns. Indeed I did want to do that and did so on a regular basis within the cloistered walls of the committee room. But this was not my primary purpose in joining the committee. I wanted to know as much as I could, in as much detail as possible, about Al Qaeda and other threats to the American people so I could more effectively pursue my concerns about our post-9/11 strategies. So the first major issue I confronted on that committee came as something of a shock—it related to the foundation of our Constitution itself. Unbeknownst to most members of the intelligence committees, to virtually all members of the Congress, and of course to the American public, the Bush administration had embarked after 9/11 on one of the greatest assaults on the Constitution in the history of our country: a warrantless wiretapping program that directly conflicted with the plain language of FISA (Foreign Intelligence Surveillance Act of 1978).

The lightning-bolt revelation of the secret program came from a highly accurate investigation by the *New York Times,* the story of which was published on December 16, 2005. It revealed that President Bush, backed by his lawyers in the Office of Legal Counsel of the Justice Department, led by John Yoo, had concocted a series of bogus justifications to allow the government, through the National Security Agency (NSA), to eavesdrop electronically on thousands of American citizens without a warrant. This was in contradiction to the Fourth Amendment to the US Constitution, the amendment that protects "the right of the people to be secure in their persons, houses, papers and effects against unreasonable searches," unless a warrant "upon probable cause" is issued. The program also directly conflicted with the plain words of the FISA law, which provided "the exclusive means" by which exceptions to the general rule could be made. The White House simply disregarded this law and first asserted absurdly that it could somehow do this under the narrowed language of the AUMF of September 2001, and, more threatening to the Constitution, under the president's general commander-in-chief powers in Article II of the US Constitution. After the government's rush to judgment on the Patriot Act and the Iraq War, this can in retrospect be seen as more of the same. The Bush administration consistently dodged any attempt to address post-9/11 challenges from a position of national unity or consensus. But that is to miss the point of how different this power grab felt at the time and how significant a blow it was to our system of checks and balances for the long term. This was a whole new level of intrusiveness, a secret government program that meant that if you got a call from your uncle in Poland, or wanted to speak to your daughter doing a junior year abroad in Leeds, England, or gave an interview to a journalist calling from overseas, or wanted to hear the personal comments of your son risking his life for his country in Ramadi, Iraq, the US government claimed that it had the right to listen in, and record essentially whatever it wanted, whenever it wanted.

The timing of the revelation was not good for the Bush administration, which was already under fire for the way in which it started the Iraq War and allowed it to drag on, and because suspicions about the questionable provisions of the USA Patriot Act were growing all over America. I found objections to the Patriot Act to be among the most consistent themes at my town meetings in Wisconsin at this time. What was even more difficult for the White House was that populist pressure from very conservative elements in states like Idaho, Montana, and Alaska began to catch on to the invasive nature of the "records" provisions of the act. When people across the country learned that there was a secret program more than four years old that could lead to unwarranted eavesdropping on them, they were not amused. It wasn't just peacenik liberals in Berkeley and Madison who were unhappy, but gun owners and libertarians in Missoula and Nome.

The timing was also bad for the administration because the story broke just as I was leading an effort, again with Harry Reid's help, to stop the reauthorization of the USA Patriot Act unless key changes were made. I had personally compiled a vote count that showed we were within one or two votes of being able to get the forty-one votes we needed to prevent cloture on the renewal bill. But when I went to bed on Thursday, December 15, I had to assume that the administration would somehow get the votes it needed. Still, I really wanted to give it a good shot. When the story that "Bush Lets US Spy on Callers without Courts" broke the next morning, we were heading into a relatively rare Friday voting session. As the news filtered through the chamber, everything changed. Chuck Schumer of New York, about whom I had held out just the slimmest of hopes, declared that this had put him over the top in terms of trusting this administration: "Today's revelation that the government listened in on thousands of phone conversations without getting a warrant is shocking and has greatly influenced my vote." Even Arlen Specter, whose job it was as the Republican chairman of the Senate Judiciary to block my efforts and get the bill passed, couldn't stomach any more, either. Specter said, "It is inexcusable to have spying on people in the United States without court surveillance in violation of our law, beyond any question." The vote was taken shortly after Specter's remarks. We prevailed.

Senator Harry Reid hurriedly called a celebratory news conference that he asked all Democratic senators to attend. Harry began the news conference crowing about the vote in terms that made even me wince when he said, "We have killed the Patriot Act." (I had spent years explaining that my goal was to fix its noxious provisions, not completely repeal it.) It was a rare if short-lived victory over the administration just before we adjourned for Christmas. It was less a product of the growing opposition to certain provisions of the act than the result of the shocking revelation of an illegal wiretapping program that had been in operation for more than four years. It now became clear to everyone except certain hard-core Bush partisans that this increasingly reckless administration would do anything to justify not only its next chosen invasion of a foreign country but also its next chosen invasion of the privacy of perfectly innocent American citizens, in violation of our nation's laws and founding document.

As the story of the Terrorist Surveillance Program (TSP) continued to break that weekend, I stayed in Washington to make as many television appearances as possible to highlight the extremity of the Bush power grab. David Gregory on NBC seemed skeptical of my alarmist tone when I tried to explain that the president can't unilaterally decide to ignore duly enacted laws of the United States. Since this emerged from a deeply classified area of our government to which even I had only limited access at this point (before joining the Intelligence Committee), it was not easy to give examples of the types of innocent conversations that could now be monitored. As the first battery of interviews concluded on Sunday I hit my rhetorical stride by suggesting that the TSP was more reminiscent of King George III than a president of the United States named George.

I returned to my apartment and turned on the television to view the reaction to the story and my comments (as politicians are wont to do). Professor Jonathan Turley of George Washington University Law School methodically laid out the possible scenarios that could make this secret program legal and concluded that none of them made the grade. Then,

on George Stephanopoulos's *This Week,* another George, George Will, surprised and delighted me by laying it right on the line. He said that the Bush
administration's scam was in a whole new league of illegitimacy, even in the
context of twenty-first-century terrorist threats. Will referred to the TSP
program as "monarchical" and pointed out that "this is what we fought a
revolution over." These and other reactions supported my initial conclusion that this was a very unusual and perhaps unprecedented threat to the
Constitution itself.

It ultimately led me to become one of the first members of Congress
since the time of Andrew Jackson to propose that a president of the United
States be censured for his conduct. As I reported to Jon Stewart on *The
Daily Show,* my daughter Ellen had called me to say, "Dad, what are you
doing? This thing hasn't been done since the 1830s." To which Stewart responded, to much audience laughter, "You're bringing it back. Here's what
I like about you, Senator. You're kicking it old school." Meanwhile, others
called for the impeachment of the president and I conceded that, although
I didn't support taking such action, this illegal wiretapping program was
exactly what the Founders meant when they included in the Constitution
"high crimes and misdemeanors" as grounds for removing a president from
office.

The administration immediately fanned out, both in person and over the
airwaves, to defend surveillance without court approval as being necessary
to win the war on terror. I had heard similar rhetoric in my race for reelection in 2004 when my three Republican opponents spent more than
$11 million on advertising that asserted that I just didn't "get it" post-9/11,
that the world had changed, and that I wasn't prepared to cede to the government the powers it needed to win the war on terror. After the revelations
of the TSP program, the administration's mantra was that people like Russ
Feingold who questioned this program suffered from a syndrome they diag-
nosed as "a pre-9/11 mindset."

When I first heard this phrase, I immediately countered with my own heartfelt view that Bush, Cheney, Rumsfeld, Yoo, and their crowd had been afflicted with a malady I described as a "pre-1776 mindset." This phrase got such a strong response in the nascent blogosphere and beyond that it came to symbolize the lawlessness of the Bush administration. I tried to take it up an esoteric notch in speeches in Nashville, Tennessee, and Ames, Iowa, by going further and calling it a "pre-1215 mindset," pointing out that these separation-of-powers issues went all the way back to when a group of his subjects forced King John of England to accept the Magna Carta limiting his feudal powers. Not surprisingly, this analogy was a dud, so I went back to my pseudo–Patrick Henry cries about this George's limitless view of his powers.

A couple of weeks after the news of the TSP broke, I became a member of the Intelligence Committee. In session after secret session, I watched General Michael Hayden, then director of the NSA, being put through his paces to explain what this surveillance program was. His explanation of these very technical matters was thorough and understandable. He was affable and credible. General Hayden went so far as to arrange for committee members to visit the highly classified headquarters of the NSA in Maryland to learn firsthand from the operators how and when they would intercept international conversations. Unfortunately, however, he stoutly defended the legality of this program, as did a parade of other administration officials. This was outrageous, given the weakness of the legal arguments in its favor. The Foreign Intelligence Surveillance Act had created a special secret court in part to handle administration requests for permission to wiretap, and Hayden acted as though this were an option they could disregard at will. This was especially absurd in light of the fact that the FISA court had already approved more than fifteen thousand requests of this kind and refused only four.

Similarly cavalier claims issued from administration mouths before the Intelligence Committee when the revelations about the use of certain torture techniques concerning Guantánamo and other post-9/11 detainees came to the fore. I remember the innocent-looking Hayden calmly describing the tactics used at Guantánamo Bay and other prisons, making the whole thing sound more like a trip to the spa gone wrong than illegal torture. I will never forget him looking up from his spectacles and wriggling his nose as he described a particular technique as just "a little jab to the tummy." I almost laughed out loud in disbelief, but then felt sick as I realized how willing our government was to be so reckless in its tactics and so dismissive of those elected to review them. Later, as I learned more details about the techniques of torture, I could more clearly see the games being played to make the American people believe that torture was necessary and was behind the information that led to the killing of Osama bin Laden.

This is a lie.

I knew that the evidence cited did not come from waterboarding or similar tactics. Although the confidentiality rules of the committee forbid discussion of all the details, I was gratified to read in an issue of the *Capital Times* in May 2011, shortly after the killing of bin Laden, a piece by John McCain titled "Torture Didn't Lead Us to Osama bin Laden." I phoned John to thank him for publicly stating this. It reminded me of a quiet moment when he and I were sitting alone in the cabin of a plane on one of our foreign trips and he said, "Torture doesn't work." It wasn't necessary for him to say, "I know." He knew.

The point about both the surveillance and torture programs, however, is that they weren't really the responses of frightened government agencies that couldn't complete a crucial mission because of obstruction by Congress or current law. It was entirely different. It was grabbing power as fast as possible in an environment that did not facilitate curbing such abuses. In this opportunistic sense, it was similar to the insertion of the FBI wish list into the Patriot Act. But in two other respects these programs were very different and more sinister: They were entirely secret *and* they were illegal, violating the clear statutes of our nation. They were part and parcel of a calculated and direct assault on our Constitution, using Osama bin Laden's attack on America as pretext.

Second only to opposition to the Iraq War was concern about the Bush administration's assault on civil liberties and the Constitution. This became an important political issue in the second half of the decade. Potential candidates for the Democratic nomination for president had to burnish their credentials by objecting to these policies. In some ways, this was politically easier than opposition to the Iraq War, since the American right had done such an effective job of associating calls for troop withdrawals with concepts like surrender and cowardice. Given the growing angst among conservatives about these government practices, a candidate for 2008 could benefit both on the left, for purposes of the primaries, and on the right, for purposes of the general election, by joining in the condemnation of the post-9/11 imperial presidency that Bush and his cohorts had constructed. After all, this was the classic challenge to big government, not in the area of taxes and government regulation, but in the area of personal privacy and respect for the checks and balances system our Founders had established.

Allies had been hard to come by for years after 9/11, but now we had such strong adherents as Senator Chris Dodd of Connecticut and former Senator John Edwards. Barack Obama joined in as well and proved a reliable vote and frequent cosponsor on our initiatives to challenge the Bush offensive. He seemed genuinely interested in the specifics of issues ranging from warrantless wiretapping to immunity from prosecution for telephone service providers who had given data to the government pursuant to these secret programs. This enhanced Obama's appeal in places like Iowa and Wisconsin and certainly added to my enthusiasm about his becoming president. I believed that here was someone who could well become something much more than just a Democrat, and of course he was not George Bush. With a proper mandate for change, Obama appeared to have the commitment to carry these constitutional issues into the heart of his agenda as a president.

I also knew that reversing the gains the executive power had acquired during the Bush years, especially under the commander in chief clause, would be extremely difficult. The general lesson of American history is that once powers are ceded to the presidency they tend to stay there and are not reclaimed. This concern was behind the largely pejorative notion of an imperial presidency. Despite Bush's unpopularity, often associated with the belief that he had abused his powers, I knew that any new president, whether McCain, Clinton, or Obama, would look at these issues very differently once ensconced in the Oval Office. There is no doubt in my mind that the weight of presidential office, accompanied by scores of military and legal advisers insisting on the strongest possible interpretation of executive power, is almost overwhelming.

While I felt that Obama was our best hope for returning the genie of extreme executive power back into the bottle, I didn't want to wait for his victory and inauguration to lay out what had to be done to reverse this dangerous trend in our federal government. On September 16, 2008, I called a hearing of my Constitution Subcommittee of the Judiciary Committee to catalog and discuss the areas of constitutional doctrine and personal freedom that had suffered in the post-9/11 years. The witnesses included Harold Koh, then dean of Yale Law School, Frederick A. O. Schwarz Jr., a leading New York attorney, and Elisa Massimino, executive director of Human Rights First. By the end of the hearing the list of concerns was a long one, and I issued a report—really a challenge—to the next president, whoever that might be. It was titled "Restoring the Rule of Law," and I resolved to grade the next president on how well he or she had done in restoring the balance.

Barack Obama became president and on his first day in office, he began to fix things. He declared torture illegal and promised to close the Guantánamo prison. But the pushback soon began and deadlines starting slipping; then he made some poor judgment calls, such as claiming that the executive branch could routinely use the state secrets privilege to block litigants from asserting their rights in federal court. The first time I issued my report card on the president there was good news and bad news. But by 2011, after my tenure in the Senate had concluded, there was almost only bad news and great disappointment for so many of us who had believed the president would shine on these issues. What most concerned me about this complacency concerning threats to our constitutional system was *who* had become willing to tolerate and even facilitate it.

———

George Bush, Dick Cheney, Senator Mitch McConnell, and Fox News were predictable in their exploitation of post-9/11 anxiety to achieve policy and political objectives regardless of the danger to our Constitution. On the other hand, I consider Barack Obama and Chief Justice John Roberts to be impressive public figures, as well as two of the finest legal minds of our time. Both graduated with high recognition from Harvard Law School and both showed a strong interest in the integrity of the law before they became perhaps the two most important leaders of our nation at this time.

I have already mentioned my concerns about some of President Obama's decisions in this area and certainly expected less from the clearly conservative John Roberts when he was elevated from the US Court of Appeals to the Supreme Court. Yet when I had the chance to question him during his confirmation hearings, I was not entirely pessimistic. I pressed him first and foremost, as did several other senators, on his view of the scope of executive commander-in-chief powers, especially in wartime. His answers to questions about such key issues as his understanding of a president's powers where a clear statute limits those powers were not exactly reassuring, but they were smooth and in concert with the crucial test proposed by Justice Jackson in the Steel Seizure Cases. Essentially this doctrine says that there is no way the president can simply do whatever he wants when faced with the kind of clear language that appears in the Foreign Intelligence Surveillance Act concerning whether a wiretap will be allowed or not. When Senator Mike DeWine of Ohio sought to engage Roberts in a focused conversation about the role of the FISA court, I expected the careful avoidance that has come to characterize all recent Supreme Court nominees' answers to virtually all questions. In effect, all you usually get is their name, rank, and serial number. I was taken a little off guard by Judge Roberts's frank preface to his answer:

> I'll be very candid. When I first learned about the FISA court, I
> was surprised. It's not what we usually think of when we think
> of a court. We think of a place where we can go, we can watch
> the lawyers argue and it's subject to the glare of publicity and
> the judges explain their decision to the public and they can

examine them. That's what we think of as a court. This is a very different and unusual institution. That was my first reaction. I appreciate the reasons that it operates the way it does, but it does seem to me that the departures from the normal judicial model that are involved there put a premium on the individuals involved.

And *then* he gave the standard noncommittal answer. Still, I came away hoping that this man of the law would know where to draw the line on executive war powers at such a crucial time in our history. Our generation (his and mine) had grown up learning and accepting that the internment of Japanese Americans during World War II was one of the greatest constitutional errors in our nation's history. So, perhaps naïvely, I believed that this man, so steeped in the law of recent decades, would be as good as we could get from President Bush; and his comment on FISA gave me heart. I voted for Roberts, and I struggle constantly with that vote. This is primarily because of his abysmal role in 2010 when he helped engineer the lawless decision in *Citizens United v. FEC*. This decision, concerning campaign finance issues, essentially created out of whole cloth the notion that corporations have the same political rights as the rest of us. Yet I still hold out a tiny bit of hope that his better angels will prevail and he will return to the constitutional instinct he showed when he learned about the FISA court.

Ultimately, the bad press around the illegal warrantless wiretapping program forced President Bush to terminate it. It was then repackaged and brought before the secret court for approval, which of course the court readily gave. In fact, it would undoubtedly have done so at the start had Bush not tried to pull a fast one, revealing his contempt not only for the court and plain law but for our system of checks and balances. The damage is done—unless somehow our constitutional structure can be repaired through a Supreme Court decision or a presidential renunciation of such extreme commander in chief powers. My hope is that a reelected Barack Obama or a more open-minded John Roberts will be the catalyst for this badly needed correction. They are relatively young men with extraordinary power to use their unusual skills to achieve a historic reversal of the Bush excesses. But it will require a bold change of course, rather than the easy alternative of continued acquiescence.

Loss of civil liberties and the undermining of our Constitution are not things that average Americans can readily discern in their daily lives. Except for those directly affected—for example, those who actually know that they are being snooped on—these intrusions will seem much more hypothetical and intangible than the monthly death toll of American servicemen and women in Iraq and Afghanistan. So I was struck by the initial intuitive concern that many people expressed about the USA Patriot Act and the revelation of President Bush's warrantless wiretapping program. As time has passed, however, these public expressions of concern have faded. Ten years after September 11, 2001, there is little serious discussion of these flawed responses to that attack. The laws, precedents, and orders used to justify these extreme measures remain largely intact. To whatever extent the Bush abuses aroused the American left, progressives, parts of the Democratic Party, and, most interestingly, parts of the conservative movement, Americans have metaphorically gone back to sleep when it comes to constitutional intrusions in the name of fighting terrorism. Criticism of Obama's failure to change much of this has been muted on the American left, embarrassingly so, given the powerful complaints that came from those quarters during the Bush years. Some elements of the Tea Party movement suddenly showed signs of caring about the Patriot Act and the imperial presidency, when a guy named Obama came into office. Given the vehemence and pervasiveness of the attacks on Obama by the right, however, it is surprising that these issues now get only a once-over-lightly from this self-styled anti-big-government movement. These are constituencies that could potentially force politicians to take their duty to uphold the Constitution more seriously, but they are somnolent, while the former constitutional law professor in the White House retreats on many of the relevant issues.

A good description of this state of affairs came from one of the first persons accurately to call out the warrantless wiretapping program for what it was in December 2005. Five and a half years later, shortly after the killing of Osama bin Laden in May 2011, Professor Jonathan Turley, mentioned earlier in this chapter, showed his commitment to keeping these issues alive when he wrote a piece titled "The Demon Is Dead; So Are Many of Our Rights," which was published in *USA Today*. On May 3 he wrote: "Bin Laden's twisted notion of success was not the bringing down of two buildings in New York or the partial destruction of the Pentagon. It was how the response to those attacks by the United States resulted in our abandonment of core principles and values in the 'war on terror.' Many of the most lasting impacts of this ill-defined war were felt domestically, not internationally." Precisely!

Turley then listed the huge and growing counterterrorism complex in government and industry, restrictions on Americans challenging searches, expanded surveillance of citizens, acquiescence to the warrantless wiretapping program, and the creation of a torture program, among other abuses that accumulated while the search for bin Laden proceeded. Turley effectively places the state of our Constitution and our civil liberties exactly where I believe them to be at this point.

> What has been most chilling is that the elimination of Saddam and now bin Laden has little impact on this system, which seems to continue like a perpetual motion machine of surveillance and searches. While President Dwight D. Eisenhower once warned Americans of the power of the military-industrial complex, we now have a counterterrorism system that employs tens of thousands, spends tens of billions of dollars each year and is increasingly unchecked in its operations. . . . There will always be terrorism, and thus we will remain a nation at war—with all of the expanded powers given to government agencies and officials.

Nor does Turley limit his critique to the Bush years. He observes that the Obama administration has moved to quash many public interest lawsuits against warrantless surveillance, refused to investigate and prosecute those who engaged in illegal waterboarding, continued military tribunals, and used "the Caesar-like authority of the president to send some defendants to real courts and some to makeshift tribunals." Turley then powerfully brought home the point that I share in this book: "The death of bin Laden is not the marker of an end of a period but a reminder that there is no end to this period. For those who have long wanted expansion of presidential powers and the limitation of constitutional rights, bin Laden gave them an irresistible opportunity to reshape this country—*and the expectations of our citizens*. . . . The privacy that once defined this nation is now viewed as a quaint, if not naive, concept."

As I read Turley's essay, I wondered if America's acceptance of these limitations reflects a view that these rights and protections are outmoded in a war-against-terror context, or, as this book suggests, that Americans have not felt the impact of these changes enough to rouse them into demanding their rights back. Whether it is the perceived obsolescence of some civil liberties or a lack of awareness, it will affect how we try to persuade Americans and their elected representatives to do something. This question takes me back to an extended exchange I had at a listening session a few weeks after 9/11.

We usually saved our listening session in Pepin County, Wisconsin, for a weekend when we could do a few town meetings and stay overnight in Pepin, a pretty little village overlooking Lake Pepin, a widening of the Mississippi River that separates Wisconsin from Minnesota. The county of Pepin is one of the very smallest in the state and sparsely populated. The village of Pepin is one of the homes of that famous little girl, Laura Ingalls Wilder, from her *Little House in the Big Woods* days. But what made us so look forward to this trip each year was the prospect of dinner at the Harbor View Café. The restaurant overlooks a beautiful harbor filled with the yachts of the well-to-do Minnesotans who sail down the river for the excellent food at this simple, restored old tavern. The atmosphere is carefree; no reservations are allowed, not even for the late King Hussein of Jordan, who came here while receiving medical treatment at the nearby Mayo Clinic in Minnesota.

Nancy Mitchell, my executive assistant, who had joined me at that first post-9/11 listening session in her home town of Beloit, would move heaven and earth to be on this annual trip. We resolved that Osama bin Laden would not be allowed to make 2001 any different. But before the drinks and good camaraderie of the Harbor View, we were off to hear what Pepin County had to say at a listening session in nearby Durand. On October 20, the eleventh speaker, Ted Krukowski, decided to take on the issues of the Constitution, civil liberties, and me directly. In an extended exchange, he gave at least as good as he got.

Ted began: "Let's start with what's been said on privacy. What's wrong with having the attorney general being able to do anything he deems necessary in order to catch people like the terrorists? Why are my privacy rights so important, if I have nothing to hide?" I responded that if we gave the attorney general that kind of authority, "there is, no doubt, sir, that we would be able to stop more crime and stop more terrorism if we had no rights, if we had a police state." Not even close to being deterred by what I thought had been a strong response, Ted said, "What's wrong with that?" I replied, "That's not America." To which Ted's rebuttal was, "Maybe we should change. There were five or six thousand lives lost and we may be able to save some in the future." I countered with a brief speech about the Founders of the country and the dangers they too faced, and Ted asked, "Did the Constitution foresee the terrorism that we have today?" I cited other times in our history where excesses led to serious denials of constitutional rights, which the nation generally later regretted, including the internment of Japanese Americans in World War II. Ted, not missing a beat, came back with "But there's no proof that didn't save lives."

I called on a woman who asked me about campaign-finance reform. I gave a long answer about how we had drafted McCain-Feingold with a sharp eye to making sure it was constitutional, noting in particular that we couldn't limit how much money someone spends on a campaign without changing the Constitution. As I glanced over at Ted Krukowski, I added, "Which I'm not willing to do for this, either. I'm consistent." Ted was sitting down but he couldn't take that. "You're pretty stubborn, aren't you?" "What's that?" Ted again: "You're pretty stubborn, aren't you?" I took the opportunity to have the last word: "Well, yeah. A little bit. Let's put it this way. When you put your hand on the Bible in the well of the United States Senate and you swear to uphold the Constitution, that makes you a little stubborn. I swore on that one. You're a little stubborn, too. Nice to have you here."

Ted's views were anathema to me and, I believe, to our nation's history. But as the years passed after 9/11, I have thought back to this exchange. More and more people simply chose to ignore the increasing diminution of our constitutional rights, taking no position on whether such steps were necessary or legal. At least Ted was thinking hard about the issue and made the effort to exercise his constitutional right to challenge his elected representative on this one. At least Ted didn't act as though this topic weren't his responsibility as an American citizen. At least Ted stayed awake.

8

Morphing Islam into Al Qaeda

I think we can do better.

On the morning of September 12, 2001, I left my apartment and returned
to the Hart Building for the first time since the attacks. In between the
Democratic Caucus and my speech on the Senate floor that day, I discovered that virtually every one of my staff members in Washington, DC, including some interns who were in their first week on the job, had simply
shown up for work and were trying to get back to normal business. We
decided to hold a meeting for all staff in my large office to try to set the tone
for the coming days of uncertainty. As I looked at the group crowded into
my office I felt great pride in these people, many of them very young and
most of them from Wisconsin. They were obviously concerned, but calm.
I said that I would understand if anybody felt unable to continue but that
we had a job to do and we would do it as well as we could. The meeting was
brief but probably reassuring for people who clearly didn't want to focus too
much on the fact that they were reporting back to work on Capitol Hill,
where Al Qaeda had tried to kill thousands of Americans, including them,
just a few hours earlier.

As the meeting concluded, a few people were a little overcome with emotion and a box of Kleenex was making the rounds. One of my staff members approached me as I was leaving and asked me if she could have a personal conversation with me, "as opposed to a professional conversation," to "tell me how she felt." This staffer was a bright young lawyer who was part of my Senate Judiciary Committee legal team. The daughter of a physician, she had been raised in upstate New York and had had a traditional small-town America upbringing. She had been serving for some time as the deputy to my top Judiciary aide, Bob Schiff, whose hands were more than full with the many projects we were working on, including campaign finance reform. This young lawyer had to take over some of the toughest issues we had pursued prior to 9/11.

One of my lifelong passions has been opposition to the death penalty and this staffer had taken the responsibility to help me advance this cause. The death penalty has been banned in Wisconsin since the late 1850s, and when I highlighted this issue for the turn of the millennium in 2000, I proposed that we leave this barbaric practice behind. We wanted a moratorium on the federal death penalty similar to the moratorium the state of Illinois had enacted after modern DNA testing had discovered that several of the inmates on death row in that state were innocent. My staffer was an enthusiastic opponent of the death penalty, too, and we had traveled to national conferences on that subject in places like Los Angeles, Chicago, and San Francisco.

She also became my lead staffer on an issue that came to be known as racial profiling. In too many jurisdictions in the 1990s and particularly in parts of New Jersey and Maryland, it was demonstrated that motorists were being stopped, not on the basis of any particular suspicion but merely because of their appearance. This drew increasing attention, and came to be known as "driving while black" or "driving while brown," depending on whether those profiled were black or Latino. As I took the Senate lead in drafting legislation on this, so did Representative John Conyers of Michigan in the House. And a new senator from New York sought aggressively to be one of the major cosponsors of the bill: Hillary Clinton and her staff met with us to discuss this issue on a number of occasions prior to 9/11. We even got John Ashcroft, the attorney general, whom I had persuaded to look at this issue as a senator, to get the president to mention racial profiling in his first address to a joint session of Congress on February 27, 2001. President Bush declared:

> As government promotes compassion, it also must promote justice. Too many of our citizens have cause to doubt our nation's justice when the law points a finger of suspicion at groups instead of individuals. All our citizens are created equal and must be treated equally. Earlier today, I asked John Ashcroft, the attorney general, to develop specific recommendations to end racial profiling. It's wrong, and we will end it in America. In so doing, we will not hinder the work of our nation's brave police officers. They protect us every day, often at great risk. But by stopping the abuses of a few, we will add to the public confidence our police officers earn and deserve.

Farhana Khera was mild-mannered, hardworking, and, given her kind manner, was one of our best-liked staff members. She was a practicing Muslim American with a Pakistani background, whose familial and social networks included Muslims all over the country as well as in Pakistan, which she had visited on a number of occasions. She wasn't the type to wear her emotions on her sleeve, but when she asked to spend a moment with me, she had almost a hunted look on her face. Farhana started to tell me about her experience on the Metro train that morning. She burst into tears when she said, "Everyone was staring at me." I also have been told that her brother had called her to say that he was shaving off his goatee and was going to wear a baseball cap now, so he could look more American. I hugged her, but couldn't begin to fathom what a shock the previous twenty-four hours had been to her and to so many other Arab and Muslim Americans. Despite being loyal Americans, they now faced the prospect of being profiled and having their patriotism questioned because of their appearance and religion. As Farhana told me about her experience I could see how one American had been suddenly transformed into "the other" and made to feel unwelcome, an object of suspicion in her own country. This didn't deter her from her work on racial profiling, the death penalty, or any other issue, and having someone with her perspective was invaluable in the following months and years. Her experience in that subway and the way it affected her, however, was a searing lesson in how difficult it would be to get Americans to adjust to the new challenges.

America initially responded to the jolting awakening of 9/11 by carefully engaging the Islamic world before invading Afghanistan to pursue Al Qaeda. We also started off largely getting it right when it came to dealing with the new tension between Muslim and Arab Americans and the rest of the nation. As I had indicated in my speech on the Senate floor on September 12, this was one of my immediate concerns. I remember feeling heartened by the administration's quick and firm warnings to all Americans not to victimize Muslims, Middle Easterners, and the religion of Islam in response to these attacks. President Bush, while addressing a joint session of Congress on September 20, 2001, said:

> I also want to speak tonight directly to Muslims throughout the world. We respect your faith. It's practiced freely by many millions of Americans and by millions more in countries that America counts as friends. Its teachings are good and peaceful, and those who commit evil in the name of Allah blaspheme the name of Allah. The terrorists are traitors to their own faith, trying, in effect, to hijack Islam itself. The enemy of America is not our many Muslim friends; it is not our many Arab friends. Our enemy is a radical network of terrorists and every government that supports them.

Republican Senator Sam Brownback from Kansas had made a similar point from the floor of the Senate on September 12, 2001: "There is another point that needs to be made. The culprits are terrorists, not the Arab people or those of the Muslim faith generally or any other group. Individuals are guilty of crimes, not classes of people. In this instance, as always, we should reject unfair characterizations or generalizations targeted at groups of people." I believe these cautions made a big difference in minimizing anti-Islamic sentiment in the months following the terrorist attacks. I received positive comments from representatives of Arab and Muslim Americans, as well as from non-Islamic South Asians, who were sometimes mistaken for Muslims. Some credited the president with real moral leadership on this issue.

Yet within the first couple of years after 9/11, things seemed gradually to change. A rational effort to distinguish one of the world's great religions from the fanatics who sought to exploit it gave way to a national discussion that tended to morph Islam into an ideological and physical threat to America. This became a tool that suited the political strategy of too many cynical players in our national government and media. Law-abiding Americans who happened to be Muslim or Arab were stereotyped, even to the point where they made others feel uneasy when they prayed before or during an airline flight. Over the last ten years this has had a tragic effect on the relationship between millions of Muslim and Arab Americans and our government, as well as the nation as a whole. In addition, there was growing evidence that anti-Islamic sentiments were affecting other non-Islamic communities. A powerful documentary, *Mistaken Identity: Sikhs in America,* showed that many Sikhs were facing discrimination, vandalism, and outright violence because of their clothing (men wear turbans, women cover their hair with long scarves). What I found particularly compelling was the way these minority communities responded to all of this. They tended not to speak of specific attacks, but seemed far more exercised by the general reduction of civil liberties that followed from the Patriot Act, screenings at airports, and increased surveillance. They were justified in their concern that the Bush administration's power grab would have a disproportionate impact on them, at least in the near term.

Even if political and media actors in America didn't actively seek to exploit emotions and sensitivities that were stimulated by 9/11, Americans have often lacked the historical knowledge to form a sufficiently positive perception of Muslims and Arabs. Unlike other groups who have come to

America in large numbers, from the Irish to the Italians, Jews, and Hispanics, immigrants from the Middle East have arrived in smaller numbers through most of the twentieth century, with the exception of large Arab communities in places like Detroit and significant Persian communities in places like Los Angeles. Americans were treated to a twentieth-century popular culture that was less than hospitable to these ethnic groups. One example is the comment to Sherif Ali attributed to the character of T. E. Lawrence in the movie *Lawrence of Arabia:* "So long as the Arabs fight tribe against tribe, so long will they be a little people, a silly people. Greedy, barbarous, and cruel, as you are." Further back, the portrayal of Arabs and Muslims is enshrined in some of our own most revered literature. In *Innocents Abroad,* Mark Twain conveyed, as only he could, the stereotype effectively and with tongue in cheek when he described Turkey: "Mosques are plenty, churches are plenty, graveyards are plenty, but morals and whiskey are scarce. The Koran does not permit Muhammadans to drink. Their natural instincts do not permit them to be moral. They say the Sultan had eight hundred wives. This almost amounts to bigamy. It makes our cheeks burn to see such a thing permitted here in Turkey. We do not mind it so much in Salt Lake, however."

Against such a backdrop, what began as a few general references to "getting back at those towel heads" soon became more directed to the religion of Islam itself. This was long after President Bush had made the fundamental mistake of referring to our fight against Al Qaeda as a "crusade." (He apologized.) I noted the obvious coordination by the White House, various conservative groups, and Fox News to mint a new term to describe what America was up against post-9/11—*Islamo-fascism.* I remember recoiling when I first heard the term on Fox News: Is it really a good idea gratuitously to insult over one billion people in the world by using such a moniker? Is this in our national security interests? After being tossed around the right-wing conservative community for years, the term was adopted in the highest levels of the White House. In fact, *Islamo-fascism* and its variants were used by President Bush himself in at least ten public statements between the fall of 2005 and summer of 2006. I remember wondering how I would have felt if a term like *Judeo-fascism* were used by government officials to describe

acts of violence by Jewish individuals such as Meir Kahane of the so-called
Jewish Defense League, who was active on the Jewish right in the 1970s and
'80s. Obviously there is no comparison between bin Laden and Kahane,
but that's not the point. What is the point is that it is an enormous mistake
to link the name of a good religion to a deeply pejorative label, even if it is
a label for a subgroup that deserves to be condemned. Nothing symbolized
for me the deterioration in our attitude toward Muslims more than the brief
use of this term. I objected to its use on September 12, 2006, when I was addressing the Arab American Institute: "We must avoid using misleading and
offensive terms that link Islam with those who subvert this great religion or
who distort its teachings to justify terrorist activities. Fascist ideology doesn't
have anything to do with the way global terrorist networks think or operate, and it doesn't have anything to do with the overwhelming majority of
Muslims around the world who practice the peaceful teachings of Islam."
Again, I was relieved by how quickly the White House responded. The word
spread that the White House would no longer use the term *Islamo-fascism.*

Reports suggested that the person who pressed most for dropping the
term was the top presidential adviser, Karen Hughes. She was one of the two
people from Texas (the other being Karl Rove) perhaps most responsible
for George W. Bush's two terms as president. Hughes had been nominated
to be undersecretary of state for public diplomacy in 2005, and she visited
me as part of the confirmation process. She was sensitive to the necessity of
reaching out to Islamic peoples around the world, so, once confirmed, she
set out to do something about it, making a successful tour of key Islamic
nations to listen to their citizens' concerns. One of the greatest thrills for
me was when she, after considering some ideas I had given her, asked me to
name the first "citizen ambassador" to accompany her. I reached back into
my past to choose my high school debate coach, Bill O'Brien, who had gone
on to be a school principal and superintendent of both public and Catholic
school systems in Wisconsin. After the trip, Bill called me and said, "For
God's sake, Russ, I was sitting in my living room in Appleton one day and
then a couple of days later I'm floating down the Nile on a barge. Then I'm
getting a friendly bear hug from a Muslim in Saudi Arabia for something I
said." Bill, a passionate Irish Catholic from Neenah, Wisconsin, who had

never been to that part of the world, took to his new role with relish. I'm sure Karen Hughes had never done anything quite like that, either. They both intuitively understood how critical these relations with Muslims are, both here and abroad, for our security and future. At the same time as I was appalled by so many other things it did, I was once again encouraged by the Bush administration's efforts in this area. It was partly for this reason that I was so taken aback by the dramatic turn for the worse our relations with Muslim and Arab Americans took after Bush left the White House.

The last couple of years have been dismal in this respect, probably the worst since 9/11. Among the mishandled matters, perhaps the most dramatic was the reaction to the application to build a mosque in the general area near the former World Trade Center. In a neighborhood full of other houses of worship, restaurants, shops, even strip joints, we had twenty-four-hour coverage that had to make even the most moderate Muslim in America feel uncomfortable. This was a local zoning issue with clear freedom-of-religion implications that are central to our country's raison d'être. Nonetheless, politicians all over America running for office in 2010 as well as President Obama were confronted with it.

Later, Pastor Terry Jones of the Dove World Outreach Center in Gainesville, Florida, decided it would be a good idea to threaten to burn a Koran at his church on September 11, 2010. After appropriate pressure from all levels, Jones backed off and was even invited to a Michigan mosque. In the words of Eide Alawan of the Islamic Center in Dearborn, "When you break bread with someone, you see them in a different light." Jones ignored the invitation and a few months later chose not to break bread, but to get out his matches and set fire to a Koran in his church after a mock trial of the holy book. Reportedly, a group based in Pakistan then put up a $2.2 million reward for his death. In the resulting unrest more than twenty people, including UN staff, were killed by angry mobs during demonstrations across Afghanistan.

We can agree that it is not always possible to prevent a misguided individual from doing misguided things like burning the Koran. But we expect better judgment when it comes to our duly elected officials. These higher standards are not being met by those state legislatures which are in the vanguard of the new movement to pass state laws prohibiting all sharia law. In the United States, American law already prevails over other laws when there is a conflict—it always has—but these new statutes go much further. Oklahoma led the way by passing a constitutional amendment prohibiting enforcement of any sharia law, even in commercial transactions between Muslims. As Aziz Huq, an assistant professor of law at the University of Chicago, pointed out, this deprives Muslims of equal access to the law, as when, for example, a butcher could no longer enforce his contract for halal meat while that same butcher could do so when providing kosher meat. And Huq effectively elaborated the broader point: "These bans increase bias among the public by endorsing the idea that Muslims are second-class citizens. They encourage and accelerate both the acceptability of negative views of Muslims and the expression of those negative views by the public and government agencies like the police."

A high-water mark of irresponsibility was demonstrated by New York Congressman Peter King's insistence on going through with an ill-advised congressional hearing in March 2011 on the threat of what he called homegrown Islamic terrorism. King claimed that American Muslim leaders had failed to cooperate with law enforcement in the effort to disrupt terrorist plots. He refused pleas to abandon his hearing, ignoring the reasonable argument that if Congress is going to investigate violent extremism, it should investigate all kinds of extremists and not just Muslims. "Singling out a group of Americans for government scrutiny based on their faith is divisive and wrong," said a letter sent by the Muslim Advocates, a group of American Muslim attorneys led by my former aide, Farhana Khera. The letter was also signed by Amnesty International, the Interfaith Alliance, and the Japanese American Citizens League. Japanese Americans, reminded of their own harsh and inappropriate treatment during World War II, have extended a hand to American Muslims. They are led by Representative Mike Honda, a Democratic Asian American who denounced King's hearings as "something similarly sinister." And to his credit, Senator Dick Durbin of Illinois had the fortitude to hold a hearing of the Constitution Subcommittee on "Protecting the Civil Rights of American Muslims." These remonstrances did not deter Representative King. He went ahead and started planning another set of hearings targeted at American Muslims, thoroughly enjoying the publicity and evidently oblivious to the insult, hurt, and resentment he has caused.

Nearly ten years after 9/11, Katie Couric, one of the best-known figures in American life of recent years, observed that there was an ongoing problem with Americans' perception of Muslims and Arabs in general and of Muslim and Arab Americans in particular. She offhandedly suggested that what we needed to correct this was the Muslim-family equivalent of the famous *Cosby Show,* which has often been credited with raising the comfort level of white America with black America, by portraying a black family as essentially the same as a white middle-class family. It is not clear that Couric's idea was meant to be serious, but it did lead a Muslim American comedian, Aasif Mandvi, to convene a group of "average" Americans to react to a prototype of a television program called "The Bill Qu'osby Show," starring himself. When the participants were asked if they thought the show was funny, they all somberly indicated that they did not. The comedian then asked what needed to be changed to make it funny and there were quite a few ideas. One was that there had to be a character in the show who was a "closet terrorist" and whom the family tried to conceal. Maybe there could be an Uncle Nayib, a Bedouin living in the basement with his livestock, another participant added. The point that Mandvi was trying to make is that average Americans would respond better to a Muslim sitcom when it includes Muslim stereotypes. That one of the first improvements the viewers suggested was a "hidden terrorist" is a window on the deep suspicion and misunderstanding that currently exists between the Muslim and Arab American communities and the broader American public.

Embedded in the response to the comedian's queries was a clue to one of the greatest barriers to Americans having a more relaxed and open attitude toward Muslims and Arabs: We don't know who they are. We have limited knowledge of the differences between Arabs and other peoples in the Middle East and South Asia and their American counterparts. Many of us are not aware that not all Arabs are Muslims or that Iranians and Pakistanis are not Arabs. More people now know of the Sunni-Shiite split in Islam, because of news coverage of the war in Iraq, but my sense is that most Americans think Muslims are all pretty much on the same side, and the "side" isn't ours. Even I, after a lifetime of interest in the Middle East, service on the Foreign Relations Committee, and a fascination with the range of world religions, lacked basic knowledge of some of these differences. I don't want to exaggerate this problem, though, for it is one that can be corrected fairly quickly, if there is a will to do that. But there has to be clear, consistent leadership that insists that we overcome this weakness in our understanding of our fellow citizens and of so many other people around the world.

The problem goes deeper than a shortage of knowledge about the ethnic and religious differences between Osama bin Laden and Iranian President Mahmoud Ahmadinejad. Not only do we have to correct the presumption that most Arabs and Muslims in America harbor strong anti-American sentiments that could lead to terrorist acts; we also have to understand how alienating the events of 9/11 were for the millions of Arab and Muslim Americans, as well as many non-Muslim South Asian Americans.

At the risk of overgeneralizing, I believe it is accurate to say that before 9/11 most observant Muslims in America were politically conservative or at least felt more aligned with the Republican Party. As I came into contact with many of them in Wisconsin and Illinois, we were usually able to find common ground on issues of good governance or promoting economic relationships with their original home countries. I particularly remember an event involving Pakistani Americans in an upscale suburb of Milwaukee in the mid-1990s. They were supporters, and I had been invited presumably because of my roles as senator and as a younger member of the Senate Foreign Relations Committee. I was cordially received but soon realized that, for the first time, I was experiencing the strict separation of the sexes—even among these prominent members of the greater Milwaukee community, most of them doctors, chemists, or businessmen. Men and women were in separate groups in the same room for the discussion and speeches, and when it came time for dinner the men were in the dining room and the women were serving or eating in other rooms of the spacious home. Although many of these individuals seemed willing to support my campaign, there were some clues as to why most Muslim Americans in that era had tended to vote Republican. It was asking a lot for these voters to support me: My positions on a woman's right to choose and gay rights, coupled with my progressive attitude about the appropriate tax burden for upper-income individuals, certainly would not have carried the day with this crowd. (All these topics were avoided that evening, of course.) Add to that my strongly pro-Israel approach, albeit moderated by my unambiguous support for a Palestinian state, and I was a little surprised to be allowed in their company. Election analyses suggest that few Democrats with my profile would have garnered much support from these Muslim Americans prior to September 11, 2001.

Given that experience with Muslim Americans in the mid-1990s, one of the most moving moments of my last campaign was just before the election. I had been asked to visit the Islamic Society of Milwaukee on the last Friday of October 2010. Over the years I had made several visits to this location on the far south side of Milwaukee, but this time I was invited not only to visit, but to shake the hands of everyone as they left the mosque at the holiest moment of the week. There was a huge sign with my and President Obama's names on it (sufficiently far enough away from the religious portion of the facility, for legal purposes), and the response I got that day may have been the most passionately positive and overwhelming of the entire campaign—more than that of the progressive crowds in Madison, or even the Jewish audiences in Milwaukee. It was an emotional response with many of the worshippers clasping my hand and saying, "You must win!" This was so very far removed from the cordial but careful reception I had received some fifteen years earlier at that event in the Milwaukee suburbs. It was as if I seemed to many of these loyal Americans a last link to a political system that had largely turned on them out of suspicion and political opportunism. Accompanying me on that day was a volunteer, my friend and former staff member Farhana Khera, the young lawyer whose life had been suddenly upended when she boarded the DC Metro on the morning of September 12, 2001.

Ten years after 9/11, I feel that we have gradually descended into an almost unconscious perception of Arab and Muslim Americans as fundamentally different from us. And they feel it. This is no way to treat fellow

Americans, and it is fraught with danger for all of us, both domestically and internationally. That is not to say our fellow citizens are adopting a more aggressive attitude toward the rest of us, but they are extremely wary about how welcome they and their children will be in post-9/11 America.

There is an absurd portrayal of this anxiety depicted in the recent English movie *Four Lions* that might resonate with Arab and Muslim Americans. The film is a zany portrayal of an inept group of four young British Muslims (including a convert to Islam) who want to become jihadists and pull off a major terrorist attack in England. It is biting satire, and not for the faint-hearted or overly sensitive. It is jarring to watch a movie where both humor and horror are combined, as one of the wannabe terrorists dressed as a Teenage Mutant Ninja Turtle is killed before he can detonate his suicide belt. The key moment of the film for me, though, comes during an open-forum discussion, when the fourth "lion," Hassan, begins heckling the panelists—a stuffy politician named Malcolm Storge and Barry, the convert.

MODERATOR. We'll take questions later, please.
HASSAN: No, no, no. You think we're all bombers, don't you?
STORGE: That is absolute . . .
HASSAN: No, no. When you see someone like me, you think
    "bomber," right?
BARRY (*to Storge*): Yes, you do.
STORGE: That is not the case.
HASSAN: So why shouldn't I be a bomber if you treat me like
    one?

I realize that this scene could be interpreted in a slightly paranoid way: If we don't treat them better, American Muslims will become more involved with terrorism. I don't believe that and hope that Americans, if they think about this, won't, either. What I do believe is that it is wrong to denigrate the rights of one segment of American society, and it may be detrimental to our own national security and economic interests not to reverse course.

———

In March 2008, my sister Dena Feingold, a leading Reform rabbi based in Kenosha, Wisconsin, arranged for me to address the Central Conference of American Rabbis at their annual event in Atlanta. Being in a room where you are one of the few persons who are not a rabbi is intimidating, at least for an American Jew. I had experienced this only once before, when Dena was ordained the first woman rabbi in Wisconsin and one of the earliest in Jewish history (there were only about fifty at the time). At her ordination in 1982, just before I started my political career, I didn't have to speak to all those rabbis. This time I did, though, and I wanted to find a topic that would interest these professional sermon givers. As I reviewed some of my work in the Senate, it occurred to me that three different groups of Americans are, at times, still alienated from their fellow citizens. I pointed out that African Americans continued to come up against barriers to their full acceptance into American society, something that dates back hundreds of years, for obvious reasons. I also wanted to highlight two other groups that had more recently and dramatically been forced into a similar situation.

For Latinos, the last few years have been unsettling and sometimes alienating as tensions over immigration from Mexico and South and Central America have grown, exacerbated now by a sour economy. On the other hand, Arab and Muslim Americans were jolted into a new status in the course of one day. Too often now these three groups share a sense of being "the other," strangers to the rest of America. If African, Hispanic, and Muslim Americans are viewed as strangers, then—I reminded the rabbis— we should follow the most-repeated directive in the Torah, that is, the command always to welcome strangers. In Leviticus it is "The stranger that sojourns with you shall be to you as the home-born among you, and you shall love him as yourself for you were strangers in the land of Egypt." And from Deuteronomy: "Love therefore the stranger, for you were strangers in the land of Egypt."

Of course no Americans should be viewed as strangers in the first place. It is simply wrong to assume that all Muslim and Arab Americans are recent or temporary visitors. This seemed to be the story Soledad O'Brien of CNN discovered for a recent broadcast, *Unwelcome: The Muslim Next Door:* "What was really interesting to me was the Muslims who were saying that the most offensive of a large range of unpleasant comments was 'Go back home!' That's the thing that gave them the most offense because they are saying, 'I am from Murfreesboro, Tennessee, what are you talking about?' "

Despite the many mistakes made over the last ten years, there are hopeful signs of a renewed awareness that this problem can be systematically addressed. On the day after Osama bin Laden was killed, I was encouraged to hear guests on MSNBC declare that this was a good time for a new relationship with Muslims. Sure enough, within a few days, the Obama administration announced a "fresh outreach to the Muslim world." But this will require a strong domestic component to eliminate the assaults on Muslim American culture and religion, and on the right to be regarded as patriotic Americans.

When the 2010 election was over, I was preparing to leave Washington for Wisconsin. My friend John Sylvester had arrived with his truck and a big U-Haul attached to it. Almost all the boxes had been packed, and there were just a few items left on my desk. I opened a lemon-yellow envelope to find a card decorated with flowers, on which a little owl was relaxing. It was from Maya Khan, a native of Kenosha, Wisconsin, and one of the youngest and newest members of my staff. She wrote: "Growing up as a young Muslim woman in Wisconsin was not easy after September 11. There were days when I found it hard to leave the house for school, because of the way my peers would treat me. But from the very beginning, I had a Senator who stood up for me. . . . You have been my inspiration through some very difficult times in my life, and will continue to be as we both move forward."

Like Farhana Khera's reaction to 9/11, Maya's note touched me deeply. In the words of one of my lifelong inspirations, Robert F. Kennedy, "I think we can do better."

9

Trivializing National Security and Foreign Policy for Political Gain

Fire hazard number one, make room for fire hazard number two.

Max Cleland served one term in the United States Senate, from 1997 through 2002. For a good part of that time he was my seatmate; that is, we sat next to each other in the very back row on the Democratic side of the Senate chamber. I had more seniority and had chosen the back row because I liked to be able to survey the entire room. Max was on the aisle, but not because he chose that. He was there because he needed maximum maneuverability to get around and carry out his work. Max was the archetype of what has become known as the wounded warrior. But the word *wounded* doesn't quite convey what this man sacrificed for his country as a soldier in Vietnam. In 1968 Max fell on a grenade and was as severely wounded as one can be and still live. He lost three of his four limbs; only his left arm remained. After years of effort and rehabilitation he had become a public figure in his home state of Georgia and was elected secretary of state in a state not well known for electing many Democrats in recent decades. Then, upon the retirement of Senator Sam Nunn, one of the most distinguished members of the Senate and former chairman of the Armed Services Committee, Max Cleland was elected to replace him.

Special ramps had to be constructed to allow Max to wheel himself into the chamber and to be able to vote or consult with other senators at "the desk," which is the center of most conversation, deal making, and general hubbub when the Senate is in session. Max could not have been a friendlier and livelier seatmate, always ready with a warm greeting or a compliment about something he had heard me say or watched me do. I remember how difficult it was for Max to cope during the infamous Bill Clinton impeachment trial, when we, as jurors, were all required to be seated in the chamber from 9 a.m. to at least 5 p.m. (with a short break for lunch) Monday through Saturday. I watched Max struggle, as we all did at times, to stay awake and get as comfortable as he could. The rest of us could rush out during a quick break to get a bite to eat or use the restroom with little difficulty, but for Max, of course, these simple actions were challenging. The schedule was clearly not easy for him, but he managed to keep it and his good humor throughout his Senate career.

Another colleague who always treated me with great courtesy was someone I was mildly surprised to find so collegial. Senator Jesse Helms of North Carolina was already the legend of the hard right long before I got to the US Senate. Along with Senator Strom Thurmond of South Carolina, these two were the political equivalent of Scylla and Charybdis to progressives and Democrats across the country as the conservative movement pressed on with its post-Reagan agenda of rolling back the progressive gains of the 1960s. Yet when I served with Helms on the Foreign Relations Committee, I found him to be a good listener and even a valuable collaborator on issues of fiscal responsibility where we were able to agree. Let there be no mistake, though: He showed a certain ruthlessness whenever he homed in on one of his favorite targets, such as the National Endowment for the Arts. I happened to be presiding over the Senate one day when he attacked the program. He displayed a blown-up picture and then described it as "a flower pot made out of a cadaver's skull with the brains scooped out and with pretty flowers planted inside." He sarcastically noted, "I think there ought to be one in every home." He took care, however, to reserve this sort of commentary for his speeches and was polite and proper in private conversations with all his colleagues.

There were times when I could believe, perhaps naïvely, that some of this collegiality was not mere veneer, but reflected genuine respect and regard for colleagues, including those who happened to be in the other party. An incident in 1998 involving Senators Cleland and Helms has come to symbolize this for me. One day I was racing through the ornate reception room of the Senate, past the portrait of my Wisconsin hero, Robert "Fighting Bob" La Follette, into the vestibule area, the last public space before one enters the Senate's restricted inner sanctum. There maneuvering himself on his motorized scooter was Max Cleland, who was struggling to make a phone call. All of a sudden another motorized scooter whizzed past me in the narrow space remaining and gently bumped into Cleland's vehicle. With a grin, Jesse Helms, who had just had double knee surgery, blurted out, "Fire hazard number one, make room for fire hazard number two," to which Max replied (as he almost always did to everyone in the Senate), "I love you, man."

I found this incident hilarious and touching at the same time. Helms demonstrated a natural ease with Cleland combined with genuine respect for his sacrifices that made me feel optimistic about how senators were interrelating. For a few months after 9/11, I witnessed what seemed to be a similar camaraderie, a dynamism based in a common recognition of the historic challenges we were facing. Yet within little more than a year after 9/11, Max Cleland, recipient of Bronze and Silver stars for valor in combat, was thrown out of the Senate by the people of Georgia after being battered by advertisements that—unbelievably—questioned this man's patriotism. He was defeated by a courtly Republican, Saxby Chambliss, whose campaign blamed Cleland for having undercut national security when he voted against a bill creating the new Department of Homeland Security. One ad, linking his image to those of Osama bin Laden and Saddam Hussein, proclaimed that Cleland "says he has the courage to lead, but the record proves Max Cleland is just misleading." Max voted against that bill (so did I) because it failed to give reasonable worker protection to DHS employees. Using the same tactics as the drafters of the Patriot Act, the backers knew they could grab a victory on some unrelated agenda because the overall bill was what was known in Washington as a must-pass. Such bills, which Congress has almost no choice but to pass, often attract riders like the one that restricted employees' rights. The Bush administration and the Republicans in the Senate, hungry to regain the majority, pounced with some gusto on the political opportunities this new climate of fear provided. Smearing Max Cleland, at a time when America really needed heroes like him, meant little in the face of this raw ambition.

The defeat of Max Cleland and the overall results of the 2002 election were early signs that any hope of a national unity government after 9/11 was fading. That possibility was to be sacrificed to partisan advantage. It is important to understand that this is not part of the same strategy that led to the deceptive entry into the Iraq War. That effort divided our nation after 9/11 but did not seem so much driven by a domestic political agenda as by a dogmatic foreign policy generated by so-called neoconservatives lurking throughout the Bush administration. It had not been demanded in any serious way at the public or popular level. The Iraq vote was a factor in some of the 2002 midterm elections, but it also presented difficulties over time for Republican and conservative candidates, including President Bush in his close reelection fight in 2004. The Bush administration used much of the political capital it had derived from being in charge post-9/11 to achieve questionable foreign policy goals of its own.

Turning the Homeland Security vote against Cleland and other Democrats, however, was an entirely different way of manipulating this national trauma. In some ways this was even more cynical, because it used a foreign policy crisis to win domestic elections and establish greater dominance for the Republican Party and the conservative movement, regardless of the relevance of the issues to our national security. What began as a sort of silver bullet to undermine Max Cleland's patriotism evolved into a whole arsenal of political weapons. These were effectively used to oversimplify foreign policy issues and to make political opponents appear weak on national security, soft on terrorism, and possibly even anti-American. President Obama was their particular and ultimate target.

Like contriving a legislative vote on a war-against-terror medal that failed to distinguish between the Iraq and Afghanistan invasions, similar games were played in Congress, especially in the mid to late 2000s. One technique was to find a relatively minor dispute that was getting a lot of media coverage and turn it into a vote on the floor to test members' patriotism or support for the troops. Simple either-you're-with-us-or-against-us votes succeeded in intimidating otherwise sensible legislators into voting aye on pointless proposals—after wasting huge amounts of time debating them. The overall effect was to trivialize the foreign policy debate. This began under the Bush administration but greatly intensified after Barack Obama was sworn in as president in January 2009. A clear example of this was when MoveOn.org took issue with General David Petraeus and questioned his candor about our situation in Iraq. At a time when it might more wisely have chosen to move on, the group chose instead to mount a "General Betray Us" campaign. It ran a big advertisement in a Monday edition of the *New York Times* condemning the four-star general. The American right purported to be outraged. But it seemed to me that they were actually rather pleased to have this unexpected albatross to hang around the necks of members of Congress who were opposed to the continuation of the war; it was good for propaganda purposes and great for fundraising from the conservative base. In short order, Republican Senator John Cornyn of Texas offered an amendment to condemn MoveOn's ad, and nervous Democrats drafted a counter-amendment condemning the advertisement that had questioned Max Cleland's patriotism in the 2002 election. The idea was that Democrats could vote to condemn the MoveOn ad, but then stick it to the Republicans on a second, tit-for-tat vote. We voted on these amendments on September 20, 2007, after many hours of pointless debate.

This was one of those times when it seemed to me that America had moved so far from its initial resolve to get the post-9/11 response right that it was embarrassing. Instead of discussing the broader terrorist threat or the merits of the Iraq War—not to mention a myriad of neglected domestic issues—we were squabbling over television ads like schoolchildren. If we

started passing resolutions condemning every disturbing or offensive statement made in the electronic media or blogosphere, we would never get anything else done. But this tactic had another, more sinister effect. It reduced
serious issues, such as the wisdom of our military approach in Iraq, to a
parlor game of who can make the other side look worse. The US Senate appeared to be less a deliberative body than a disparate group playing gotcha.
As strongly as I felt about the way Max Cleland had been treated, and as
inappropriate as MoveOn's name-calling seemed, when the roll was called I
couldn't stomach voting for either amendment and voted no on both. I was
soon to discover that the trivialization of our national security debate was
just beginning.

The way presidential overseas trips are now characterized is another example. I could swear that we Americans used to have a different view of
presidential visits. Whether it was John F. Kennedy declaring, "Ich bin ein
Berliner," or Richard Nixon stunning us with his bold visit to "Red China,"
or Ronald Reagan in Berlin telling Mikhail Gorbachev to "tear down this
wall," most of us, regardless of party or ideology, felt some pride in a president who would go abroad to represent us as a nation at critical moments
in history. Maybe the combination of so many pressing domestic issues and
the greater frequency of presidential trips to everything from G20 conferences to commemorations of various anniversaries has devalued these visits.
How did we get to the point, though, where the leading story coming out
of President Clinton's attendance at Yitzhak Rabin's funeral was one about
Speaker Newt Gingrich whining that President Clinton didn't talk to him
on Air Force One and asked him to deplane on a back set of stairs?

In an era of instantaneous blogging, emails, and tweeting, even the
smallest fact or piece of gossip can become news, and presidential foreign
trips, with their phalanxes of journalists, are no exception—nor should
they be. It seems, however, that something more insidious is undermining
President Obama's worthy efforts to repair the damage done to our international reputation by the Bush-Cheney administration. Well received abroad,

his Cairo speech, intended to help restore good relations with the Arab world, was met with derision at home: He was accused of apologizing inappropriately when, in the words of Fox News, "America has nothing to apologize for." A trip to Indonesia was postponed several times between 2009 and 2010. This was partly because of justifiable pressure on the president not to leave Washington while critical legislation was pending. I had the distinct impression, though, that the White House was just as concerned about the political optics as it was with the legislative mechanics of postponing a first presidential trip to one of the largest Islamic countries in the world.

This disturbing trend seemed to find a new low when the president visited India in 2010. Not only is India the largest democracy in the world, but it also has a large Islamic population of some 160 million. India is becoming one of the most vibrant and important economies in the world, a competitor, but also an opportunity. This is what the executives of Harley-Davidson in Milwaukee told me on many occasions as they fantasized about being able to sell their motorcycles to the Indian market. Even more important, as we try to solve the problem of Al Qaeda and its role in Pakistan and Afghanistan, is understanding that Pakistan's attitude toward Al Qaeda and Afghanistan has less to do with us than with its perception that it has a potentially existential problem with its adversary, India. Given our international challenges, it is hard to imagine another country more worthy of visiting at this point. Regardless, the president was subjected to a barrage of criticism. Fox News and other indiscriminate critics of the administration mocked the size of his entourage, wildly exaggerating its size and cost. They suggested that the president and first lady's participation in traditional dancing with some Indian children was somehow undignified or inappropriate, instead of the informed, respectful diplomacy it was. It is a sad commentary on our inability to understand how much work we have to do to improve our international standing.

There have been consistent attempts by various right-leaning, conservative, and Tea Party–related commentators to discredit President Obama by twisting his candid comments about how America might on occasion have better played her role. Any such statement is immediately turned into an unpatriotic apology. A list produced by the Heritage Foundation in June

2009 featured "Barack Obama's Top 10 Apologies: How the President Has Humiliated a Superpower." The compilers of this document were unable to find even one example of the use of the word *apology* in the president's speeches. So they had to go about simply claiming that his statements were apologies. For example, they characterized his statement in France that "America has shown arrogance" in some of its international alliances as an abject apology. The president's comment to a Muslim audience on satellite network Al Arabiya that "we have not been perfect" is included as another example. My favorite for its absurdity is Obama's acknowledgment that "we went off course" in our pursuit of the war on terror, a comment he made in a speech given at the National Archives in May 2009. Never missing an opportunity to cozy up to the right this time around, Mitt Romney marched right down to the Heritage Foundation and shamelessly blasted the president's Cairo appearance as Obama's "apology tour in June of 2009." Romney was so excited about this conceit that he entitled his new book *No Apology: The Case for American Greatness*. It includes such gems as "Never before in American history has its President gone before so many audiences to apologize for so many American misdeeds, both real and imagined." Tim Pawlenty, former Minnesota governor, jumped on the same bandwagon, chiming in with an anemic attempt to sound Reaganesque: "Mr. President, stop apologizing for our country." Coupled with the mockery of the president's overseas diplomatic tours, this tactic seeks to place the president on the constant defensive, to make him appear incompetent, and even un-American. It exploits and expands the absurd claims by some that the president is a practicing Muslim, who was actually born in Kenya, not Hawaii as the Honolulu newspapers reported at the time of his birth. This approach is not limited to trying to undermine our confidence in the president, though. It follows a broader theme on the right, known as American exceptionalism.

While the repetition of the term *American exceptionalism* was noticeable on Fox News and other outlets a few years ago, it became much more common during the 2010 election cycle. There are obvious antecedents for this in the early notion that America has a divine role, not only as the ideal experiment in government and nation building, but also as the dominant nation in the world. The expansionist version, Manifest Destiny, accompanied the Monroe Doctrine in the first half of the nineteenth century to articulate America's providential mission to expand from the Atlantic seaboard to the Pacific. Later, President Theodore Roosevelt grounded some of the most aggressive foreign policy in American history—including military adventurism—in his idea of a Roosevelt Corollary to the Monroe Doctrine. These doctrines were principally focused on the Western Hemisphere. But these days the potential scope of American exceptionalism is global. Its most powerful expression in modern times is Ronald Reagan's evocation of the classic notion from the time of the *Mayflower* of a so-called shining city on the hill.

The notion of American exceptionalism is effective in part because there is little on the face of it that is offensive. It can mean different things to different people. For my part, I regard with pride America as unique and exceptional. I am particularly open to the emotional appeal of a special role for America and Americans, just as I have always been cognizant of the notion of the Jewish people as the chosen people. As an American and a Jew, I value these affiliations; they have always motivated me to try to be a worthy example of both American and Jewish ideals. So when political figures on the right speak of American exceptionalism, they know they are connecting with traditional notions of America's destiny that warm the heart of any patriot, including my own. They also know that it immediately places on the defensive anyone who raises questions about this doctrine, as I am about to do.

It seems that the purveyors of the American exceptionalism slogan fail (or willfully refuse) to understand that American exceptionalism could appropriately be phrased in a positive manner as a call for American leadership. They, however, are not concerned with employing the best parts of it to support a serious foreign policy for the twenty-first century. Rather they see its purpose as the opposite, to thwart serious attempts to reposition our country as a leading nation in a far more complex world. It is principally for domestic political consumption for congressional and especially presidential elections. The conservative version of American exceptionalism has become a password of sorts for candidates who want to prove their credentials to right-wing America. I experienced this in my reelection campaign in 2010. My opponent carefully avoided essentially any discussion of foreign policy, including Afghanistan and Iraq. He tried to stick to his domestic story of jobs and budget reduction. It was a real surprise then, when he suddenly ran two weeks of radio advertisements with a theme of American exceptionalism on Milwaukee's big conservative talk-radio stations. Clearly he had been advised that he had to check that particular box with the right to establish his bona fides. He targeted that particular audience with his new message and didn't bother to repeat it to the broader Wisconsin public.

Following this playbook was of even more consequence as the long battle got under way for the Republican nomination for president in 2012. American exceptionalism was on conspicuous display at the Conservative Political Action Conference held in Washington in February 2011. Each potential candidate made sure those words were uttered several times, with suitable pauses for applause. There were subtle but telling differences in tone: Some, like former Senator Rick Santorum, did so with his usual bombast. Others, like former Speaker of the House Newt Gingrich, were notably reckless in their approach. It was almost amusing to hear mild-mannered Tim Pawlenty firmly declare his belief in American exceptionalism. Just a few weeks before, Pawlenty had tried to reinvent himself in a new tough-guy image by rudely—and uncharacteristically—referring to the president as a "chicken." It was even more out of character when he adopted the term *American exceptionalism*. Anyway, as a Wisconsinite who grew up with many Norwegian Americans, I always thought Minnesotans believed in Swedish exceptionalism.

American exceptionalism has been joined to other conservative notions—that global warming has little or nothing to do with human activity (sunspots are the most likely culprit) or that President Obama is a socialist—to form an ideology of the right that no candidate is wise to question. This might be a vote winner at home but it could be instructive to give some thought to how this doctrine might be perceived by others around the world. American exceptionalism is too often promoted on its own, without modification by any statement of respect for other cultures, and can come across as arrogant, unfriendly, and offensive. To emerging superpowers like China and India, it has the flavor of Rudyard Kipling's "White Man's Burden" of the former British Empire, which once dominated one-fourth of all humanity. To those in the turbulent nations of the Middle East, it must have echoes of President George W. Bush's gaffe about crusades. Although it is an understandable sentiment, in its current incarnation American exceptionalism post-9/11 does not help. It undermines our national security interests by encouraging rather than reducing resentment toward America and Americans. The foolishness of constantly shoving the term *American exceptionalism* in the faces of other peoples of the world seems as obvious as when a child is told by its mother or a teacher that it is not nice to brag and that people won't like you if you do. What has happened to useful notions such as "walk softly and carry a big stick," as articulated by President Theodore Roosevelt, or the idea of showing humility, so often stated by President George W. Bush? We are an exceptional nation and I expect we will continue to be the leading nation in the world. But we are less likely to remain in that position if we wake up only briefly from our slumbers to shout, "We're number one!" and then go back to sleep.

Russ Feingold and John McCain *(Mary Murphy Irvine)*

Taller Buddha of Bamiyan, before and after destruction by Taliban in 2001
(left: UNESCO/A. Lezine; right: Carl Montgomery)

Russ and his father, Leon Feingold, late 1960s
(Sylvia Feingold)

Sylvia Feingold, Russ's mother, late 1990s
(Courtesy of Russ Feingold)

Russ Feingold with former President Richard M. Nixon at the
US Capitol in 1993 *(Mary Murphy Irvine)*

Mohamed Atta

Former United States Attorney
General John Ashcroft

Ambassador Richard Holbrooke

Admiral William Fallon

Russ Feingold with Senators McCain, Clinton, Graham, and Collins, and members of the armed services in Kabul, Afghanistan, in 2005
(Courtesy of Russ Feingold)

Russ Feingold with Badger soldiers in Camp Fallujah, Iraq, in 2005
(Courtesy of Russ Feingold)

Russ Feingold with "Packer backer" Wisconsin troops in Kabul, Afghanistan, in 2005 *(Courtesy of Russ Feingold)*

John McCain addressing Kuwaiti emirs at banquet in 2006
(Courtesy of Mark Kirk)

Russ Feingold jotting notes while traveling in a military helicopter over Iraq in 2006 *(Mark Kirk)*

Russ Feingold, Senator McCain, Senator John Thune, Governor Tim Pawlenty at banquet with vice president of Iraq Adil Abdul-Mahdi in 2006 *(Mark Kirk)*

McCain Codel of 2006 holding a press conference with the president of Iraq, Jalal Talabani *(Courtesy of Mark Kirk)*

Russ Feingold touring a school in earthquake-damaged Pakistani Kashmir in 2008 *(Sarah Margon)*

Russ Feingold with a local Pakistani leader in 2008 *(Sarah Margon)*

Russ Feingold with Sheikh Sharif Sheikh Ahmed in Djibouti in 2008, just prior to Sharif becoming president of Somalia *(Evan Gottesman)*

Russ Feingold being greeted
by King Abdullah and Queen
Rania of Jordan in Amman in
2006 *(Mark Kirk)*

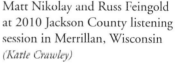

Matt Nikolay and Russ Feingold
at 2010 Jackson County listening
session in Merrillan, Wisconsin
(Katie Crawley)

Pig Roast pink pig and Russ
Feingold in Endeavor, Wisconsin,
in 2009 *(C. Y. Ferdinand)*

President of Angola,
Jose Eduardo dos Santos
(Ricardo Stuckert/PR, Agência Brasil)

President of Indonesia,
Susilo Bambang Yudhoyono

Former Tunisian president,
Zine al-Abidine Ben Ali
(Presidency of the Nation of Argentina)

10

Economic Collapse and the Loss of International Focus

... the president's real name is Soetoro; he changed his name to Barack Hussein Obama.

I had been invited to a new kind of Tea Party months before, so I certainly wasn't expecting adulation at my Jackson County listening session in January 2010. Almost exactly a year earlier, within days of President Obama's inauguration, the atmosphere at town meetings had become pretty heated. There was now only occasional respite from the harshness and incivility exhibited by some members of many audiences in almost every corner of the state. Wisconsinites were, and in many cases still are, hurting from the sudden economic collapse of fall 2008. But this didn't mean that most of the discussion and complaints were about the faltering economy, whose fault it was, or what should be done about it. Rather, the dominant topic in the first half of 2009 was what Obama would do as president, whether on climate change, health care, or taxes. An alternative, and rather popular topic, was the absurd claim that the president was not legally entitled to serve, because he had been born outside of the United States. I first experienced this foolishness at a town meeting in Richland County in July 2009, when some constituents were warming to the idea of turning listening sessions into confrontation sessions. I had a hard time believing that the so-called birther movement would get much traction or would last very long, given the wide range of other items on the conservative agenda, let alone on the nation's. But it did. One conversation, illustrative of the new mood in my listening sessions, sticks in my mind.

The meeting in Merrillan, Wisconsin, was well attended and started with comments about cap-and-trade legislation and the power of the oil companies. When Jim Franks was called on he did begin with a statement that he worked in a nonunion shop and didn't like what he called the special deal the unions got in the health-care bill, which had recently been passed by the Senate. I made some comment about how so many more people were showing up to these meetings to complain about issues that existed before Obama became president, and wondered why they hadn't been mentioned before. Jim explained, "Okay. Here's the deal. I'll tell you exactly what it is. I don't trust the president that's in office." I responded, "Ah, I think that's an honest answer." Jim went on, "He's a shady character. There's a lot of secrets going around. He talks about being transparent, but there's no transparency with this guy." And then he got to the heart of his argument. "My first thing I have to say is, do you know that the president's real name is Barry Soetoro? He changed his name to Barack Hussein Obama." "I've never heard this one," I responded. "What is Soetoro?" Mr. Franks informed me that "Barry Soetoro is his real name."

This exchange, with its reference to Obama's Indonesian stepfather, was just an odd interlude for me. But it was just too much for Matt Nikolay, my longtime aide, friend, and regional coordinator. Matt, a native of Abbottsford, a town in the same general region, usually made a point of keeping his mouth shut during the listening sessions. Of all my regional coordinators, he had the least tolerance for my occasional tendency to engage with confrontational constituents when it might be wiser just to listen. Matt would give me a jab in the ribs or whisper, "C'mon now, Rusty," in his folksy Wisconsin way in hopes of getting me back on track. But this time it was Sunshine, as some female staffers liked to call my intermittently grumpy aide, who couldn't put a lid on it. Matt emitted a phony loud cough so he couldn't be heard by everyone else, turned to me in disgust, and said, "Why wouldn't he just call himself Bill Smith?" For Matt, me, and all the staff members who attended the listening sessions in 2009 and 2010, this sort of exchange became commonplace. Maybe it wasn't as irrelevant as describing a thong to Carl Levin during the Clinton impeachment trial in 1999, but these meaningless discussions seemed so far removed from the international and domestic problems we were facing that it was hard to fathom. It was then I began to ask myself if America was in some sort of denial, to be discussing fantastic stories about our president rather than the enormous challenges that confronted us.

The beginning of the Obama administration marked a dramatic shift in the national conversation about our priorities and our future. While there were inklings of this after the economic collapse in late 2008, the real change began in early 2009. After September 11, 2001, there had been years of intense debate about America's position in the world and the right way to combat Al Qaeda. That debate was too often distorted by its failure to consider Al Qaeda in an honest and informed manner, the Bush administration's chicanery on Iraq being the most egregious example. Nonetheless, there was discussion about the dangers that could result from a failure to stay alert to our national security and related international issues. As the election year of 2008 unfolded, much of the debate in Congress, the content of the Sunday television talk shows, and a great deal of talk on the long presidential campaign trail revolved around Iraq, Afghanistan, the military, the handling of terrorist suspects, and, to a lesser extent, the nature of Al Qaeda and its affiliates. The enormous economic shock in September introduced a wide range of urgent new subjects that overshadowed the international issues. The big bank bailout, the need to re-regulate Wall Street, the plight of the suffering automobile industry, home foreclosures, and the flagging economy all required our attention. This recalibration of our national attention was necessary, inevitable, and completely appropriate. One would have expected, then, that the first months of the Obama years would involve an intense dual national debate about both our domestic and international challenges. From the start, President Obama did his best to be a leader who stayed on top of the international issues, including a long and thoughtful review of our Afghanistan policy in the context of the challenge of Al Qaeda. I could not have disagreed more with his decision on this matter, but the balance he achieved at the outset between domestic and global concerns impressed me and held the promise that America would meet the difficult challenge of walking and chewing gum at the same time at this crossroads in our nation's history. But it was not to be.

The president's decision—a correct one I believe—to make health-care reform the biggest expenditure of political capital in his first two years in office naturally led to that issue occupying a huge portion of the government's and public's attention. But health-care reform and pressing economic issues, not to mention questions about the president's birthplace, need not have been combined in such a way that they effectively obliterated any serious concentration on the post-9/11 national security issue. Part of the blame for this goes to those on the left, progressives, and other Democrats who suddenly muted or altogether stopped their intense opposition to the war in Iraq and suppressed their growing concerns about the continuing commitment in Afghanistan. We now had a Democratic president and control of both houses of Congress, so the political advantages of excoriating George Bush and the Republicans for a wayward foreign policy were largely gone. This change was disappointing and did not speak well of the sincerity of some of Bush's harshest critics. But something far more calculated and sinister came into play as soon as the new president was sworn in. Knowing that recovery from the worst economic downturn since the Great Depression would be slow at best, a powerful and well-heeled group took calculated action. They wanted this presidency to fail from the outset and so they brilliantly and ruthlessly exploited the deep public anxiety that was symbolized, if not accurately represented, by the new Tea Party movement.

In the beginning, a central feature of this new conservative strategy, for which the Tea Party was either the vanguard or a tool, was an attempt to limit national debate to the distressed economy. Ignoring the fact that the origins of the economic crisis lay in the Bush administration's fiscal policy, or lack of it, they blamed continuing financial woes on Obama. His overall agenda was stigmatized as socialist; later his health-care program was to be described as the greatest threat to our freedom in our lifetime. It is interesting that once-popular topics such as guns, God, and gays (and of course abortion) were dropped; some had even credited the Bush and Republican successes in 2004 to their vocal position on these issues. Another critical tactic was to observe virtual silence on the international and national security issues that had been so problematic for the Bush administration.

Just a few weeks into Obama's term, I hosted a private bipartisan meeting with Democratic Senator Jeff Bingaman and Republican Senator Lindsey Graham in my office. The topic was the future of the various state-based health-care proposals each of us had made in the past to restart a debate that had stultified since the failure of Bill Clinton's big plan and the Republican tsunami in 1994. It didn't take long for me and Jeff to realize that we really had to wait to see what the president would announce, since Obama had already indicated that health-care reform was to be his top priority in the near term. Lindsey Graham, affable as always, and candid as often, said that was just as well because "the decision's already been made to bring Obama down on health care." This was long before this particular strategy became apparent, but by July, sure enough, the very conservative Senator Jim DeMint of South Carolina came right out in public and said, "If we're able to stop Obama on this, it will be his Waterloo. It will break him."

So much for the honeymoon. Obama had been elected by a healthy majority at a time when many Americans were panicked about their economic future and found themselves in what seemed to be an increasingly unfriendly world. Instead of working with the president, this partisan group decided that Obama was to be treated as though he were the enemy, a vulnerable Napoleon, rather than a new president whose leadership we sorely needed. Whether the health-care bill or the economy or the rise of the Tea Party movement or any combination of them will be Obama's Waterloo in

November 2012 is yet to be seen. What is clear is that this political strategy worked like a charm in the 2010 elections, when the conservative movement made unprecedented gains and took over the House of Representatives, erasing a significant deficit. Indeed, the fact that I have the time to write this book now, instead of working in the US Senate, is a testament to the effective exploitation of the political environment in 2009 and 2010.

But the point here is that one major side effect of the stop-Obama strategy was to turn the national conversation inward. Efforts to engage the public or even my colleagues on the challenge of Al Qaeda and international terrorism became the equivalent of talking to a brick wall. September 11 was long ago, the economy was in shambles, we hadn't been attacked in the homeland successfully since 2001, and the costs of the foreign interventions were astronomical and apparently unending. The country had indeed been induced into another dangerous slumber when it came to the rest of the world.

Some date the origin of the Tea Party to October 3, 2008, when the TARP (Troubled Asset Relief Program) bill was signed, effectively bailing out the banks and Wall Street. I was one of the very few members of Congress to oppose the bailout and I did receive some favorable comments about that. But in the fall of 2008, this sentiment seemed to be coming from more liberal constituents. A more accurate date to mark the birth of the Tea Party is November 4, 2008, the day America elected Barack Obama as its forty-fourth president. The early Tea Party rallies got a lot of attention and certainly fascinated the media. A favorite and well-publicized Tea Party tactic was directed particularly at town hall meetings—they set out to destroy or at least constrict meaningful conversations at the meetings that so many members of Congress usually held during congressional recesses. While I had only three listening sessions left in the final two months of 2008, I noticed an immediate increase in the number of conservative Wisconsinites who attended the meetings, mostly to talk about the nation's debts and deficits.

Then at the Walworth County listening session just four days after the president was sworn in, Matthew Hartlaub became the first to ask me if I would like a copy of the Constitution. In the next two years I was offered copies of the Constitution or asked if had read it on many occasions. It is curious that not one of the people who now questioned my knowledge of the Constitution had come to a single town meeting from 2001 to 2009 to raise concerns when the Bush administration was savaging the Constitution. In retrospect, it is evident that tactics to discredit the new president, question his legitimacy, and accuse him of promoting a socialist agenda were being auditioned for coming confrontations with members of Congress.

Then, on or around February 19, 2009, the movement got its name. CNBC reporter Rick Santelli called for a tea party in Chicago to oppose President Obama's plans to relieve the housing crisis. Right after this, Tea Party rallies sprung up across the country leading to more organized gatherings in state capitols all over the nation on April 15, tax day. Because I had town meetings all year round, rather than only during the August recess, I was an early observer of the new movement. One of the biggest myths in American politics is that this was primarily about Obama's health-care plans. No, it was not, although, as Lindsey Graham had warned, that was considered the best weapon to undo the president. The president had just barely moved into the White House when we started receiving tea bags at our offices in Wisconsin—and most of us were big coffee drinkers. By March we were still getting tea bags in the office, but now angry men and women who adorned the brims of their hats with dangling tea bags started turning up at listening sessions in northwestern Wisconsin. They sure didn't seem to like the cut of my jib. The generally civil attitude of Wisconsinites toward me and the others in the room began to deteriorate. At both the Brown County listening session on March 28 and the Manitowoc County listening session on April 17, a couple of people kept shouting out comments, contrary to the usually respected ground rules for the meetings. My state director, Jay Robaidek, a generally low-key native of this part of the state, made note of this: "I recall thinking how odd that behavior was at the time because we had not seen it before." I had seen it before, but only a couple of times, during the heated debate over partial-birth abortion in 1997 and 1998, before Jay's long tenure with me. But it was indeed rare.

One of the first indications of how different these town meetings would be from ones in prior years came in the summer of 2009 in one of the most progressive and green-oriented counties in the state, Crawford County. In the midst of endless apple orchards in the nonglaciated hills of western Wisconsin, a good crowd gathered in Gays Mills, a place significantly populated by people of my vintage or older who liked to describe themselves as aging hippies. They were generally supportive of my work, especially on environmental matters. This was a place where Al Gore's warnings about global warming would seem to have been almost religiously heeded. But on July 18, 2009, in the Gays Mills Community Center, in a community that had just been devastated by a flood, Rodney George of nearby Soldiers Grove said, "I just want to make a statement that I do not believe in global warming. It's a scam." The room erupted in applause. I was stunned. This man was from a town that had made national fame when it moved its entire downtown up the hill after a flood decades ago, and had created one of the first solar-power communities in America.

And then in a more conservative county, Waushara, later that month, I had my first experience of the willful attempt to rewrite recent history, to blame all that is wrong on Obama. Richard George of Waupaca sat at the front of a pretty agitated crowd at the Wild Rose Lions Club building and clearly didn't like much of what I had to say. He held up a sign accusing Obama of being a socialist. When I called on him, he said, "Senator, I wondered what your opinion is on Obama trying to turn our beautiful country into a fascist state by trying to take over the auto industry, take over the banks, take over the insurance industry, take over the health care. It's no longer socialism, it's pushing communism." Reacting to his suggestion that the bank bailout had occurred on Obama's watch, I failed to resist the temptation to say, "It's funny, I could have sworn that happened under George Bush. I've heard of history being rewritten, but how does history get rewritten that fast?" I continued, "Okay, Obama may have come to

Washington to vote for it and I voted against the bank bailout, but it wasn't under Obama." To which an anonymous constituent yelled out, "Who was it?" I could not believe that I had to spell it out for them. I said it was Bush. But Mr. George had had enough. He got up from his front-row seat, flung his makeshift sign into the air, and stalked out of the room.

The big push at the town meetings by the Tea Party and their sympathizers came in August. We began to encounter well-coordinated efforts to take over the meetings. There was an obvious nationwide pattern of harassment that would ensure that anyone who spoke up for or even expressed a willingness to consider Obama's initiatives would find their town meeting experience a very unpleasant one. We had witnessed enough at earlier meetings to see this coming and C-SPAN was already broadcasting similar encounters in places like Virginia and Pennsylvania. We obtained a copy of "Rocking the Town Halls—Best Practices: A Political Action Memo," a manual for disrupting town meetings. It was written by a Bob MacGuffie and produced by a Fairfield County, Connecticut, group calling itself "Right Principles: Unapologetically American." They boasted of having successfully "conducted an action at Congressman Jim Himes's Town Hall meeting in May 2009." The memo suggested that the tactics used against Himes "could be useful to activists in just about any district where their Congressperson has supported the socialist agenda of the Democrat leadership in Washington." Their goal was candidly stated: "Our objective was to 'pack the hall' with as many of our people ready to challenge the Congressman, put him on the defensive, and give him a reality check from we-the-people."

They happily reported that their techniques "immediately made Himes uncomfortable" and that he "clearly left the hall staggered, as the meeting, billed as a progress report for his economic solutions, clearly did not go as he had planned." The memo then "humbly submits" a "potential playbook" with some perfectly reasonable suggestions on how to build a crowd and prepare specific questions. But then it said, "Use the Alinsky playbook, of which the Left is so fond: freeze it, attack it, personalize it, and polarize it." The yelling out that we had begun to experience was specifically recommended:

You need to rock-the-boat early in the Rep's presentation. Watch for an opportunity to yell out and challenge the Rep's statements early. If he blames Bush for something or offers other excuses—call him on it, yell back and have someone else follow-up with a shout-out. Don't carry on and make a scene—just short intermittent shout-outs. The purpose is to make him feel uneasy early on. . . . The goal is to rattle him. . . .

The conclusion is triumphant. "Just imagine what we can achieve if we see to it that every Representative in the nation that has supported the socialist agenda has a similar experience!"

Now, let there be no question: I would defend at any cost the right of the Right Principles group to express themselves at a town meeting and I can congratulate them for their doggedness and discipline. That is in fact what the First Amendment is all about. As a representative and a lover of history, I was intrigued by this new phenomenon. My staff got a little worried about me when I seemed occasionally to enjoy jousting with people who had absolutely no intention of giving me credit for anything I had ever done or said. Maybe I had spent so many years receiving positive feedback for holding these meetings that I was ready for a rumble or two. There can be no doubt that my supporters and I got quite a bit more than that, however.

The anticipated health-care bill was becoming the central focus of the attacks by August 2009 and it continued as such well into 2010, after the bill was actually proposed, passed, and signed into law. These tactics put off many people who had regularly come to my listening sessions. Constituents who used to prepare comments or questions for me every year would now sometimes pass when I called out their names or would not fill out a speaker's slip in the first place, once they'd assessed the mood in the room. Many looked worried or even fearful as they watched how I would handle the situation. Very few people find being booed by an angry crowd good fun.

One person who had the guts to take this on was Dr. Bob Horswill, who attended most of the Iron County listening session in Mercer, Wisconsin, on August 19. He was a member of a prominent family from Janesville, my own hometown at the other end of the state, and his dad had been the high school principal there. Bob had been a family physician in the Mercer area for decades. By the time his slip came up, he had already witnessed one of the most contentious town meetings I had ever held. Dr. Horswill seemed to be a person worth listening to when he explained, "Been in practice for forty-one years. Finished grad school in Madison in sixty-eight. We need a single-payer system." Some of my uncharacteristically silenced regular attenders actually applauded. Bob added, "I've worked with the military, in military hospitals, the VA, the small clinic down in Hurley part-time. I'm on Medicare. You know, it's pretty good. We need Medicare for everybody." Bob got a little more applause and the angry part of the crowd was a bit quieter for a moment, in a rare exception to the belligerent reception that kind of comment usually got in the second half of 2009. Maybe it was just too much, even under the Right Principles manual, to heckle a guy who may have been involved in the birth of your child or the comforting of your elderly grandmother. Bob finished his comments, looked unhappy, and then just slipped out of the back of the hall.

The assault in Mercer on Obama's not-yet-existent health-care program then resumed in earnest. Every myth imaginable was trotted out in a carefully orchestrated attack: There would be death panels for the elderly, your personal bank accounts would be fully accessible to the government, everyone's Medicare benefits would be cut. We were forced to defend a list of provisions that simply did not exist. In the absence of an actual proposal for me to cite, these determined advocates could simply claim of any imaginary proposal that they "had heard it was going to be in there." No one could have imagined a more unpopular piece of legislation.

And by no means did everybody get the grudging respect accorded Dr. Horswill in Mercer. This was the experience of one Norwegian (and I don't mean a Norwegian American; I mean a Norwegian who was visiting Wisconsin) who spoke up at a listening session in what has to be the most Norwegian place outside of Oslo. Early that same August 2009, we traveled to western Wisconsin for town meetings and drove to the tiny town of Chaseburg. The people in this area of the state are legendary for their affection for everything Norwegian. The ancestors of many who still live and farm in this region had settled in this land of sweeping valleys and picturesque hills in the nineteenth century, and helped make Wisconsin famous around the world as America's Dairyland. The cafes in town are often decorated with the delicate Norwegian flower patterns known as *rosemaling*. You can order *lefse,* a flatbread, and sometimes even lutefisk, whitefish soaked in water and lye until it becomes pungent and gelatinous. (Only a few non-Norwegians ever acquire a taste.) Golf course logos are likely to portray Viking ships, and the most common form of humor is still the latest Ole and Lena joke, a genre that features a challenging marital relationship between a couple of Norwegians. When told in a halting Norwegian accent, even off-color Ole and Lena jokes take on a charm that makes them funny, even in mixed company. So as I surveyed the exceptionally large crowd that had gathered in Chaseburg, the last thing I expected was the response this young man got as he spoke to the group.

There were 108 in attendance, and the room in the village hall was filled well beyond its capacity. Clearly most of the folks in the room weren't from Chaseburg, but that's not to say they weren't from the general area. As was so often the case that August, the crowd was full of intense-looking people who seemed ready for a fight—very different from the respectful, calm speakers who had been attending town meetings in this county for the previous sixteen years. As in Iron County and just about everywhere else at the time, the largest share of criticism was directed at the imagined health-care bill that Fox News and the right-wingers on the Internet had assured people would be passed by the Congress and signed by the president. After the usual list of fantastical items that were sure to be in the bill was repeated several times, I came upon a slip from someone with a name even more Scandinavian than the scores of Olsons, Nelsons, and Moens who lived in this area. I called out "Stian Bjerkvold" and a pleasant-looking young man stood up at the very back of the room and began. "I am from Norway," he said. I confess that I was grateful to think that this kid might provide some respite from the hostile atmosphere in the room and said, to laughter from the crowd, "There are no Norwegians around here at all." Stian, who was a foreign-exchange student from Hov, continued: "I compliment you, sir, and I compliment members of Congress and especially President Obama. We love what you are trying to do, sir, to create universal health care for everyone." One constituent yelled out, "This is our country." Undeterred, Stian politely added, "We have done that in Norway for a long time." Stian was greeted with a round of exceptionally raucous booing, tempered by a little subdued applause. I managed to regain a little control when I said, "I can't believe I'm in western Wisconsin and you're booing a Norwegian. That's impossible. Let him talk." This raised a little laughter, and the crowd cooled down for a minute to let Stian reiterate his comments and conclude by saying, "You have my warmest support, sir." What a nice, gutsy young man, I thought, as I called out the name of the next speaker. But as the people of this region love to say after a long day at work or after lifting a heavy crate, "Uff-da." If foreign-exchange students were going to be the only ones willing to speak out publicly for health-care reform, then we were in deep trouble. So many Wisconsinites had clamored for this sort of change for years. Now they seemed intimidated by the tone at the town meetings, first remaining silent and then not attending at all.

Indeed, strong support for universal health care had almost always been the most frequent single discussion point at my town meetings from as far back as 1995. The September 11, 2001, attacks did not displace health care; it was only the growing dismay at the toll of the Iraq War that finally knocked support for health-care reform out of its top slot in the mid-2000s. In 2007, 435 people talked about foreign policy and national security issues; health-care matters ran a distant second at 290. By 2008, health care was nearly equal with international issues at my listening sessions, and almost every single comment on that subject was in support of significant health-care reform legislation. Concerns about our post-9/11 international strategy were still in first place as Wisconsin awakened to the drain on our domestic resources that these international miscues would cause for America in general. Then came 2009.

Not only was the number of people in attendance the largest I had experienced in sixteen years, but the mood and content had completely shifted. More than one thousand people commented on health care. It was number one again, all right, but this time there were hundreds of harshly negative comments about federal legislation in this area. Foreign and military affairs as a topic slipped to third after health care and the economy. It got a mere 256 comments by comparison. As the Tea Party rose in 2010, I saw fewer and fewer of the constituents who had come every year to talk about health-care reform. Foreign matters slipped to fourth place when it attracted only 149 comments out of 2,350, the largest number of total comments I had fielded in eighteen years. In the middle of two wars and continuing Al Qaeda threats, as well as scores of other related issues, from Guantánamo to torture to better-made Humvees, all of this had faded from public discourse. In the midst of an economic crisis, we were witnessing the effective constriction of public debate into just a few topics. We weren't hearing much about abortion, which had always been a big topic and now wasn't even in the top ten. We were hearing precious little about the power of the oil companies whose record profits had sent constituents into a rage when gas prices kept rising. And, less than ten years after 9/11, we were hearing almost nothing about events throughout the rest of the world and our role in them.

When we voted on the health-care bill in the Senate on Christmas Eve and I headed out for a brief holiday break, I knew 2010 would be a very tough year. The electorate was clearly infected with an almost across-the-board anti-incumbent fever. Many senior congressmen and our own state governor were not inclined to run for reelection in this environment, so, after eighteen years in the Senate, I essentially became the incumbent to defeat in Wisconsin. I also knew that my town meetings would be at least as heated in 2010 as they had been in the second half of 2009 and feared they would be focused for a long time on the passage of the health-care bill, to the exclusion of just about everything else.

I was right.

In fact, wanting to gauge how much difficulty we were in, I chose to hold one of my first listening sessions of the year in one of the toughest counties. The Waukesha County listening session on January 11, 2010, was packed. The audience was intent on discussing not only the evils—imagined or otherwise—of the health-care bill but also my political future. In addition to the confrontational comments of most of the speakers I called on, anonymous voices yelled out things like "Do like Dorgan and Dodd!" referring to two of my Senate colleagues who had chosen not to run for reelection rather than face a very tough campaign fight. One particularly popular speaker, Natalie Freed, let me have it for "not listening to the views of the people" and added a warning: "We are fed up and you better get your résumé ready." This received thunderous applause. Her comment was featured in a television advertisement against me and Natalie was lionized at the state Republican convention that May. I came to expect to be on the defensive at these meetings, until some of those supporting my views decided it was safe to return around April 2010. I even had a good laugh at myself, when someone dressed in a huge pink pig outfit appeared at the back of the room at my 2009 Marquette County listening session. I automatically assumed this would involve a representation about something Obama or I had done to destroy the country. Instead, as I found out at the end of the meeting, that pig was only promoting the upcoming Endeavor Pig Roast and wanted its picture taken with me. I smilingly complied.

Perhaps the most poignant example of how far the listening sessions had drifted from the issues of the mid-2000s came in the person of one Tom German. Tom was an older man from the conservative town of Brillion, Wisconsin, in the Fox River Valley. Despite having some obvious difficulty in walking, Tom made it to my town meetings year after year all over the state, apparently driving long distances just to speak his piece on the same topic, over and over again. I first remember seeing Tom at town meetings on April 1, 2002, just months after 9/11. At the one in Oshkosh, Tom kicked off his comments with this: "Welcome to Oshkosh, Senator. I appreciate your help against bovine growth hormone. It was the last time we agreed [laughter from the crowd]. I came today because I'm afraid that with campaign finance, that I will lose my free speech. It sounded like you wanted to deal with these terrorists—I call them coward cockroaches—by bringing them over here for trial."

Tom went on to attend listening sessions all over the state for almost ten years. I even got him to smile once, when I noted that the only guy who attended more listening sessions than Tom German was me. And he was right: The last thing we'd agreed on was that dairy cows should not be injected with BGH. From 2001, Tom would come to a meeting somewhere in the state and patiently wait his turn. He would always manage to get to the front of the room, so when he was called upon he could turn to face the whole crowd. He would hold up a big book full of color photos of the 9/11 attacks and open it to two pages showing the Twin Towers in flames. Sometimes he'd turn to me and accuse me of aiding and abetting the terrorists. Perhaps the most memorable example of this was in Brussels, Wisconsin, in 2006. Tom's opening shot was "You've politicized the war for political gain. Nineteen thirty-eight. Neville Feingold or Russ Chamberlain. What are you going to do when they come for you?" Other times he would lecture the crowd, "See, you've forgotten all about this," when he would point to the 9/11 photographs. After a couple of years he added to his repertoire a little sign that said, "If we don't win the war on terror, nothing else matters."

Before mid-2009, I would often have to ask the crowd not to boo Tom. I'd say that I was glad he drove long distances to participate, pointing out that he was never rude in his tone. By my calculations, Tom attended twenty-seven listening sessions. But after Barack Obama was inaugurated, he encountered a completely different scene. At last the rooms were packed with his people, not with antiwar Democrats or advocates for universal health care. Now he was, at least in theory, surrounded with like-minded conservatives, who certainly shared his view that Obama and I were too soft on the terrorists. One would have expected him to receive a rousing reception when he excoriated me for my foreign policy views while alternating between his photo book and his sign. Instead there was only a smattering of polite applause; judging by the look on his face, he expected more.

But Tom hadn't gotten the memo—literally. After all, Right Principles' "Rocking the Town Halls" memo provided a clear rulebook that meant sticking to attacks on Obama's and the Democrats' domestic socialist agenda, not some foreign policy or antiterrorist stuff. It was only after Tom trudged back to his seat and I called on another person who would stick to the script that the crowd would get fired up again. Tom and I saw the post-9/11 challenges very differently but at least he thought they deserved to be discussed consistently throughout the ten years following 9/11. Tom stayed alert and asked that we all do the same. Unfortunately, our political environment had narrowed and turned the conversation almost entirely inward, and Tom's warning was being ignored.

PART 3

AWAKENING AMERICA

Members of Congress Engaging Other Countries

You see we have moved up six spots in the corruption rankings.

The Senate Foreign Relations Committee holds most of its major public hearings and meetings in the cavernous and simply decorated hearing rooms in the Dirksen Senate Office Building. The committee also has some of its smaller meetings in the far more cramped quarters of Room S-116, conveniently located just one floor down from the Senate floor in the Capitol. To enter the room you pass through the magnificent corridors designed by the great Italian artist Constantino Brumidi, who literally gave his life to decorating our Capitol. He died as a result of a fall from scaffolding while he was painting the Great Rotunda. The first time I passed through the corridors and the double doors into the ornate committee room, in January 1993, I saw a huge oval table, large enough for all the members of the committee as well as a stenographer and a witness or two. As the youngest member of the Senate and the most junior member of the Senate Foreign Relations Committee, I was uncertain where I should sit for my first meeting. A staff member said, "Senator," and pointed to a place on the table with a shiny gold plate embossed with MR. FEINGOLD. I pulled out the chair and took my seat, my dream of being a member of the Senate Foreign Relations Committee now realized.

Most proceedings in this historic room are open to the public if you can fit yourself in among all the senators, staff, and press usually crammed into the space. A longtime tradition of the committee, however, transforms the room into a beautiful parlor. Heads of state and other top foreign officials are formally greeted by the Senate in this setting under the auspices of the committee. These sessions are private, and are usually held in the middle of the week when most members are in Washington. The conference table is covered with a fine tablecloth and set with elegant Senate china and silver. A program embossed with the names of the senators and their foreign guests is placed at each setting. There are dishes of pastries, cakes, and fruit, and committee members and their guests are served by formally dressed waiters, who pour coffee from silver pitchers. When the foreign leader enters the room, everyone gathers for an official photograph. Then committee staff escort the media out of the room and an entirely off-the-record session ensues. The chairman and ranking member each make brief remarks of greeting, and then each senator according to seniority (but alternating by party affiliation) is given the chance to ask the guest of honor one question. I found these sessions to be among the most interesting and useful of my career in the US Senate. It was in this room where, while sipping coffee, I observed in person the incredible intensity of Robert Mugabe of Zimbabwe; the gentle, almost jolly demeanor of the Dalai Lama; the somber and fierce mien of Hosni Mubarak of Egypt; and the supremely confident style of Benjamin Netanyahu of Israel.

These were serious sessions, but I am able to report a couple of lighter moments. Not long after the great peace agreement on the South Lawn of the White House in 1993 at which King Hussein, Yasir Arafat, and Yitzhak Rabin came together for the first time to begin what many thought would resolve the Middle East dispute, Rabin was invited to one of these coffees. He was delayed, so while several senators waited for him to come through the double doors, we had a chance to make small talk with the always affable Jesse Helms, then the ranking member of the committee. Robyn Lieberman, my foreign relations staffer at the time, was well-versed in all things relating to Israel, and when she heard people referring to the prime minister as "Rabeen" (as most of us did), she pointed out that in Israel his name sounds more like "Robben." Soon the doors opened and, as the prime minister of Israel slowly walked in with a dour expression on his face, Jesse Helms said right out loud, "Well, the red, red robin comes bob, bob, bobbin' along." Rabin groaned, shook a few hands, and took his place for the coffee. This was surely an unusual way to greet a distinguished foreign dignitary, but it pales in comparison to what came into Joe Biden's head—and out of his mouth—when he was asked to welcome the king and queen of Jordan to one of these events.

After the death of his father King Hussein, and his ascendancy to the throne of the Hashemite Kingdom of Jordan, King Abdullah became one of the youngest key world leaders. His queen, Rania, is an even younger monarch of Palestinian origin, from one of the most significant and restive groups within Jordan. Together they made for one of the most striking couples in the world, but in my every encounter with them, their youth and attractiveness were at least matched by a serious and concerned demeanor when addressing issues important to Jordan and the rest of the Middle East. They visited Washington in May 1999, early in their reign, and, in addition to their White House visits, they graced one of our committee coffees. After the photos and the standard comments of greeting from Chairman Helms, it was ranking member Biden's turn to greet the royal couple. Joe decided it was a good time to articulate what all the male senators in the room were thinking but had no intention of voicing. He said, "Your Majesty, I see you have the same excellent taste in choosing a partner that your father had." (This was a reference to King Hussein's American-born Queen Noor.) I kept my gaze down for a moment and then looked up to see an uncomfortable king and queen. Mercifully, Biden quickly moved on to more serious material but I then caught the eyes of two of the most senior Democrats on the committee, Chris Dodd and John Kerry. It was one of those moments we've all been through—God, please don't let me burst out laughing. Dodd and Kerry were having the same problem. When I regained composure,

I couldn't help but think that in another place and time, any commoner who spoke that way about a monarch's wife would have been disposed of immediately.

I tell this story with respect and even affection for Joe because once he got down to business on almost any topic relating to foreign policy he spoke knowledgeably and sensibly. From the time he entered the Senate at the age of thirty in the early 1970s, he had chosen to make the Foreign Relations Committee one of the defining aspects of his long political career. There is no question that this experience influenced Obama's decision to choose Biden as his running mate. Barack had worked with Biden on international issues and knew that one of the biggest criticisms he himself would receive in the 2008 campaign was that he lacked international experience. Biden was the perfect antidote for this, but he was one of very few members of the House or Senate who could have filled that bill in this era. Despite the illuminating coffees and occasional interesting committee hearings, the few members of Congress sitting on these Foreign Relations Committees often did not devote a great deal of time to investigating issues, unless they comprised the foreign policy crisis of the moment. Compared to most members of Congress, however, the committee members were much more engaged in this role that the Founders clearly intended should be central for all members of the Senate. Giving the Senate exclusive powers to approve all ambassadors and all treaties was a major departure from the royal dominance of foreign policy that the English Crown had enjoyed. An awareness of world events and our role in them would presumably be considered part of any senator's job description. Unfortunately, there is little expectation within the Senate that senators should know much about foreign issues; expectations are even lower among the public at large. In fact a particular interest in the rest of the world is likely now to attract the criticism that a senator is spending too much time on foreign matters and not worrying enough about the people back home. I regret to say that far too many Senate members and their staff calculate pretty early on that you don't get much political bang from being well-versed on issues involving another part of the world. This has been true in many phases of our nation's history, but this insularity is highlighted in the sound-bite, thirty-second-attack milieu that masquerades as political discourse these days. Yet this may be the time in our nation's history when we can least afford to regard international expertise and activism as an unnecessary frill for the elected representatives of the most powerful nation on earth.

Upon entering the United States Senate in 1993, after a campaign that touched only tangentially on foreign policy, I had to make some decisions about which committees I would seek to join. As an observer of the Senate's unique powers over nominations and international treaties, I had imagined being a member of both the Judiciary and Foreign Relations committees. The Judiciary Committee had continued to enjoy high visibility and prominence at this time, particularly because of the increasingly contentious nature of Supreme Court nominee confirmation hearings and proceedings. The Foreign Relations Committee, however, had declined in status compared to the dramatic role it had played at various times in the past, including the 1960s. Senator William Fulbright's decision to highlight the problems with the Vietnam War had played an important role in defining the growing unpopularity of that conflict.

As I sought—or was simply offered—advice about the committee-choice decision, certain insiders in Washington, DC, as well as a few back home in Wisconsin tried to persuade me to join committees that would help me raise money for my next campaign. Having just won an election against a big fundraising incumbent by railing against this type of Washington thinking, I found these suggestions insensitive or even offensive. I had also campaigned on my belief that the growing federal deficit was an important issue for the country, so I sought to join the Budget Committee as well as the Judiciary Committee. Since I was a new Democratic senator with no seniority, however, none of these requests came through in my first Congress. Accordingly, Majority Leader George Mitchell called me, apologized, and offered me the choice of any one of the following committees: Banking, Commerce, Armed Services, or Foreign Relations. He needed an answer right away. I distinctly remember deciding to reject the political advice not to join the Senate Foreign Relations Committee because, I was told, it was in decline, wouldn't be good for raising money, and wouldn't do me any good at home. I chose that committee, not only because of its role in helping shape American foreign policy throughout much of our nation's history but also because my instinctive reaction to the way people talked about the committee was to wonder why the Senate of the most powerful nation in the world would give international matters such short shrift.

One of my first tasks on the committee was to list my preferences for subcommittees, most of which are based on geographic regions such as Europe or Latin America, rather than on topics such as antiterrorism or nonproliferation of nuclear weapons. I was told by one or two senators and a couple of staffers that, given my low seniority, I would probably "get stuck" on the Subcommittee on African Affairs at first, but could later move on to more glamorous assignments. This struck me as just as unfortunate as the advice to pick one's committees based on their fundraising potential. In this case, however, I started to think about how misguided it was for a superpower essentially to ignore an entire, complicated continent that had played such an important role in World War II and in Cold War debacles like the power struggles in Congo and Angola. The prevailing attitude seemed to be that now that the Soviet Union was no longer a problem, we wouldn't have to give serious attention to the lost cause of Africa.

For me, this was a wake-up call. One of my political predecessors and heroes, former governor of Wisconsin and US Senator Gaylord Nelson, had advised me that many senators knew their own areas of interest very well and it behooved me to pick something about which very few senators knew much and then make myself the Senate's expert on the topic. I was concerned about the dismissive attitude toward Africa and noticed that only a few senators, such as Paul Simon of Illinois, Nancy Kassebaum of Kansas, and Richard Lugar of Indiana, had taken Africa seriously. So I decided not only to become a member of the Africa subcommittee but pledged that I would stay on that subcommittee for as long as I was in the US Senate. I did so for a full eighteen years and certainly reaped the benefits of learning more about what is now an increasingly relevant part of our world.

My experience with the Subcommittee on African Affairs highlighted the low importance placed on international issues by the Senate in general and the lack of focus of the full committee itself on such unresolved and clearly potentially explosive issues as, for example, those simmering between India and Pakistan. I began to grow pessimistic about how we would fare internationally if we were perceived by much of the rest of the world as uninterested in, unaware of, or even dismissive of the needs, disputes, and aspirations of the peoples and nations of an ever more interconnected and complex world. I slowly began to understand that this could develop into a national security issue for America. Wouldn't we become the object of blame for much of what was wrong in the eyes of the international community, if we did not live up to our responsibilities to lead or at least to understand? And the word *resentment* kept running through my mind. If we as a nation, with our wealth and military power, appeared to want simply to gloss over these matters, would we not be the object of growing resentment from many quarters and thereby reap the whirlwind when this emotion turned to action?

During my eighteen years I discovered that the title of senator might have almost more status abroad than it does now at home. A visit, a letter, or a phone call from the right person could help to free an imprisoned journalist thousands of miles away, or to encourage something as wide-ranging as political reform. All things being equal, most other countries would prefer to have good relations with the most powerful nation on earth and are prepared to make modest adjustments to keep that relationship in balance. This gives each and every member of the Senate some leverage to effect change in other countries and reinforce our relationship with them. As I developed my knowledge of the rest of the world during my time on the Foreign Relations Committee, I could see that my ability to make a difference became greater, too. Indeed, in the stultifying partisan atmosphere that has bogged down the Senate in recent years, I found that foreign relations work provided some of the most rewarding opportunities to actually get something done.

Sometimes you can make the difference by passing legislation to pressure regimes to stop abusing their own people. This is what Republican Majority Leader Bill Frist and I did, when we proposed the 2001 Zimbabwe

Democracy and Economic Recovery Act in response to Robert Mugabe's near destruction of that country. This act stated that the United States would endorse sanctions against the Zimbabwean government and would "support the people of Zimbabwe in their struggle to effect peaceful, democratic change, achieve broad-based and equitable economic growth, and restore the rule of law." Other times sending a communiqué at the right time might have a big impact. In 2006, President Obasanjo of Nigeria proposed a bill to overturn the constitutional limitation to two terms of presidency, so that he could run for a third term. This move was disappointing. Obasanjo, though flawed, was a huge improvement over the kleptomaniacal Sani Abacha, who had been the dictator over that nation until his sudden death in June 1998. Whether relatively popular African leaders who had been elected in fairly legitimate balloting and had accepted term limits would actually stick to that limitation became one of the most important tests for political transition and stability in many countries, especially in Africa. So, when the Nigerian parliament defeated the president's bill, I sent off a letter on June 7, 2006, to the Speaker, congratulating the parliament and its members for standing up to the president on this constitutional issue. I learned that at one point during a contentious debate in that legislature over the distribution of oil revenues—the hottest issue in that divided nation—Senator Ken Nnamani, the president of the National Assembly, interrupted the proceedings to read what he called an important message from a United States senator. My letter read: "I am writing to congratulate you on your recent decision against the proposed amendment to the Constitution that would have extended your country's presidential term limit. Your decisive action is an important step forward for the health of your country's democratic institutions."

The interruption helped defuse the oil debate *and* Obasanjo stepped down without a hitch when his second term ended. I am well aware that my letter was only one factor in this outcome, but as my mother might have said in the Yiddish accent she had heard while growing up in Denver, "It didn't hoit." Even more effective than bills and letters and meetings in offices in Washington, however, were face-to-face meetings with leaders and other key figures in their own nations.

My first Codel as a US senator in 1994 included a substantial visit to Angola, after a brief stopover in Liberia. Angola is a country rich in natural resources and potential but is one of the worst victims of the Cold War as well as its own inner turmoil. Almost from the moment of its independence from Portugal in 1975, Angola had been consumed by a brutal civil war. It involved its so-called Marxist-Leninist regime supported by the Soviet Union fighting an anticommunist insurgency backed by the United States and South Africa. One of the disastrous consequences of this conflict was a large population of amputees, injured by the land mines that had been planted by both sides in the rich farmland of that country. Much of the populace had fled to the city to avoid the endless war, and now more than fifty thousand amputees lived in the country, most in the overcrowded capital of Luanda. As we arrived we saw many teenagers and younger kids with missing legs or arms. Oddly, their injuries were not always immediately evident, because some were carrying AK-47s that, at first glance, appeared to stand in for the missing limb. We visited a refugee camp where the squalor was almost unimaginable—refugees were crowded into tiny shacks of rusty corrugated metal; the water was polluted; dirt was everywhere; there was little sanitation and no electricity; and unhygienic conditions had led to outbreaks of disease. Hundreds of smiling children in rags would run up to us to have their picture taken and to beg for something to eat or keep. Yet the president of that country, Jose Eduardo dos Santos, who had been in power since independence and remains so as of this writing, lived in palatial splendor only a short distance from that teeming camp. His regime has been notoriously corrupt from the start, siphoning off billions of dollars of foreign aid and much of Angola's natural wealth. He implicitly justified that and his heavy-handed rule by reminding his constituents of the excesses of his late opponent Joseph Savimbi and his UNITA insurgent movement.

When Senators Paul Simon, Harry Reid, and I were finally offered an audience with the president, we took a hair-raising drive in a motorcade to the outskirts of town where his palace sprawled over many acres. We were escorted on both sides by trucks loaded with armed Angolan soldiers who hung off the sides of their vehicles, sometimes jumping off to shove the crowds back. We sped by the grim refugee camp to arrive at the gates and majestic drive to the palace. As we drove through, we could see the gardens bursting with color, and beyond them the Atlantic glimmered a beautiful light blue. Well-fed peacocks were strutting freely around the grounds, obviously enjoying a much better life than the refugees down the road. We were escorted to a spacious waiting room dominated by a huge watercolor of a baobab tree, the symbol of Africa especially in the postcolonial era. When we were taken into the president's office, we were greeted by a cool and calm Dos Santos, dressed in a Nehru jacket. His attire was a subtle reminder that we had ended up on opposite sides during the Cold War, as his government had sided with the Soviets. Now that the Cold War was over and our former alliance with apartheid South Africa largely irrelevant, we were trying to normalize our relations with his country. It was a low-key conversation but, as I always did in these sorts of meetings, I interspersed a tough question or two among the pleasantries and discussions of areas of common ground. I pressed Dos Santos to explain why Angola was rated one of the most corrupt countries in the world. He constructed an evasive answer that blamed the war and refugee influxes; shortly thereafter he politely showed us the door.

Five and a half years later I returned to Angola on my trip to Africa with Richard Holbrooke. The refugee camps were just as depressing, although many amputees now had prosthetic legs or arms—producing them had become a thriving business in Angola. The war still raged on. And Dos Santos's estate was still as grand and as discordant with the rest of Luanda as it had been the last time we were there. Holbrooke and I passed the gardens and the peacocks, saw the same watercolor, and then met with a slightly grayer, quieter president. As soon as I made my introductory remarks, Dos Santos smiled and said, "You see we have moved up six spots in the corruption rankings," referring to Transparency International's annual ranking of corruption in countries. That was still an outrageously bad ranking, but he wanted me to know they had improved. Apparently it mattered to him to prove to one US senator who was paying attention that Angola was moving in the right direction.

My 2005 congressional visit to Indonesia (where I had spent time with Admiral Fallon) had a completely different kind of impact. Before our trip to Aceh, I was able to spend an hour with the powerful president of that nation, Susilo Bambang Yudhoyono. One of the first foreign policy issues I ever encountered in my political career was the question of whether the island known as East Timor, a former Portuguese colony, should be given its independence from Indonesia. This is not exactly the first thing you expect to be discussing at a Badger football game, but that is just where I learned of this dispute, when I was a candidate for the Senate in the early 1990s. The incumbent, Senator Robert W. Kasten, had apparently become a fan of the harsh Indonesian regime under Suharto. He not only turned a deaf ear to the pleas of human rights advocates who exposed the brutal Indonesian crackdown on the East Timorese, but was also reported to be key to the success of Indonesia's arms requests to the United States when he sat on the Senate Appropriations Committee. When some Madison-area ETAN (East Timor and Indonesia Action Network) activists handed me some material at that Wisconsin football game, I became aware that about 250 East Timorese pro-independence supporters had been massacred by Indonesian soldiers as they marched from the Motael Church in Dili to the nearby Santa Cruz cemetery for a memorial service. There was no question that this was true— the Indonesian army's violence had been secretly filmed. I learned more, and after I defeated Kasten in 1992, I became one of the leading proponents in the Senate for East Timorese independence. I joined others, who were usually from states with Portuguese ethnic populations such as Massachusetts and Rhode Island.

These efforts, although somewhat removed from my particular interest in Africa, got me more involved in Indonesian affairs. After 9/11, I became interested in Jemaah Islamiyah, an ally of Al Qaeda, and its origins in Indonesia. But I was also troubled by the regime's treatment of people living in the Aceh region. Then I became concerned about the military's purported role in an incident on the eastern part of Indonesia, the shrouded Papua region, where several Americans had been shot and killed near a big mining operation. By the time I had my meeting with President Yudhoyono in 2005, I had such a wide variety of discussion points that I wasn't sure where to begin. And, because the opportunities for such contact are rare, advocates for human rights and other concerns were desperate for their issues to be discussed, too. In these meetings one always has to find a balance between the easier diplomatic topics on areas of mutual agreement and the trickier areas of tension that can weaken a bilateral relationship. When I sat down with the president, whose accommodations in this massive, resource-rich nation were far more subdued than those of Dos Santos in another former Portuguese colony, I made sure something entirely different was covered early in the meeting, and then got to as many of the other topics as I could in the time allotted me.

Indonesia is critical to our military and shipping needs in the Strait of Malacca but it also has a strong, historic relationship with Iran. Officials between those two nations meet and cooperate with one another all the time. At the same time Indonesia is eager to cultivate a strong relationship with us. So I took the opportunity to confront Yudhoyono by asking him, "Why was Indonesia one of only five countries not to vote to refer Iran to the Security Council for its activity in developing nuclear weapons?" Yudhoyono looked surprised, but in his mild way he explained that their abstention was temporary, designed to give Iran a little more time; Indonesia would probably be in favor of referral the next time around. And that's exactly what they did. Again, I have no delusions that this was solely the result of my pointed question, but I do know that the president took note of the fact that one of the most persistent critics of Indonesia's human rights record had chosen to prioritize curbing Iran's nuclear weapon ambitions, because of the threat this posed to us and the rest of the world. I believe it mattered to him that I had traveled to his country, was there in his office, and had obviously made it my business to include Indonesian matters in my US Senate work. Perhaps he thought that if he gave me the right answer and some action on Iran, I might go a little easier on my criticism of the Indonesian military's excesses. Of course, I did nothing of the kind. But showing him that I was paying attention to what was happening on the other side of the world from the United States gave me the credibility to press him on a vital national security issue.

These encounters with world leaders on their own home territory can be invaluable. This is, of course, why we have ambassadors and embassies as well as State Department officials. Even presidents sometimes make these trips. What I'm arguing is that a level of congressional involvement can help our government establish common ground with others while simultaneously pursuing concerns and disagreements that may be more delicate for other officials to convey. This has worked many times. A good example is the effect that people like Republican Senator Richard Lugar had when they put pressure on the apartheid regime in South Africa—they were able to make a difference, even during the Reagan administration.

On the other hand, it is also necessary to recognize that there are limits to this kind of congressional activity. An effective member has to tend to an enormous range of general domestic issues as well as those peculiar to one's own state (the dairy industry was my subspecialty for twenty-eight years). It is true that some members become a little too comfortable in DC, where they are treated with great deference so long as they are in office, and they don't always spend enough time in their own home states. But if a senator wants to commit to living at home, commuting, and then doing extensive town meetings or other constituent outreach, as I did, the recesses are the only time other than weekends when I could really cover a lot of ground. Just as meeting with world leaders in their home countries has value, I believe that seeing constituents in *their* hometowns has real merit. After subtracting the time needed to be in Washington for votes and the ever-expanding legislative sessions, such a schedule leaves little time for many foreign trips.

Unfortunately, some members have managed to abuse the system that allows them to travel the world, making unnecessarily lengthy trips or trips that were less substantive than they should have been. I remember in 1999 sitting in the bar of the Miekles Hotel in Harare, Zimbabwe, one afternoon between meetings, and hearing some American officials there complaining about an entourage of some twenty members of the House that had just blown through the region on what appeared to be a safari tour masquerading as a Codel. It was alleged that, on his Codels, Senator Arlen Specter and his staff had demanded that squash games be arranged for them in every capital; on other Codels staff sometimes had to haul huge quantities of shopping items onto official government planes to meet the retail therapy needs of spouses who had accompanied members on the trips. These practices did little to enhance our image abroad and have ensured that such trips are frequently and derisively called junkets, even if they're in the middle of eastern Congo during one of the deadliest wars in human history.

Despite these limits, I believe this country cannot afford to have a Congress that is largely populated by people who do not think foreign policy is part of their job. It is. No one can be expected to have a comprehensive knowledge of foreign affairs, although the late Congressman Stephen Solarz of New York was reputed to have a detailed knowledge of the political situation in every country of the world and spent most of his time overseas. That is not what I recommend. What I do recommend is a better division of labor and the creation of a public expectation that each member of the Senate and perhaps of the House will develop special knowledge of at least one other nation. This should be in addition to the usual committee assignments. An informal system should be established to ensure that every senator or representative is assigned a country. I believe this would be well received: Most members should find this assignment motivating and would welcome the opportunity to list this expertise as an official responsibility. Constituents would become aware of, and sometimes interested in, the country assigned to their representative. I know that on the few occasions when the topic of Africa came up at my listening sessions, Wisconsinites were happy to learn more about that continent from someone who had been there and knew what he was talking about. When an important foreign issue or crisis arose, congressional members would turn to the colleague assigned to that area for advice. These issues are sometimes generated by ethnic groups from a member's own state, for example by Ethiopians in Seattle or Poles in Milwaukee. This knowledge could enhance the stature of the member, improve what will hopefully be bipartisan cooperation on foreign policy, and strengthen the hand of that member when he meets a foreign leader to discuss sometimes contentious policy issues.

When George Bush tried to justify the Iraq invasion in his State of the Union speech on January 28, 2003, he claimed that "the British government has learned that Saddam Hussein recently sought significant quantities of uranium from Africa." (This unfortunate statement became known as the famous "sixteen words.") I was puzzled. When we then heard that the country of Niger in northern Africa had supposedly supplied yellowcake (a concentrated form of uranium) to Saddam Hussein for his nuclear program, something didn't ring true. Based on my knowledge of Niger, my immediate instincts were to doubt this. In December 1999, Richard Holbrooke and I had spent a long time in the tiny airport in Niamey with Lieutenant Colonel Mamadou Tandja when he was president-elect. It was two in the morning, during a refueling stop on our way home. The president-elect, dressed in white flowing robes and a white hat, spoke at length about his economic plan and complained that Niger could not choose its neighbors, worrying mainly about Libya and Muammar Qaddafi. When Bush made his accusation, my first thought was that President Tandja doesn't seem like the type to work with Saddam Hussein. Not only did I have a brief chance to know the man, but I had also taken the measure of his personality and intentions in his own environment. It later became clear that Bush's claim was based on what turned out to be forged documents. This is a valuable lesson for our executive branch and for our country. Members of Congress must be part of the awakening to the rest of the world that the post-9/11 environment requires of all of us.

The direct engagement of members of Congress in foreign matters is not without its risks. Obviously, we cannot have 535 separate foreign policies. I have observed members of Congress develop too-sympathetic relationships with flawed foreign officials of regimes whose legitimacy is questionable and who might be involved in corruption or brutal human rights violations. Such was the case when former Democratic US Senator Carol Moseley Braun of Illinois became close to Sani Abacha, the dictator of Nigeria in the 1990s. Some attribute her defeat after only one term to that relationship. But the risk of the occasional misjudgment of that kind is worth taking; it is more important that our lawmakers are engaged and informed about world affairs.

A more incorrigible problem is that whatever congressmen do know about another country might be spoon-fed to them by hired lobbyists in Washington. Second only to the booming antiterror and corporate lobbying that has arisen to exploit 9/11, the business of foreign governments employing highly paid prominent Americans to lobby for their policies is sadly one of the true growth industries in our nation's capital. I first noticed this unsettling practice, when a delegation from Zimbabwe asked if they could present their government's viewpoint to me to counter my tough line against the abuses in that country. I agreed to the meeting and found it heartbreaking to listen to one of the great leaders of the civil rights movement, Andy Young, repeat almost every lie that Robert Mugabe had manufactured in his desperate attempt to prevent democratic reform in his country.

Potentially more insidious is the institutionalized use of Washington power brokers, lobbyists, and former members of Congress as key figures of expertise and influence for a foreign country. For many years, Mark Siegel, partner in the Locke Lord Strategies lobbying firm employed by the Pakistani government, has been the main link between Washington leaders and the Pakistani dynasty of, first, Benazir Bhutto and now her widower, President Asif Ali Zardari. In mid-May 2011, it was reported that, as Pakistan's top lobbyist, Siegel's "job [was] to convince US officials not to take out their anger on the country despite the fact that Osama bin Laden spent at least five years living in relative comfort outside Islamabad." I am not suggesting that foreign countries or political movements should not employ representatives in Washington, but that one should treat their advice with caution. Although always wary, I have benefited on many occasions from American representatives who facilitated meetings with, for example, the late heroic Sudanese leader John Garang in the early 1990s, and with Morgan Tsvangirai, as he courageously stood up to Robert Mugabe and made contact with those of us in America who wanted him to have a fair chance to lead his party to power. The problem is that movements like Tsvangirai's rarely have the resources to match the financial power of corrupt government treasuries that can afford to keep expensive Washington-based lobbyists on retainer, attending political fundraisers, and generally participating in the Washington social scene. In a context where members of Congress have neither the time nor inclination to delve deeply into these matters, the big hitters representing repressive and undemocratic governments often have the most influence. This diminishes the quality of our overall foreign policy and tends to encourage relationships with rulers or parties who do not deserve unending fealty from the United States of America.

Foreign nations should not have such an influence over America's foreign policy, and former administration officials and members of Congress should be officially barred, either permanently or for a lengthy period of time, from accepting huge payments to act as their lobbyists. Their disproportionate power is derived from the fact that they were once elected by the people of this country and thereby have unusually strong contacts in Washington. Even before they leave office, the incentive of a lucrative contract in the future can consciously or unconsciously affect the way congressmen behave toward foreign governments. There is a related problem with current officials going easy on big corporate interests in anticipation of the large paychecks that await them on lobbying epicenter K Street after their government stint ends. Instead of waiting to see which foreign power will pay for their services, members of Congress should, as an accepted part of their job, be given the encouragement, support, and time to visit foreign countries and make their own judgments in person.

The Arab Spring that began in late 2010 is an excellent example of this problem. Our relatively unreserved ties with President Ben Ali in Tunisia, where the Arab Spring first blossomed, is an illustration of this. The most dangerous foreign policy scenario is when former administration officials and members of Congress themselves become the direct lobbyists for unsavory foreign powers. In May 2010, John McCain and I tried to get ahead of what we could both see was the excessive crackdown on human and democratic rights in Egypt by the Mubarak regime. On May 24, 2010, I spoke on the Senate floor to raise the issue of Egypt's recent extension of Emergency Rule—laws that extended police powers and legalized censorship—which had been in place almost continuously since 1967: "Continuing to provide uncritical support to an authoritarian regime undermines our credibility as champions of political and civil rights and creates tensions, particularly in the Muslim world, which are ripe for exploitation. Those tensions, in turn, threaten our own national security."

McCain and I then introduced a resolution to highlight this concern. Given the bill's bipartisanship and fairly mild language, most of us assumed it would have a fairly easy ride through the Congress. But it was not to be. As Eric Lichtblau reported in the *New York Times* in March 2011, after Tahrir Square and Mubarak's departure from power, "one of the most formidable lobbying forces in town" for years had been an "elite band of former members of Congress, former diplomats in Middle Eastern nations." Lichtblau reported, "Just last year, three of the biggest names in the lobbying club— Tony Podesta, Robert L. Livingston and Toby Moffett—pulled off a coup for one of their clients and helped stall a Senate bill that called on Egypt to curtail human rights abuses." Moffett, a former liberal Democrat congressman from Connecticut, told his former colleagues that the bill "would be viewed as an insult" by an important ally. And so, unlike the better-known McCain-Feingold campaign finance bill, the Feingold-McCain Egypt democracy bill went down in flames as the 111th Congress adjourned. In order not to insult a repressive regime, we insulted an entire democratic movement that was just beginning to emerge in the Arab world.

12

Americans Reaching Out to the
Rest of the World

Where in the world is Tunisia?

When I was teaching law at Marquette University Law School in the spring semester of 2011, I picked up a copy of the February 3 *Marquette Tribune*, the student news. An undergraduate, Brian Harper, had written a column titled, "Where in the world is . . . Tunisia?" His compelling confession of his lack of knowledge of the rest of the world mirrored my own feelings at different times, from my first studies abroad in England to my first weeks on the Senate Foreign Relations Committee. Brian wrote that the first question he asked himself "after hearing about the recent wave of political protests in Tunisia was probably the same many Americans asked: where is Tunisia? . . . If Tunisia were that big of a deal . . . it would have been featured more prominently in the news before these protests. Is it even an ally of the United States? Apparently not a very important one." Mr. Harper cited data about the deficiencies in geographical knowledge among eighteen- to twenty-four-year-olds (which I'm sure would be reflected in the broader population) and then worried that this was based on "the false assumption that anything that does not entertain us or affect our lives in a direct way is of little, if any, importance." In my favorite line in this well-written column, Brian noted that "though we may not know how to spell Kazakhstan, we do know how to spell Kardashian." His conclusion focused more on the economic and human benefits of being aware of and knowledgeable about the rest of the world, rather than on national security implications, but his words apply to each of these considerations. "We are connected to the rest of the world in ways few of us can fully fathom, from the shoes we wear and coffee we drink to the cell phones we carry and the tweets we post."

I must be one of the few current or former elected officials from the United States to have visited Tunisia not once but twice, in 1994 and then again in 2005. The first trip was a congressional delegation to Africa led by the late Senator Paul Simon of Illinois. After seeing harrowing sights in war-torn Liberia and Angola, we flew all the way across the Sahara Desert for a calmer conclusion to the trip in a beautiful and stable nation led by our alleged friend President Zine al-Abidine Ben Ali. Then eleven years later, in 2005, Senator John McCain led a delegation of five senators to Afghanistan, Iraq, and Pakistan and decided that Tunisia would again be a good place to decompress and connect with an ally in the Middle East. As we travelled from our hotel or from our ambassador's beautiful residence in nearby Carthage on both trips, the capital, Tunis, appeared to be thriving, safe, and especially stable with its lively markets overlooking the Mediterranean Sea. Both times we were given a generous audience with President Ben Ali in his magnificent offices, where he made sure we knew of his friendship with the United States as well as of his actions—so rare in the Middle East—for better relations with the state of Israel.

On both occasions I confronted the president as diplomatically as I knew how about abuses under his regime. Both times my questions were about the imprisonment of political foes and the severe restrictions on journalistic freedom in Tunisia. In 1994 he had responded firmly, and not particularly defensively, "These people are with terrorist groups." He said that he would look into these matters, but we had to be mindful that these prisoners and journalists were associated with our "mutual enemies." On the second occasion we were all impressed that Ben Ali was well prepared, specifically referring to my similar questions from eleven years before.

The president seemed to do everything he could to appear calm, dignified, and reasonable. The setting in which he presided fit the bill. Somehow, however, many of us at both meetings agreed that "he looked kind of like a thug." I remember that his hair seemed much blacker and shinier the second time I saw him. Ben Ali seemed to be falling a bit short of looking the part of the regal father of his nation that he wanted to be. Yet he seemed a strongman, fully in control of his nation for as long as he wanted. In fact he was planning to continue his legacy but had been waiting patiently for a son and heir for many years. On that second visit I was able to greet this powerful Arab president, perhaps a bit presumptuously, with a "Mazel tov." He understood the Hebrew term and grinned broadly—a son had recently been born and his dominance and family's control of Tunisia looked secure for the foreseeable future. Had it been so, perhaps Brian Harper may never have heard of Tunisia despite the antidemocratic and repressive regime that Ben Ali had inflicted on this ancient nation for decades. Six years later the president had to flee the country in a big hurry.

Tunisia is also connected to the larger point about the danger of America's lack of awareness about the rest of the world. Repressive regimes help encourage some Muslims, particularly young Muslims, to sometimes turn to causes such as Al Qaeda. President Ben Ali was not all wrong about the presence of terrorist influences in his country. In what seemed a great coincidence to me, the first major attack for which Al Qaeda took credit after the events of September 11, 2001, was an explosion in Tunisia in April 2002 that killed a reported nineteen people, including fourteen German tourists. The terrorist attack seemed calculated to destroy one of the most ancient synagogues in the world, on the Tunisian island of Djerba. I had never heard of this synagogue before my first visit to Tunisia, but Senator Simon, knowing my Jewish background and that my sister Dena Feingold was a rabbi, had asked me whether we should include a brief visit to Djerba on this trip. When we arrived at the dusty site, we were quickly ushered into the beautiful interior of the house of worship. Tradition has it that it dates back over 2,500 years. We were greeted by, of course, a Mr. Cohen, a local tailor, who had special responsibilities in the synagogue. We enjoyed a good tour, followed by an informal lunch where the participants assumed that Paul Simon, the son of a Protestant minister, was Jewish. It was a touching encounter with one of the oldest continuous (but tiny) Jewish communities in the world. If you had told me that this very spot would be the next target for Al Qaeda after 9/11, I would have been astonished. What was even more surprising is that virtually no one in America seemed to pay any attention to this attack in North Africa, even though it came so soon after our own great national tragedy. After all, it wasn't Afghanistan, or Pakistan, or Iraq, and, by the way, "where in the world is Tunisia" indeed?

Writing a book about America's place in the world and our understanding of that role was something I'd wanted to do long before September 11, 2001. As soon as I became a member of the Senate Foreign Relations Committee in 1993, I began to feel there was a large gap in our national discourse as well as in the deliberations and discussions within the halls of Congress. But, with my schedule as a senator and role in helping raise my two daughters, Jessica and Ellen, I had never gotten to the point of writing even one word of such a book. In any event, why would I think I had anything interesting to say on this topic at the very beginning of my eighteen-year tenure on that committee? It was in part because when I joined the Senate, I quickly learned how little I really knew about foreign policy and the rest of the world—despite being a thirty-nine-year-old, who had had the benefit of a strong education that included living overseas for two years. I toyed with the idea of writing a book titled something like "The First Post–Cold War Member of the Senate Foreign Relations Committee." While not a really gripping title, it reflected some of my feelings about my own relationship with the rest of the world then. It also considered America's place in the world as of 1993 and how this country was largely ill-prepared for the events that were to follow, culminating on September 11, 2001.

I had not exactly been trained to be one of only nineteen people, out of more than 250 million Americans, to serve on the Senate Foreign Relations

Committee. In this regard, I think it's fair to say that I was much like most Americans at the time, largely oblivious to the rest of the world. The Foreign Relations Committee was the preeminent legislative body dealing with global affairs for a nation that was then indisputably the only superpower in the world—membership should have called for someone with more serious international credentials than I had. But my generation had grown up in the post–World War II, bipolar world that pitted the United States and the West against the communist bloc led by the Soviet Union. We understood the overriding concern of American foreign policy to be the free world's struggle to stem the spread of communism. Not only the seemingly endless war in Vietnam, but virtually all events from Congo to Castro were discussed in terms of this simple dichotomy. We did not usually delve into the more subtle differences between the countries and regions that had become the war-game playing fields for this great global struggle. While I greatly enjoyed following and absorbing what I could of world events, they were not my primary concern, nor that of most of my friends, relatives, teachers, and mentors. America was in tumult throughout my middle school, high school, and college years. Of course, much of the most significant tension in this era related to the war in Vietnam. Even that distant conflict, however, was usually viewed as part of a larger domestic burden that included the civil rights movement and subsequent race riots, horrifying assassinations, and the emergence of both the environmental and women's movements. All these events encouraged America to turn decidedly inward even as the twin threats of the Soviet Union and Communist China seemed to loom ever larger.

My own educational and career choices reflected this inward-looking trend. My brilliant mother, Sylvia, was fluent in five or six languages but had little opportunity to use them as a mother of four and a full-time real-estate abstracter in Janesville, Wisconsin. I was proud of her linguistic abilities but rejected her advice to take Latin and to become conversant in some modern languages. The closest I ever came was specializing in driving various dedicated language teachers crazy as I tried to attract attention from the principally female student body in high school French classes. I took the view that knowing another language was unnecessary and probably a waste of time, though it might be fun. Americans in our era figured that any people we needed to communicate with, even in other countries, would know enough English for our purposes.

Then, when choosing classes at the University of Wisconsin–Madison, I often picked history and political science courses that had a foreign focus, but most of my friends and I were more concerned with trying to get into law school; we expected to have careers with a principally domestic focus. This was very different from the focus of many of our contemporaries, not only in Great Britain, Germany, and France, but also in places like Russia and India. People of similar ages in those nations knew a lot more about us than we knew about them.

After college and law school, I spent several years practicing law in Wisconsin. I then sought elective office and in 1983 began a ten-year stint as a member of the Wisconsin State Senate representing a largely rural district surrounding much of Madison. I loved the job and the district I served, but the steady diet was dairy policy, the home construction market, and especially the burden of local property taxes to pay for schools. The Madison City Council itself had been occasionally derided as having its own distinct foreign policy because of all the resolutions it passed on international matters, but in so doing it was different from almost all the rest of the state. Foreign matters were of little concern to me and my constituents. This was not only because my job was to be a state senator. People in my area and state and, I'm sure, throughout the nation, usually discussed national and local issues in casual conversations. So while it is often said that all politics is local anywhere you go, I believe America's tendency to put international matters on the back burner is exceptional.

We also have a hard time paying attention to more than one issue at a time. When I was preparing to return to Wisconsin at the end of my last term in the Senate, I became even more aware of the twenty-four-hour-news phenomenon that has come to dominate America's electronic media. In the Senate I received a steady flow of information on every imaginable subject—the highlights and minutiae of legislative work, international events, or plain gossip. That is not to say that anyone could make sense of it all or that what was important was always skillfully distinguished from what was not. What I especially noticed as I left the Senate to enter private life was what I would call the lurching nature of general news coverage. It's as if the competition to provide the best and most comprehensive coverage of the hot story of the moment crowds out other important but less urgent stories. So, we were riveted for a few days in late 2010, when the people of Tunisia anticipated the Arab Spring and dramatically ousted their long-standing dictator Ben Ali. Just as the pundits began to consider whether this phenomenon would spread to other countries, particularly in the Islamic world, the shooting of Congresswoman Gabrielle Giffords and others in Tucson horrified the whole country and led to near-exclusive attention to that story for a couple of weeks. When the Giffords story began to wane, the demonstrations in Egypt and the removal of Hosni Mubarak took over and provided some of the most dramatic television footage any of us had ever seen. And then, in mid-February, when I began to hope that that story would lead to a period of calmer and more reflective analysis of the events unfolding in the Middle East, I turned on CNN to see familiar images on the screen. Candy Crowley teased the next story, "What you are seeing is not happening in Cairo. It's Madison, Wisconsin." Of course I was aware that the protests against Governor Scott Walker's brutal effort to strip public employees of most of their long-standing collective-bargaining rights was big news in Wisconsin. What seemed incredible, however, was the speed with which this story was broadcast wall-to-wall on every major news broadcast regardless of the ideological slant of the outlet. The Wisconsin protests were soon pushed out of view, however, when Japan's earthquake and resulting nuclear disaster moved to center stage.

That important domestic stories from Tucson and Madison managed to obliterate most international coverage is completely understandable and appropriate. It is human nature to want to know more about what is happening in one's own backyard, especially when the stories are as dramatic as these. It is possible that the media were merely tracking events in appropriate proportions. I have a feeling, though, that we Americans suffer from a sort of attention deficit disorder when it comes to keeping our focus on foreign events that can directly affect our lives and our country's future. We are not trained to follow these events closely and often lack the knowledge of these distant countries to be able to understand why they should matter to us. My own realization of how insular we are came in the mid-1970s. When I became a student at Oxford University, after graduating from the University of Wisconsin, I noticed the way the BBC and the print media in the United Kingdom closely and consistently followed unfolding events in what was then known as Rhodesia, one of the most racist societies in modern history. As black Africans rose to demand their freedom and ultimately their independence as Zimbabwe, it was evident that ordinary people in Britain were alert to and interested in events that Americans largely ignored. Of course, Britain had been a colonial power in Africa, the white settlers who had been running Rhodesia were mostly British, and I was in Oxford, where people tend to have a more international outlook than most other places. Those may be grounds to dismiss this example, but in a way that only reinforces the point—we do not have a colonial background or the geographic proximity that compels us to report or follow events like this closely. We have never felt the need to know much about current events outside the United States, and therefore we have not developed the skills to evaluate them, or even pay much attention to them. This is not a criticism but an observation that we leave ourselves in a vulnerable position if we do not have the public capacity to process international events that are important to our economic and national security. To continue to play a leading role in the world, and to be safe at home, we have to develop these abilities in government, education, and the media.

Perhaps foremost among the abilities we Americans need to cultivate is the knowledge of foreign languages. I know only English and a smattering of French, so I have to admit to my own failings in this area. They say that it's very hard to learn a language later in life, but if there's an experiment somewhere to see if someone approaching sixty can still become fluent in some foreign language, sign me up. A failure to learn other languages can be viewed as arrogant, possibly even rude. Some might expect that any well-rounded person today really should know another language or two. But it is more urgent than that. I am convinced that it is actually a threat to our national security and our leading role in the world if we continue to believe that we can be safe and powerful without learning how to communicate with other people in the world.

There were no weapons of mass destruction to be found in Iraq when we invaded in 2003. What can be found there, however, is the site of the biblical Tower of Babel, on the plain of Shinar, near Al-Hillah, capital of Babil province. One of the most interesting stories in the Old Testament tells of God's anger with early mankind's arrogance in attempting to build a magnificent tower, "whose top may reach unto heaven." With a common language they had a good chance of completing the project, but God confounded their plans by condemning them to speak in a multitude of languages, so they could no longer understand one another. Iraq is also the site of the great Babylonian kingdom of Nebuchadnezzar II. Before we showed up, Saddam Hussein had tried to emulate his famous predecessor by reconstructing the ancient royal palace, hoping that his ostentatious modern structure would ensure his reputation as "protector of Iraq, who rebuilt civilization and rebuilt Babylon." When I was with the John McCain delegation in 2006, I had a chance to make a helicopter-assisted survey of this incredible combination of ancient ruins and modern folly. When we were back on the ground and attended a meeting with local officials, we learned that Babil province was no longer considered to be one of the safest places to take military tourists in post-invasion Iraq, as it had been until recently. The local governor seemed distraught about the increase in violence and the presence of insurgents in his area. After we covered this ground, though, I wanted to get a sense of just how aware the Iraqis were of the biblical significance of this general area—after all, here were the original sites of the Hanging Gardens of Babylon; Nebuchadnezzar's palace; the lion's den from which Daniel emerged uneaten; the miraculous fire walk of Shadrach, Meshach, and Abednego; and possibly Ur, birthplace of Abraham. I asked if they had ever thought about the tourist potential of this area, if peace could be established. This question had to go through an interpreter, of course, and we didn't get very far. I wished I had had the ability to speak Arabic and more time, so the meeting could include a positive discussion about the region's future, rather than just military matters. Whether I ever learn another language is of no great import; what is more important is whether our younger Americans do.

Developing a radically different attitude toward foreign language skills is no simple matter. As a state senator, I tried to follow other states' lead in the 1980s, when it came to passing legislation on languages in schools. At the urging of Sally Cullen (formerly Mackinnis), my seventh-grade French teacher at Marshall Junior High, I introduced a bill to establish incentives to include foreign language teaching in Wisconsin schools' core curriculum. Such things did not seem so urgent to most other legislators in that pre-9/11 era, and the bill did not pass. Another impediment was the skepticism most of us shared about heavy-handed state or federal mandates that affected our school curricula at the elementary and secondary level. I believed then and still do that, with important exceptions such as special needs, local control of education is preferable in a free and diverse society. Even then the federal government can play a limited role: When a national education need is identified, offering voluntary federal grants to interested school districts is a good way to jump-start change. This was done with some success under the Clinton administration to encourage smaller class sizes and after-school student programs. In suggesting such a national initiative I'm well aware of the limitations, particularly the financial ones. As of this writing there could not be a worse time to ask school districts and states to find money for new programs—even with federal grant money, which is usually time-limited, matching or continuing funds would have to be found at the local level. Nevertheless, I think it is urgent that we make a national commitment to encourage school districts to become more focused on the importance of foreign language skills.

In my day most of us studied a single second language for many years and emerged from school not even close to being fluent. In my case it was six years of French. My failure in that department was no fault of my French teachers (Sally Mackinnis and then Helen Brace at Janesville Craig Senior High School), who were professional and enthusiastic instructors. Apart from my own lack of commitment to the language, teaching methods then provided no real opportunities for me to develop fluency. The numerous discussions I've had with teachers and students since then suggest that not enough has changed. It is now generally recognized that the best way to learn a language is through immersion. There are a variety of means to achieve that: living in a country where the language is spoken, being around native speakers, and watching TV programs, listening to words and music, or reading books in that language. There are serious economic implications to implementing language immersion programs, but investing in more effective language teaching is something to which we should aspire.

Our need for greater linguistic skills has changed dramatically over the last fifty years. It has also become more urgent. In the mid-1960s I was offered a choice of French, German, Spanish, or Latin. Our national security and international outreach requirements today are vast, and so are the number and variety of languages embraced by those priorities. Spanish has become more important in our multicultural society; Chinese, Hindi, and Russian can assist our relationships with those world powers; in the context of national security Arabic and Pashto are even more important, for they provide us with an opportunity to understand a more complicated and dangerous world; the old European languages remain useful for travel, work, and international relations; even the classics, Latin and Greek, can help with learning other languages and just about any other subject. I have often heard officials in our intelligence community in Washington and abroad complain about the difficulty of gathering or decoding information that is crucial to our safety. That is precisely because we simply do not have enough Americans trained in these languages. In fact, this became part of the practical argument for eliminating the ridiculous "don't ask, don't tell" policy against gay and lesbian Americans in the military. I also know that many young people are taking this matter very seriously at the collegiate level, as I saw, for example, when I spoke at the commencement ceremony for Wisconsin's Lawrence University in June 2011. We simply need more Americans who are willing to make linguistic diversity an important part of their education and lives. Forty years ago I would have been happy if I had mastered French; now I wish someone had invented a microchip for my brain that could instantly give me new linguistic skills. I am not an expert on languages, but I do know that we need to tackle this problem in a far more systematic way than we have since our wake-up call in 2001.

In the 1960s, the national campaign to warn people about the dangers of smoking didn't eliminate the practice, but it did make smoking a central part of our national health discussion, and led to positive results compared to many other countries in the world. About the same time, President

Kennedy identified lack of physical fitness as a nationwide problem and launched a program to improve the situation. This was successfully publicized by the famous challenge to hike fifty miles in twenty hours, a challenge issued decades before by Theodore Roosevelt to the Marine Corps. Many other Americans were inspired to take up that challenge. Although we still have problems with our diet and child obesity, Kennedy's initiative began a whole new era of health clubs, attention to diet, and exercise regimens that have made America in some respects a healthier nation. Now we need our president and other leaders to reinforce the idea that learning a language is a good way to serve your country, whether as a soldier, a musician, a diplomat, or a businessperson. We can no longer rely, as I did, on the hope that someone will know English if anything important comes up—no matter where we are in the world.

As a senator, I had a pretty demanding travel schedule, especially when I was in Wisconsin. I came home virtually every weekend and loved having a little free time just to do errands around Middleton, the town I've lived in since 1979. In 2007, Middleton topped *Money* magazine's Best Places list for communities of its size in the entire country and I can only agree. The town is well planned, family friendly, and has beautiful hiking areas, but it could use a few more restaurants. So I was excited when a new Malaysian restaurant opened downtown. We already had plenty of good beer, brats, and cheddar cheese, but this was the only place in town where I could get a meal wrapped in banana leaves. I soon became one of its best customers.

During one recess, I was in town in the middle of the week and headed straight over to Malay China for lunch. Only a couple of tables were occupied, an early sign that my Malaysian getaway wouldn't last long. As I sat down with my food a man approximately my age (early or mid-fifties) called out to me from across the restaurant. "How's Ellen?" He had been one of my younger daughter's teachers at Middleton High School. He was with three other casually dressed middle-aged men who had also been teachers at the high school. After catching them up on the recent history of my two daughters, I asked them what they were up to. The answer was something along the lines of fishing and hunting and taking it easy; apparently they had all retired early and already seemed a little bored with all that spare time. They were a little gray—so was I—but appeared to have decades of potentially active life ahead of them. I remember thinking that these experienced and personable teachers could have so much to offer young people in another country, perhaps one where America's reputation had soured. I had the sense that they would probably enjoy the opportunity to work abroad for maybe a few weeks a year, as a satisfying and even patriotic contribution to amend America's shaky reputation in too much of the world. That would still leave plenty of time for hunting, fishing, and Packer games. Actually, Malaysia is just the kind of place where we need guys like this to dispel the negative myths about America and the American people.

We need to reverse the unfortunate trend of the last few years to downplay our international relationships, and we need to accomplish that at all levels. The federal government has a big role to play, of course. It sends ambassadors and other diplomats around the globe to support our relationships abroad. There is an outreach role, too, for members of Congress, who have particular opportunities and obligations to learn more about foreign matters. There is also a part for what is known as public diplomacy; that is, official American government programs: The broadcasts of the Voice of America and the Iftar dinners held during Ramadan in our embassies in countries with significant Islamic populations are good examples. More is required and it should involve calling on every American to find a way to engage in private or citizen diplomacy. We need a national movement that equates involvement in international affairs with effective patriotism. The president down to leaders at the local level should encourage other Americans to see that efforts at reaching out to the rest of the world are critical to our own national security. This doesn't necessarily mean supporting greater foreign aid or any other specific programs, although that can be a part of it. The overall effort is enhanced by language proficiency, but it does not have to depend on that. Rather, we should do all we can to facilitate the efforts of Americans, whether they have other languages or not, who are interested in providing practical help to other nations. Since 9/11, I have spent a fair amount of time both inside and out of the Senate promoting programs to assist adult Americans to spend even a small portion of their time, perhaps annually, to travel to foreign countries to assist in everything from best agricultural practices to the protection of cultural artifacts. A fair amount of informal activity has been initiated on this front, but far more is needed. We need a formal call—not a mandate—at the national level to ask every American to think about this. A broader-ranging foreign policy is sorely needed now, more than ten years after 9/11.

Our history is filled with citizen efforts that literally helped to change the world. Americans participated in table tennis tournaments in the early 1970s and we all know that this so-called Ping-Pong diplomacy helped us reestablish long-severed ties with mainland China. In 2008, the privately funded New York Philharmonic's concert tour to North Korea may not have cut through that international Gordian knot, but, as the *Economist* reviewer James Miles wrote, "For at least 90 minutes in a theatre in Pyongyang it was possible to believe that 55 years of cold-war hostility were coming to an end." Cuba is another potential example. Instead of limiting people-to-people exchanges, as the Bush administration did with Cuba in 2004, we should be encouraging them. The passage of Fidel Castro from active leadership presented us with a golden opportunity to promote democracy and new relations through a free exchange of people and ideas. Our decades-old policy of curtailing travel to Cuba has had little discernible impact on Cuba's leadership. Individual exchanges, however, can make an impact by offering meaningful opportunities for citizen dialogue, a chance for countries to get to know each other from the bottom up. One of the best members of Congress and my former colleague Congressman Jim McGovern of Massachusetts said it well when he reported from a meeting with Fidel Castro that the two words in the English language he feared most are "spring break." This is not about proposing nostalgic spring-break revivals for those of us in the over-fifty crowd; it is about acknowledging that democracy travels best in person. And it is something that flows from our memories of the inspirations of our youth; for me, particularly of John F. Kennedy.

As a child in the early 1960s, my first impressions of the federal government were of the Kennedy administration. For so many of us, the Peace Corps—proposed by Hubert Humphrey in 1957, and symbolized by the young President Kennedy, who promoted and signed it into law in 1961—showed us exactly how America should seek to relate to the rest of the world. The Peace Corps' stated mission is to pursue three simple goals:

1. Helping the people of interested countries in meeting their need for trained men and women.
2. Helping promote a better understanding of Americans on the part of the peoples served.
3. Helping promote a better understanding of other peoples on the part of Americans.

In the era of the so-called ugly American, the Peace Corps presented a milder, more acceptable face of our nation abroad. I have encountered scores of people who point to their Peace Corps experience with pride and nostalgia. More than that, their service provided them with a lifelong interest in and commitment to the nation where they served. I could see this developing in current volunteers, when I met an enthusiastic group at a dinner in Dakar, Senegal, in February 2000. I noticed it in my political supporters and staff members who had served. They frequently spoke of how they felt their work in the Peace Corps had made a difference not only for themselves and the people they served, but had also improved the image of the United States in their host country. Year after year one of my constituents, Judy Figi, a former Peace Corps volunteer from my hometown, Janesville, would come to my annual Rock County listening session to speak about the situation in the African nation of Sierra Leone, a topic that contrasted in an interesting way with our usual discussions of health-care reform and the war in Iraq. Judy would give us a progress report on the efforts to rebuild that nation after it had been brutalized by the Charles Taylor–backed Revolutionary United Front (RUF). She had served in the Peace Corps there several decades before, when Sierra Leone suffered serious poverty but at least enjoyed relative peace. Her distress at the horrors inflicted on Sierra Leone by the

RUF was matched only by her subsequent joy when the Peace Corps was able to return to Sierra Leone several years after the war.

Equally memorable was a meeting on another trip to Africa, when I was chairman of the Senate Foreign Relations Committee's Subcommittee on African Affairs. Among other countries in eastern Africa, we visited Tanzania, a comparatively stable African nation. One of our meetings was in Dar es Salaam with a distinguished group of women members of the Tanzanian national legislature. The conversation was lively and covered substantive issues. Almost every woman there credited her success in male-dominated Tanzania to knowing English, and they specifically acknowledged the Peace Corps' role in teaching them. Such encounters made me an enthusiastic supporter of President George W. Bush's proposal to expand the Peace Corps again, which was skillfully guided through Congress by Senator Chris Dodd of Connecticut, a former Peace Corps volunteer himself and for many years its best friend in the Senate.

Over the years the Peace Corps has grown in other ways and now accepts older Americans—including seniors—as volunteers. As effective as the Peace Corps is, even in its enlarged state it can only begin to tap the incredible resource that exists in the talents and experience of ordinary American people. Joining the Peace Corps usually involves a multiyear commitment that many potential volunteers may not be willing or able to make if they are in the middle of a career or looking after a family. Like the retired Middleton teachers I met at the Malaysian restaurant, there are many other Americans who would probably jump at the chance to spend a few weeks, perhaps for several years in a row, sharing their expertise in a country that has requested assistance and where our image could be improved. Whenever I mention this concept to any audience, from a Rotary Club to a group of nurses, people in the room nod approvingly and obviously begin imagining themselves doing this kind of work, rather than listening intently to whatever my next topic is.

Damon Szymanski is my nominee for a role model for short-term volunteering. He was a dairy farmer from Pulaski, Wisconsin, who came to Washington in 1993 to talk with me about a small federal international development program: Volunteers in Overseas Cooperative Assistance (VOCA).

We met in the beautiful reception room just outside the Senate chamber. He wanted to share the experience of his recent visit as a volunteer to one of the newly liberated former Soviet republics. His role was to teach better practices to dairy farmers there. He observed that the milk he found at the first farm he visited had "so much bacteria in it, it could almost walk to market by itself." I've repeated this story many times, and it has never failed to bring down the house with an audience of cheeseheads at a town meeting anywhere in America's Dairyland. The audiences got the point every time; they knew the stages that dairy science had to go through to establish Wisconsin's world prominence in this industry. While this exchange with Damon had had an impact on me even before 9/11, when he came back to see me again some ten years after our first meeting I was impressed to learn that he had sold his farm so that he could devote more time to his volunteer work. By then he had visited some fifteen different countries and helped dairy farmers all over the world. When I first met him he was still running a dairy farm, so two or three years in the Peace Corps was not an option for him then. But he was able to carve out smaller amounts of time each year to share his valuable skills. Since 9/11, I have often spoken of Damon and imagine legions of dairy farmers, teachers, violinists, car mechanics, plumbers, and construction workers going out into the world to do something equally useful. It is a vision that has already been realized by many but should be available for more. I see this as part of a call to duty on behalf of America, a call to patriotic service at almost any stage of life that would be challenging, fun, and personally satisfying.

Encouraging citizen diplomacy does not have to mean the creation of a new, heavy-handed federal bureaucracy that would impede the efforts and spirit of volunteers who are already reaching out to other parts of the world. A lighter touch would work. I have thought for some time that the federal government could help facilitate these efforts in a way that makes it clear to all Americans that volunteer activity abroad really helps us integrate into the world in a better way. For this reason I introduced the Global Services Fellowship Act Program on May 23, 2007. It calls on the secretary of state to establish a grant program to fund fellowships that promote international volunteering opportunities "as a means of building bridges across cultures, addressing critical human needs, and promoting mutual understanding." We must also create an online database of all existing international exchange and volunteer programs, including the many spearheaded by churches, synagogues, mosques, and other religious institutions. The grants from the Global Services Act should be made in conjunction with these other projects, or could even help fund them. I am still hopeful that legislation of this kind will pass in the relatively near future. The enthusiasm for such programs was demonstrated at the national level in December 2009 at a conference of nearly three hundred leaders from twenty-three countries and more than 160 organizations, colleges, and universities. This gathering of international volunteer service leaders featured an address by my former colleague Harris Wofford, senator from Pennsylvania and former director of the Peace Corps. Harris, one of the best-liked and respected members of the Senate and a national leader on volunteerism, urged participants to action noting that "good intentions are not good enough to achieve a 'quantum leap' in policies and resources for international volunteer service." And, as worthy as current programs are, a quantum leap is precisely what we need in order to expand our connections to the rest of the world. Especially in the difficult economic times we are experiencing now, a federal boost in facilitating and funding would go a long way to leveraging more and more citizen volunteers. My guess is that once people start volunteering they will find it rewarding and perhaps, like Damon Szymanski, even continue it on their own or through other resources. What is missing is a clear national call for this kind of patriotic service.

It's time for all of us to wake up and recognize that America can never be a world apart again. We prospered on this land largely free of the ancient feuds and restrictions that afflicted so much of the Old World. We were able to feel almost as if we were on a huge island protected by vast oceans in eras when transport and communication could not so easily override those barriers. That is over now. We must all do our part to help our country adjust to the realities of the post-9/11 world, and of the third century of our nationhood. Instead of seeing this as a problem, we can learn to view it as a challenge. We cannot meet this challenge if we simply stay here in America; as if seeming rich and powerful is sufficient in this world of rapid and unpredictable change. We have to get to know the rest of the world better and it has to get to know us better. That is why I consider international people-to-people outreach more important and appealing now than at any other time in our history. Experiences we have with people and cultures outside of our own stay with us forever. And each person from another culture or country who has that encounter with one of us, whether here or there, is having a similar experience.

The Pew Global Attitudes Project found that "those individuals who have traveled to the US have more favorable views of our country than those who have not." I'm certain the same would be true of most people who have never been here but have met Americans volunteering in their own home countries. The Pew study also notes, "The image of America tends to be more positive among those who have friends and relatives in the US whom they regularly call, write to, or visit. . . . People with friends or relatives in the US are generally more likely to have a favorable opinion of the country than those who do not have personal connections in the US." How can these connections be made? Well, the relatives can take care of themselves. And we can continue to do our best to ensure good relations with visitors who travel to the United States. To build up the world's good opinion, we must also go to their countries on a regular basis—not in the capacity of tourists staying in the best hotels, but as potential friends, advisers, and allies. Through a more personal outreach we have an opportunity to reestablish our nation's role as a champion of freedom and democracy, and to enhance respect for the values we represent. In so doing, we are likely to derive pleasure from these life-affirming experiences and have opportunities to forge human bonds among ordinary people, disarm narrow-minded ideological opponents, and strengthen both the values and security of this country. It is time for us to reflect both our confidence and our humility as we support the common aspirations of an increasingly interconnected and interdependent global world.

Conclusion

What we need is an armed guard that will wake up when the fire first starts or, better yet, one that will not permit a fire to start at all.

Those who have worked with me over the years know that phoning me anytime after dinner is usually a dicey proposition. When I was in college, one of the reasons I never took a foreign language was that all the classes in languages were at 7:55 a.m. I tried pretty hard not to have a class before the 11 a.m. slot, so I could study late after dinner and then go out to some of the great spots around the University of Wisconsin–Madison. Time marched on and now my idea of a good schedule is getting up at five or six in the morning with the birds, the quiet, and coffee. If I feel like going to bed at nine, eight, or even seven, I just do. So it was with a bit of trepidation that my longtime aide and current research assistant on this book, Jeremy Tollefson, phoned me at home late in the evening of May 1, 2011. He hadn't done that a single time during the many months we had been working on this book. Jeremy hesitantly said, "Sorry, but you might want to turn on your TV. The president is about to speak—sounds like they got bin Laden." I was excited, fascinated to hear the details, and pleased.

Friends who knew I was writing this book asked me what this milestone meant for the project, which I was describing as an attempt to critique the way we have responded to many of the issues raised by the 9/11 attacks and to suggest some better approaches. What they seemed to be asking was, Doesn't this mean that the Al Qaeda–terrorism chapter is pretty much over? And given the power of bin Laden's image and his ability to evade capture in Afghanistan and Pakistan for almost ten years after, this question makes sense. This larger-than-life, frightening creature, like something out of a scary movie, had been vanquished. For some, including me, it was a bit like hearing the account of the deaths of Adolf Hitler and Eva Braun in the depths of the Führerbunker. There was a dramatic feeling of closure, something like the triumph of good over evil. And I shared that feeling. What I began to predict, though, was that bin Laden's demise would not bring a sense of urgency about being prepared for similar threats in the future. I feared that many would assume that Al Qaeda, its franchises, and sympathetic imitators were now more or less incapacitated. That was past history, and we were now free to move on to our myriad domestic problems.

A little over a month after bin Laden's death, Jeremy and I spent a weekend in Appleton, Wisconsin, at the festivities around Lawrence University's 2011 graduation. He had been a student there and I was receiving an honorary degree. It was an interesting weekend and one of the highlights was dinner on Saturday night at the home of university president Jill Beck. The guests included Jerald Podair, a distinguished history professor and one of the most popular instructors at the university. We were all gathered for drinks in the living room and when asked what I was doing, I launched into my *While America Sleeps* summary. I mentioned my fear that America would lapse again into ignoring the threat of Al Qaeda and international matters generally. Podair looked at me and said, "Maybe that's our default position." Having carefully watched the reaction to the death of bin Laden in the last few months, I think Professor Podair is right. Maybe it *is* our nature to return to that complacent position, given our history and experiences, but it does not bode well for a nation that can never again say it wasn't warned.

It is fair to ascribe some of this reaction to the tremendous economic difficulties we are experiencing at home. As of this writing, we have had the grim employment report for August 2011 showing no job growth at all for the first month in a long time. Accordingly, the predictions that the successful elimination of bin Laden would cinch Obama's reelection were short-lived; its effect on popularity polls lasted only a couple of weeks. The president's higher approval ratings soon began to plummet and his political base was becoming frustrated. The Republicans and the right kept pummeling him, knowing it's not too hard to blame the man in the Oval Office for all that is wrong when the economy simply won't turn around. More credible candidates started to emerge for what now seemed a more attractive Republican presidential nomination. As early as June 8, 2011, newspapers stopped commenting on the incredibly presidential way Obama handled the bin Laden attack, but were instead saying things like this headline in the *Milwaukee Journal Sentinel* that day: "Obama Feels Heat of Cooling Economy." The economy, however, is not the only reason we are heading for the second presidential election in a row where the important international issues we face after 9/11 will almost certainly get short shrift. The Republicans believe that if they focus solely on the economy and downplay Obama's foreign policy, which has had some major successes, they can look forward to another triumphant night like the one in November 2010. Also, from the moment the president announced the death of bin Laden, far too many leaders, experts, and media figures began to talk as though there was no further threat from Al Qaeda. We are being lulled into not being concerned about threats like Al Qaeda; it is almost like giving us psychological permission to let international matters take care of themselves. It's a lulling or, if you will, a lullaby seducing us back to our default position.

Within days of the announcement of the death of Osama bin Laden, the postmortems for Al Qaeda and the terrorist threat began in earnest. On MSNBC's *Morning Joe*, reporter Jon Meacham minimized the organization's impact, lamenting that "it just takes one moment for them. You know? It's not a sustained war-like operation. They get lucky once and innocent people die, and so this is the tragedy of history, the tragedy of this conflict." On the Wednesday following the raid in Pakistan, *USA Today* ran a story headlined "Al Qaeda Losing Relevance," by Shadi Hamid, the director of research at the Brookings Doha Center. This followed a series of articles and interviews prior to the bin Laden killing that claimed that the Arab Spring of the preceding four months had already made Al Qaeda less appealing to disaffected Arabs and Muslims throughout the Middle East, Africa, and Southeast Asia. Hamid wrote on May 4, 2011, "As Americans celebrate the death of Osama bin Laden, there is a risk we will exaggerate his importance in death as we did in life." Hamid further explained, "In recent years, Al Qaeda, while retaining its ability to wreak havoc, has become an increasingly marginal actor on the Arab stage," and noted that in the early weeks of the recent Arab uprisings, "Al Qaeda remained quiet, seemingly unsure how, or even if, it could spin events to its advantage." Hamid's piece is balanced, however, and he wisely warns, "As regimes wage war on their own people, Arabs might begin to lose faith in the effectiveness of non-violence. In such an environment, al-Qaeda might yet get a second wind."

Such balance seemed lacking in much of the domestic commentary assessing the impact of bin Laden's death. *FP: Foreign Policy* ran an article called, "Why Is It So Hard to Find a Suicide Bomber These Days?" It claimed that "leading terrorists regularly complain: Why aren't more Muslims resisting the onslaught of the West? What more provocations do they need before they heed the call to arms?" We can certainly hope this is the case, but a campaign to persuade Americans that Al Qaeda and its ilk are no longer a threat seems premature. Most troubling is the way that comments like Peter Beinart's of *The Daily Beast* may be taken. In what must have been an attempt to be dramatic, Beinart wrote—within hours of bin Laden's death—a column provocatively titled, "The War on Terror Is Over." He writes, "But we have more to be grateful for than this one villain's demise. We must give thanks for something broader: The war on terror is over." In fairness, Beinart qualifies his statement by admitting that there may still be some attacks and we should continue to track terrorist cells. He also points out that the excesses of the past ten years have often been done in the name of the "war on terror," something with which I strongly agree. The problem is that Beinart goes on to claim that "terrorism does not represent the greatest threat to American security; debt does, and our anti-terror efforts are exacerbating the problem." As a long-serving senator who was regularly called a deficit hawk, I concur with the enormous importance of fiscal responsibility—but not to the exclusion of the urgent need to get serious about international threats to our security. Beinart concludes with another ill-considered statement: "The war on terror is over; Al Qaeda lost. Now for the really hard stuff, let's hope we haven't deferred it too long." Now for the hard stuff? I am uncomfortable with a message that encourages the American people to breathe a sigh of relief that Al Qaeda is gone, and then turn back to domestic issues. Our attention to international matters has been deferred too long. This is no time to say you can forget about it again.

The Obama administration has seemed a little overconfident in its pronouncements on this subject, too. I say this while acknowledging that we all owe President Obama an enormous amount of gratitude not only for eliminating bin Laden but for developing a coordinated military, intelligence, and diplomatic strategy to deal with Al Qaeda and its allies. This is a vast improvement over that of the Bush administration. In addition to bin Laden, Atiyah Abd al-Rahman, Al Qaeda's new second in command, was killed in Waziristan soon after he started that job. Many other successes in diminishing Al Qaeda's power can be attributed to the Obama administration, although some do not or cannot get much attention because of classification rules. Having said that, I'm concerned about the tone of the statements coming from this administration, for they seem unnecessarily triumphant and are likely to send out the wrong message to the rest of the world and especially to Americans. On July 26, 2011, the *Washington Post* reported that "US counterterrorism officials are increasingly convinced that the killing of Osama bin Laden and the toll of seven years of CIA drone strikes have pushed al-Qaeda to the brink of collapse." Then, on September 1, 2011, the Associated Press published an article titled, "US Counterterror Chief: Al Qaeda Now on the Ropes," which began: "On a steady slide. On the ropes. Taking shots to the body and head. That's how White House counterterrorism chief John Brennan described Al Qaeda on Wednesday as he offered the first on-record confirmation that Al Qaeda's second-in-command was killed last week in Pakistan." Brennan was quoted as saying, "There's not another bin Laden out there. I don't know if there's another Atiyah Abd al-Rahman." I wonder—do we really know this and if so, why say it? What troubled me even more were the comments of one of the persons I most respected and admired in my years in the US Senate, Leon Panetta.

Leon Panetta is a very competent and accomplished public servant. I have had the pleasure of working with him when he was a leading congressman, a director of the Office of Budget and Management, White House chief of staff, and director of the CIA. Now he's the secretary of defense. He excelled in all these roles, but as CIA director he was head and shoulders above any other CIA director I had the chance to work with when I was a member of the Senate Select Committee on Intelligence. It is reported that the internal leadership and the rank-and-file at the agency agree with that assessment. So I did a double take when I read a story that appeared in July 2011: "Panetta Appears to Link al-Qaeda Presence with Iraq Invasion." He was said to have told troops at Camp Victory, the largest US military outpost in Baghdad: "The reason you guys are here is because on 9/11 the United States got attacked. And 3,000 Americans—3,000 not just Americans, 3,000 human beings, innocent human beings—got killed because of al-Qaeda. And we've been fighting as a result of that."

Not in Iraq we haven't. Why would one of the most distinguished leaders of our time lapse into this kind of language at the very moment when the American people and those Americans who fight to protect us need real clarity about our foreign interventions? I can understand that Leon was probably trying to reassure the troops that what they are doing is necessary, worthwhile, and appreciated—all of which is true. But our country has a tendency to accept fabrications that oversimplify our foreign policy choices, and we need to resist this temptation to minimize or dismiss errors that have been made since 9/11.

Indeed, as we bring our troops back from Iraq and begin to withdraw from our overcommitment in Afghanistan, we must avoid two tendencies. One is to perpetuate the dual myth that invading Iraq was somehow connected to Al Qaeda and that the length and depth of the Afghanistan invasion was justified because the 9/11 attacks originated there. The second is propagating the myth that Al Qaeda and related entities are in their last throes, unlikely to reappear or threaten us in any significant way again. Just days after administration officials were predicting the imminent demise of Al Qaeda, one of its key officials, just-retired director of the National Counterterrorism Center Michael Leiter, told an audience at the Aspen Security Forum, "We still have pockets of Al Qaeda around the world who see this as a key way to fight us," referring to the possibility of the chemical or biological attacks that Osama bin Laden had been fond of promoting. He added, "The potential threat from Al Qaeda in the Arabian Peninsula is very real," and pointed to a likely strategy of a series of smaller attacks rather than the big-bang approach favored by Osama bin Laden. In my experience, Michael Leiter ranks with Leon Panetta in his skills in intelligence and counterterrorism. I found in my work with him that he was consistently honest, detailed, and accurate. Leiter's assessment should be taken *very* seriously.

A little before the tenth anniversary of the 9/11 attacks, a suicide bomber detonated a vehicle packed with explosives outside the United Nations headquarters in Abuja, the capital of Nigeria. At least eighteen people were killed. Boko Haram, a Nigerian-based Islamist insurgency, claimed responsibility on the BBC's Hausa language radio broadcast in northern Nigeria, the most Islamic portion of this huge country. Before this, Boko Haram had attacked only domestic targets, following a pattern not unlike that of the GSPC (Salafist Group for Preaching and Combat) in Algeria before it became Al Qaeda in the Islamic Maghreb. For years there have been suggestions that Boko Haram had already formed ties with Al Qaeda, and this surely signals an intensifying of that relationship or an intention to use Al Qaeda–like tactics against Western and international targets throughout Nigeria. One local expert, Dr. Jibrin Ibrahim, commented in the *New York Times* that "what's really alarming is the level of planning and organization that has gone into it. . . . The whole issue about Boko Haram is that we know very little about them." These words were very similar to the comments made about Al Qaeda's pre-9/11 attacks, and this news story gave me the same chill I felt when the USS *Cole* was attacked in 2000 in Yemen.

This time it's Nigeria. Not Afghanistan. Not Iraq. Not even Yemen or Somalia. This is the same Nigeria where the Christmas Day bomber was raised in a prominent family. This is the same Nigeria where in early 2001 I first saw those kids with postcards of Osama bin Laden on the streets of the ancient Islamic city of Kano. This is the same Nigeria where we didn't even have a permanent diplomatic presence in the vast northern, predominantly Islamic part of the largest country in Africa. This is the same Nigeria where one of our top officials was more concerned about what kind of steaks he could get in Kano than he was in trying to delve into the complexities of Islamic disaffection in this region. We must dedicate ourselves to a more developed relationship with other nations. We must make the governmental and personal commitments that allow us to better understand what is happening in a place like Nigeria. As Dr. Zbigniew Brzezinski said on MSNBC the day after Osama bin Laden was killed, "I think we are in a position to ask ourselves, can we in some way if not put an end then at least greatly reduce what was mounting over the last decade, namely a bigger and deeper conflict between America and the world of Islam. This is a chance." But declaring victory over Al Qaeda and ignoring sinister developments in places like Nigeria won't do it. We must launch a decade of outreach, learning, and development of new ties that will allow us to understand the rest of the world better.

In 1940, an undergraduate at Harvard College had the temerity to expand on Winston Churchill's *While England Slept*. In his senior thesis he addressed some of Churchill's claims about the failure of England properly to rearm in anticipation of Germany's military buildup after the First World War. It was later published as *Why England Slept*. In it the young John F. Kennedy wrote, "Now that the world is ablaze, America has awakened to the problems facing it." He added, "We cannot escape the fact that democracy in America, like democracy in England, has been asleep at the switch." Ten years after 9/11, I think we would all agree that this nation was asleep at the switch when it came to the gathering threat of Al Qaeda, and that it is our mission to stay alert into the future. I don't think we have adequately done so. In the words of that future president, "To say that democracy has been awakened by the events of the last few weeks is not enough. Any person will awaken when the house is burning down. What we need is an armed guard that will wake up when the fire first starts or, better yet, one that will not permit a fire to start at all."

ACKNOWLEDGMENTS

I wish to first acknowledge my late parents, Leon and Sylvia Feingold, whose love and guidance prepared the way for what has thus far been an eventful and happy life. They instilled in me an idealism and optimism about life and this great country that has always sustained me. The members of my family, both immediate and extended, as well as so many friends, have only added to those feelings and their support has been remarkable. Most of all, I thank and send my love to my daughters, Jessica and Ellen. I am so proud of their achievements and the women they have become. They treat their dad very well. Together we now enjoy an expanded circle of family and friends including Alex Dewar, Matthew and Jen Brack, my son-in-law Jeff Lieberson, and my new grandson, Isaac Benjamin Feingold Lieberson ("Izzy").

The role I played in some of the events described in this book could never have happened without the steadfast support, hard work, and creativity of the hundreds of staff members who have worked with me since 1982, in both official Senate offices and on our political campaigns. Their dedication and laughter made the journey exciting and fun. Three people who have been working with or advising me since the very beginning deserve special mention: Nancy Mitchell, my executive assistant and former legal secretary, has worked with me in one capacity or another every day for more than thirty-two years—she has defined both loyalty and friendship in my career and my life. Sumner Slichter was at my side for every vote I took in twenty-eight years as a legislator, and I didn't vote until I sought his wise counsel. And John Sylvester is the truest of friends, an exceptional political mind, and the best ally the hardworking people of Wisconsin have ever had.

I also received a boost from a great Wisconsin institution. I want to express my gratitude to Dean Joseph Kearney, Associate Dean Matthew Parlow, and all the faculty, staff, and students at Marquette University Law School in Milwaukee, for the opportunity to try my hand at teaching law both semesters during 2011. It is a great learning environment with strong community ties and support. The welcome given to me at Marquette allowed me to enjoy and give the classes the attention they deserve while also grappling with the challenge of writing this book.

As to the book itself, I want to thank those who made this book and its publication and promotion possible. Bob Barnett, who Mary Irvine understood was the best "book lawyer" in the business, represented me well. He helped provide the advice and resources to allow this book to be written with the attention to detail for which I was hoping. And it surely helped that this was a joint Badger project, since he and his wife, Rita Braver, are among the most active and loyal alumni of our common alma mater, the University of Wisconsin–Madison.

Sean Desmond has been a superb editor and coach. When Sean first visited me in Washington, DC, in late 2010, he immediately grasped what I wanted to convey in this book. Never missing a beat, he helped me learn a different kind of writing compared to the "legal" style I've usually employed. His edits were direct when necessary but he also went out of his way with his good humor to encourage me along the way. I thoroughly enjoyed the experience of working with him. I also want to thank Campbell Wharton of the Random House Speakers' Bureau, who is focusing on making sure somebody reads this book. I'm looking forward to the opportunity to take it on the road.

Three people really created this book with me. I did the writing but they joined me on an almost daily basis for the eight-month effort of refining and improving it. First, Mary Irvine. The idea of my writing a book was hers and so was the skillful implementation of a plan to get somebody to publish the thoughts of a recently defeated politician. I've already detailed in the previous pages some of her exceptional work as my chief of staff in the United States Senate. On this project, she was the first to see each portion as I completed the roughest of drafts. Her feedback was timely, clever, and especially encouraging, as I had never tried to write a book before. Given her sense of humor, I would love to say any errors in judgment are entirely hers, but they are of course mine.

Second, Jeremy Tollefson. This young man, a native of Middleton, Wisconsin, moved without a hitch from working for me in the US Senate for six years to becoming my research assistant on this book. He was dogged in his attention to detail and accuracy and his research was first-class. I also benefited from his good humor as all the different elements of this book came together through his fine work.

Finally, Dr. Christine Y. Ferdinand, the Fellow Librarian at Magdalen College, Oxford University. Christine volunteered to serve as the copy editor for my draft of the book before submission of the manuscript to Crown Publishers. She put in hundreds of hours carefully editing each page of my sometimes haphazard writing, managing gently to point out, for example, that using the word *just* thirty-five times in one chapter might be a bit much. Her substantive understanding of what I was trying to achieve with this book was *just* as valuable. Most of all, though, walking with her, sometimes hand in hand, through the University Parks in Oxford, the Mall in Washington, DC, the Big Bay State Park on Madeline Island, and the Pheasant Branch Creek in Middleton, Wisconsin, while we discussed both the minutiae and the broad themes of the book, was music.

I end by thanking the people of the great state of Wisconsin for the honor and privilege of serving them in the United States Senate for eighteen years. It was a rare and joyful adventure.

Russ Feingold
Middleton, Wisconsin
September 11, 2011

SOURCE NOTES

INTRODUCTION

The introduction is based on interviews with the following people: Nancy Mitchell, April 8, 2011; Mary Irvine, Jan. 28, 2011; Sumner Slichter, Jan. 28, 2011; Bob Schiff, Feb. 18, 2011; Jenny Hassemer, April 11, 2011; Trevor Miller, March 29, 2011; Mary Frances Repko, Feb. 22, 2011; Bill Dauster, Feb. 22, 2011; Tom Walls, Feb. 12, 2011; Rea Holmes, Feb. 12, 2011; Steve Driscoll, Feb. 12, 2011; Farhana Khera, Feb. 16, 2011.

The introduction draws on the following published sources: Winston S. Churchill, *While England Slept: A Survey of World Affairs 1932–1938* (New York: G. P. Putnam's Sons, 1938); John F. Kennedy, *Why England Slept* (New York: Wilfred Funk, 1940).

CHAPTER 1: A Quiet, Almost Smoldering Determination

This chapter is based on interviews with the following people: Mary Irvine, Jan. 28, 2011; Sumner Slichter, Jan. 28, 2011; Farhana Khera, Feb. 16, 2011; Bob Schiff, Feb. 18, 2011; John Sylvester, April 29, 2011.

This chapter draws from the following town hall meetings: Rock County Listening Session, Beloit Public Library, Beloit, WI, Sept. 20, 2001; Dodge County Listening Session, Horicon City Hall, Horicon, WI, Oct. 1, 2001; Sauk County Listening Session, Sauk Prairie District Education Center, Sauk City, WI, Oct. 1, 2001; Waupaca County Listening Session, Manawa Middle

School, Manawa, WI, Oct. 6, 2001; Door County Listening Session, Sturgeon Bay City Hall, Sturgeon Bay, WI, Oct. 7, 2001; Kewaunee County Listening Session, Algoma City Hall, Algoma, WI, Oct. 7, 2001; Walworth County Listening Session, Michael Fields Agriculture Institute, East Troy, WI, Oct. 15, 2001; Outagamie County Listening Session, Appleton City Hall, Appleton, WI, Dec. 27, 2001.

This chapter draws on the following published sources: Alison Mitchell and Richard L. Berke, "After the Attacks: The Congress; Differences Are Put Aside as Lawmakers Reconvene," *New York Times*, Sept. 13, 2001; Alison Mitchell and Katharine Q. Seelye, "A Day of Terror: Congress; Horror Knows No Party as Lawmakers Huddle," *New York Times*, Sept. 12, 2001; Alison Mitchell and Philip Shenon, "After the Attacks: Congress; Agreement on $40 Million for Aid and a Response," *New York Times*, Sept. 14, 2001; Barry Schweid, "White House Rebukes Israel: Critique," *Washington Post*, Oct. 5, 2001; Johanna McGeary, Massimo Calabresi, Margaret Carlson, James Carney, Michael Duffy, Mark Thompson, Douglas Waller, and J.F.O. McAllister, "Odd Man Out," *Time*, Sept. 10, 2001; "Reluctant Warrior," *The Observer*, Sept. 30, 2001; Anthony Lewis, "Abroad at Home: Progress and Problems," *New York Times*, Sept. 29, 2001; Kevin Hermening, "Hold Back Nothing in Avenging Terrorism," *Wisconsin State Journal*, Sept. 19, 2001; Senator Russ Feingold (WI), "Terrorist Attacks against the United States," *Congressional Record*, 107th Congress, 1st Session, Library of Congress, Sept. 12, 2001, S9318; CRS Report for Congress—Authorization for Use of Military Force in Response to the 9/11 Attacks: Legislation History, Federation of American Scientists; "Text of Bush's Address," CNN, Sept. 11, 2001; "Transcript of President Bush's Address," CNN, Sept. 21, 2001; "Bush State of the Union Address," CNN, Jan. 29, 2002; "President Bush Says Taliban Paying a Price," CNN, Oct. 7, 2001.

CHAPTER 2: A Growing Climate of Fear in the Capital

This chapter is based on interviews with the following people: Mary Irvine, Jan. 28, 2011; Sumner Slichter, Jan. 28, 2011; Steve Driscoll, Feb. 12, 2011; Rea Holmes, Feb. 12, 2011; Mary Frances Repko, Feb. 22, 2011; Trevor Miller, March 29, 2011; Tom Walls, Feb. 12, 2011; John Sylvester, April 29, 2011; Bob Schiff, Feb. 18, 2011; Nancy Mitchell, April 8, 2011.

This chapter draws from the following town hall meetings: Walworth County Listening Session, Michael Fields Agricultural Institute, East Troy, WI, Oct. 15, 2001; Pepin County Listening Session, Durand Senior Center, Durand,

WI, Oct. 20, 2001; Chippewa County Listening Session, YMCA, Chippewa Falls, WI, Dec. 1, 2001.

This chapter draws on the following published sources: Tom Daschle, *Like No Other Time: The 107th Congress and the Two Years That Changed America Forever* (New York: Crown, 2003); Tom Daschle, "The Unsolved Case of Anthrax," *Washington Post*, Oct. 15, 2006; Tom Walls, "I Keep Forgetting That I Was a Victim of Attempted Murder," *isthatlegal*, Oct. 26, 2006; Brian Kates, "We Get $5-a-Head for Security: N.Y. Is Top Terror Risk but Ranks 49th in Aid," *New York Daily News*, Nov. 24, 2003; Matthew Rothschild, "Protestors Detained in Milwaukee: Are You on the No-Fly List?" *The Progressive*, April 27, 2002; Sara Kehaulani Goo, "Sen. Kennedy Flagged by No-Fly List," *Washington Post*, Aug. 20, 2004; David Snyder, "Muhammad and Malvo Indicted in Md.," *Washington Post*, June 17, 2005; "Sniper Accomplice Says Mentor Had Extortion and Terror Plan," *New York Times*, May 24, 2006; Ian Urbina, "Washington-Area Sniper Convicted of 6 More Killings," *New York Times*, May 31, 2006; N. Zeke Campfield, "Anthrax Scares Spread Across Madison, Country," *Badger Herald*, Oct. 14, 2001.

CHAPTER 3: The Iraq Deception

This chapter draws from the following town hall meeting: Dodge County Listening Session, Horicon National Wildlife Refuge, Mayville, WI, Feb. 9, 2003.

This chapter draws on the following published sources: "Bush State of the Union Address," CNN, Jan. 29, 2002; "Transcript of President Bush's Address," CNN, Sept. 21, 2001; Dai Richards, "Blair's War," *Frontline*, PBS, April 3, 2003; Patrick E. Tyler with John Tagliabue, "Czechs Confirm Iraqi Agent Met with Terror Ringleader," *New York Times*, Oct. 27, 2001; "Hijacker Did Not Meet Iraqi Agent," BBC News: Americas, May 1, 2002; Bob Woodward, "With CIA Push, Movement to War Accelerated: Agency's Estimate of Saddam Hussein's Arsenal Became the White House's Rationale for Invasion," *Washington Post*, April 19, 2004; "President Bush's Address to the United Nations," CNN, Sept. 12, 2002; Jules Witcover, "What about the War Powers Act?" *Baltimore Sun*, May 1, 2002; Transcript of "Applying the War Powers Resolution to the War on Terrorism," hearing before the Subcommittee on the Constitution, Federalism, and Property Rights of the Committee on the Judiciary, US Senate, 107th Congress, 2nd Session, Government Printing Office, April 17, 2002; Transcript of "Hearing to Examine Threats, Responses, and Regional Considerations Surrounding Iraq," Hearing before the Committee on Foreign Relations, United States Senate, 107th

Congress, 2nd Session, US Government Printing Office, July 31 and Aug. 1, 2002; "Bush: Don't Wait for Mushroom Cloud," CNN, Oct. 7, 2002; Senator Russ Feingold (WI), "Authorization of the Use of United States Armed Forces against Iraq," *Congressional Record*, 107th Congress, 2nd Session, Library of Congress, Oct. 9, 2002, S10147–S10149.

CHAPTER 4: A Game of Risk

This chapter draws on the following published sources: "History and Strategy of Risk: The Game of Strategic Conquest," Hasbro; "Transcript: Sen. Lieberman, Rep. Hoekstra on 'FNS'," Fox News, Dec. 27, 2009; "Bush Makes Historic Speech aboard Warship," CNN, May 1, 2003; Senator Russ Feingold (WI), "The Fight against Terrorism," *Congressional Record*, 108th Congress, 1st Session, Library of Congress, May 13, 2003, S6037-S6039; Transcript of "Madison Civics Club Speech," Russ Feingold, Nov. 18, 2006; Robert Burns, Associated Press, "Mullen: Afghanistan Isn't Top Priority," *USA Today*, Dec. 11, 2007; Rick Maze, "Senate Supports One Medal for Terrorism War," *Army Times*, Oct. 14, 2003; Rick Maze, "Campaign-Medals Bill Clears Senate, Heads to White House," *Army Times*, May 18, 2004; Vince Crawley, "Bush Signs Bill Creating Separate Iraq, Afghanistan Campaign Medals," *Army Times*, June 8, 2004; Senator Russ Feingold (WI), "National Intelligence Reform Act of 2004," *Congressional Record*, 108th Congress, 2nd Session, Library of Congress, Oct. 6, 2004, S10530–10531; Glenn Thrush, "Russ Thanks Russ," *Politico*, Jan. 5, 2010; Joseph Conrad, *Heart of Darkness;* "Kenya Terror Strikes Target Israelis," BBC News: Africa, Nov. 28, 2002; "Al Qaeda Claims Credit For Kenya Attacks," CNN, Dec. 2, 2002; *The World Factbook*, "Indonesia," CIA; "Bali Death Toll Set at 202," BBC News: Asia-Pacific, Feb. 19, 2003; "Bomb Wrecks Top Jakarta Hotel," BBC News: Asia-Pacific, Aug. 5, 2003; Thomas P. M. Barnett, "The Man between War and Peace," *Esquire*, April 2008; Mark Mazzetti, "US Is Intensifying a Secret Campaign of Yemen Airstrikes," *New York Times*, June 8, 2011; Mohammed Ibrahim, "More Clashes in Somalia; Minster Is Killed," *New York Times*, June 10, 2011; Jeffrey Gettleman, "Somalis Kill Mastermind of 2 US Embassy Bombings," *New York Times*, June 11, 2011.

CHAPTER 5: In for a Penny, in for a Pound

This chapter draws from the following town hall meetings: Dodge County Listening Session, Horicon National Wildlife Refuge, Mayville, WI, Feb. 9,

2003; Dunn County Listening Session, Dunn County Government Center, Menomonie, WI, April 23, 2003; Eau Claire County Listening Session, Fall Creek Village Hall, Fall Creek, WI, April 23, 2003; Sauk County Listening Session, River Arts Center, Prairie du Sac, WI, April 12, 2003; Waushara County Listening Session, Plainfield Community Center, Plainfield, WI, April 17, 2003; Juneau County Listening Session, Juneau County Courthouse, Mauston, WI, April 21, 2003; Rock County Listening Session, The Gathering Place, Milton, WI, May 28, 2003; Taylor County Listening Session, Jump River Community Center, Jump River, WI, Aug. 6, 2003; Waupaca County Listening Session, Iola Community Center, Iola, WI, June 25, 2005; Forest County Listening Session, Newald Community Center, Newald, WI, Aug. 3, 2005; Green Lake County Listening Session, Marquette Village Hall Gymnasium, Marquette, WI, Aug. 18, 2005; Door County Listening Session, Liberty Grove Town Hall, Liberty Grove, WI, Aug. 1, 2005; St. Croix County Listening Session, Star Prairie Community Center, Star Prairie, WI, Aug. 26, 2005; 2003 Listening Sessions End-of-the-Year Report; 2004 Listening Sessions End-of-the-Year Report; 2005 Listening Sessions End-of-the-Year Report; 2006 Listening Sessions End-of-the-Year Report.

This chapter draws on the following published sources: Aftab Borka, "Al Qaeda Suspected of Pakistan's Marriott Bombing," *Reuters*, Sept 21, 2008; "Bin Laden Tape: Transcript of Osama Bin Laden's Speech," *Worldpress*, Oct. 30, 2004; William Safire, "The Way We Live Now: On Language; Guns, God and Gays," *New York Times*, Jan. 25, 2004; "Delegation of Senators Hold Live Press Conference in Iraq," CNN, Feb. 19, 2005; "Transcript for Feb. 20: Guests: Sens. John McCain, R-Ariz; Hillary Clinton, D-N.Y.; Katty Kay, BBC; Andrea Mitchell, NBC News; Dana Priest & Robin Wright, the *Washington Post*," MSNBC, Feb. 23, 2005; "The Toll of War: US Troop Fatalities in Iraq Since March 2003: A Month-by-Month Count of US Troops Killed in the Conflict," National Public Radio, Aug. 4, 2009; Marcia Davis, "Rep. Jones, Resolving to Follow His Heart," *Washington Post*, June 17, 2005; Gail Russell Chaddock, "On Iraq War, Senate Leader Harry Reid in Cross Hairs," *Christian Science Monitor*, April 27, 2007; "To Require the Redeployment of United States Armed Forces from Iraq in Order to Further a Political Solution in Iraq, Encourage the People of Iraq to Provide for Their Own Security, and Achieve Victory in the War on Terror," S. Amdt. 4442, Roll Vote No. 181, *Congressional Record*, 100th Congress, 2nd Session, Library of Congress, June 22, 2006, S6335; "To Provide for a Transition of the Iraq Mission," S. Amdt. 1098, Roll Vote No. 167, *Congressional Record*, 110th Congress, 1st Session, Library of Congress, May 16, 2007, S6166; Russ Feingold, "More US Troops to Afghanistan?" *Christian Science Monitor*, Oct. 24, 2008;

Senator Russ Feingold (WI), "Liberia," *Congressional Record,* 108th Congress, 1st Session, Library of Congress, July 9, 2003, S9111.

CHAPTER 6: An Old Wish List of the FBI
This chapter is based on interviews with the following people: Mary Irvine, Jan. 28, 2011; Bob Schiff, Feb. 18, 2011.

This chapter draws on the following published sources: "Uniting And Strengthening America Act," S. 1510, Roll Vote No. 302, *Congressional Record,* 107th Congress, 1st Session, Library of Congress, Oct. 11, 2001, S10604; Senator Zell Miller (GA), Presiding Officer, Transcript of Senate Floor Proceedings, "Uniting and Strengthening America Act," S. 1510, Roll Vote No. 302, C-SPAN, Oct. 11, 2001, 11:55 p.m. EST; Senator Russ Feingold (WI), "Terrorist Attacks against The United States," *Congressional Record,* 107th Congress, 1st Session, Library of Congress, Sept. 12, 2001, S9318; *Kennedy v. Mendoza-Martinez,* 372 US 144 (1963); Transcript of "Protecting Constitutional Freedoms in the Face of Terrorism," Hearing before the Subcommittee on the Constitution, Federalism, and Property Rights of the Committee on the Judiciary, US Senate, 107th Congress, 1st Session, US Government Printing Office, Oct. 3, 2001; "Uniting and Strengthening America Act," S. Amdt. 1899, Roll Vote No. 299, *Congressional Record,* 107th Congress, 1st Session, Library of Congress, Oct. 11, 2001, S10575; "Uniting and Strengthening America Act," S. Amdt. 1900, Roll Vote No. 300, *Congressional Record,* 107th Congress, 1st Session, Library of Congress, Oct. 11, 2001, S10577; "Uniting and Strengthening America Act," S. Amdt. 1901, Roll Vote No. 301, *Congressional Record,* 107th Congress, 1st Session, Library of Congress, Oct. 11, 2001, S10586; Senator Tom Daschle (SD), "Uniting and Strengthening America Act," *Congressional Record,* 107th Congress, 1st Session, Library of Congress, Oct. 11, 2001, S10574; Senator Russ Feingold (WI), "Uniting and Strengthening America Act," *Congressional Record,* 107th Congress, 1st Session, Library of Congress, Oct. 11, 2001, S10575; Amy Goodman, "Sen. Russ Feingold: Dems Platform on Iraq a 'Mistake'," *Democracy Now: The War and Peace Report,* July 29, 2004; Brian Lamb, Transcript of "Russ Feingold: Democratic Senator from Wisconsin," C-SPAN, Feb. 6, 2005; Tom Curry, "For His Foes, Ashcroft Became Symbol of Lost Liberties: Attorney General Seemed to Relish Giving His Adversaries a Partisan Ear-Twisting," MSNBC, Nov. 9, 2004; Eric Lichtblau, "Ashcroft Mocks Librarians and Others Who Oppose Parts of Counterterrorism Law," *New York Times,* Sept. 16, 2003; "Transcripts: The

Roberts Confirmation Hearings," *Washington Post*, Sept. 13–15, 2005; "Foreign Intelligence Surveillance Act Court Orders 1979–2010," Electronic Privacy Information Center; "A Review of the Federal Bureau of Investigation's Use of National Security Letters," US Department of Justice Office of the Inspector General, NPR, March 2007.

CHAPTER 7: A Pre-1776 Mindset

This chapter is based on interviews with the following people: Mary Irvine, Jan. 28, 2011; Sumner Slichter, Jan. 28, 2011.

This chapter draws from the following town hall meeting: Pepin County Listening Session, Durand Senior Center, Durand, WI, Oct. 20, 2001.

This chapter draws on the following published sources: Tom Curry, "For His Foes, Ashcroft Became Symbol of Lost Liberties: Attorney General Seemed to Relish Giving His Adversaries a Partisan Ear-Twisting," MSNBC, Nov. 9, 2004; Eric Lichtblau, "Ashcroft Mocks Librarians and Others Who Oppose Parts of Counterterrorism Law," *New York Times*, Sept. 16, 2003; Dahlia Lithwick, "Pulling the Plug: Alberto Gonzales Browbeats the Critically Ill," *Slate*, May 15, 2007; Senator Ron Wyden (OR), "Small Business Additional Temporary Extension Act of 2011," *Congressional Record*, 112th Congress, 1st Session, Library of Congress, May 26, 2011, S3386; James Risen and Eric Lichtblau, "Bush Lets US Spy on Callers without Courts," *New York Times*, Dec. 16, 2005; Senator Chuck Schumer (NY), "USA Patriot and Terrorism Prevention Reauthorization Act of 2005," *Congressional Record*, 109th Congress, 1st Session, Library of Congress, Dec. 16, 2005, S13718; Senator Arlen Specter (PA), "USA Patriot and Terrorism Prevention Reauthorization Act of 2005," *Congressional Record*, 109th Congress, 1st Session, Library of Congress, Dec. 16, 2005, S13714; "Patriot Act Extension Filibustered," *Washington Times*, Dec. 17, 2005; Transcript of "Russ Feingold: Senator Feingold Is Calling for Censure of President George W. Bush for His Illegal Use of Domestic Wiretaps," *The Daily Show with Jon Stewart*, March 22, 2006; "Foreign Intelligence Surveillance Act Court Orders 1979–2010," Electronic Privacy Information Center; John McCain, "Bin Laden's Death and the Debate over Torture," *Washington Post*, May 11, 2011; Transcript of "Restoring the Rule of Law," Hearing before the Subcommittee on the Constitution of the Committee on the Judiciary, US Senate, 110th Congress, 2nd Session, Government Printing Office, Sept. 16, 2008; "Transcripts: The Roberts Confirmation Hearings," *Washington Post*, Sept. 13–15, 2005; Jonathan

Turley, "The Demon Is Dead; So Are Many of Our Rights," *USA Today*, May 3, 2011; John McCain, "Torture Didn't Lead Us to Osama Bin Laden," *Capital Times*, May 18–24, 2011.

CHAPTER 8: Morphing Islam into Al Qaeda

This chapter is based on interviews with the following people: Mary Irvine, Jan. 28, 2011; Farhana Khera, Feb. 16, 2011; Bob Schiff, Feb. 18, 2011.

This chapter draws on the following published sources: "Text of President Bush's 2001 Address to Congress," *Washington Post*, Feb. 27, 2001; "Transcript of President Bush's Address," CNN, Sept. 21, 2001; Senator Russ Feingold (WI), "Terrorist Attacks against the United States," *Congressional Record*, 107th Congress, 1st Session, Library of Congress, Sept. 12, 2001, S9318; Senator Sam Brownback (KS), "Terrorist Attacks against the United States," *Congressional Record*, 107th Congress, 1st Session, Library of Congress, Sept. 12, 2001, S9318; Vivanti Sarkar (dir.), *Mistaken Identity: Sikhs in America* (2000); David Lean (dir.), *Lawrence of Arabia* (1962); Mark Twain, *Innocents Abroad* (New York: American, 1869); "Remarks by the President upon Arrival," The South Lawn, George W. Bush White House Archives, Sept. 16, 2001; "President Discusses War on Terror at National Endowment for Democracy," Ronald Reagan Building and International Trade Center, Washington, DC, George W. Bush White House Archives, Oct. 6, 2005; "President Commemorates Veterans Day, Discusses War on Terror," Tobyhanna Army Depot, Tobyhanna, PA, George W. Bush White House Archives, Nov. 11, 2005; "President Addresses Troops at Osan Air Base in Osan, Korea," Osan Air Base, Osan, Republic of Korea, George W. Bush White House Archives, Nov. 19, 2005; "Press Conference of the President," James S. Brady Briefing Room, George W. Bush White House Archives, March 21, 2006; "President Attends Pennsylvania Congressional Victory Committee Dinner," Sheraton Philadelphia City Center, Philadelphia, PA, George W. Bush White House Archives, March 21, 2006; "President Bush and Prime Minister Blair of the United Kingdom Participate in Joint Press Availability," East Room, George W. Bush White House Archives, May 25, 2006; "President Bush and Prime Minister Rasmussen of Denmark Participate in Joint Press Availability," Camp David, George W. Bush White House Archives, June 9, 2006; "Press Conference of the President," Rose Garden, George W. Bush White House Archives, June 14, 2006; "President Bush and Secretary of State Rice Discuss the Middle East Crisis," Prairie Chapel Ranch, Crawford, TX, George W. Bush White House Archives,

Aug. 7, 2006; "President Bush Discusses Terror Plot upon Arrival in Wisconsin," Austin Staubel International Airport, Green Bay, WI, George W. Bush White House Archives, Aug. 10, 2006; "Call for Bush to Stop Using 'Islamic Fascists': Feingold Says Term Offensive and Unconnected to Global Terrorism Fight," MSNBC, Sept. 12, 2006; Niraj Warikoo, "Some Muslims Plan to Welcome Pastor Who Burned Quran," *Standard Examiner*, March 25, 2011; Aziz Huq, "Defend Muslims, Defend America," *New York Times*, June 19, 2011; "Interfaith Alliance and Colleagues Raise Concerns about Rep. Peter King's Planned Hearings on 'Radicalization of the American Muslim Community,'" Interfaith Alliance, Feb. 1, 2011; David Nakamura, "Japanese Americans: House Hearings on Radical Islam 'Sinister,'" *Washington Post*, March 8, 2011; Felicia Sonmez, "Senate Judiciary Panel Sets Hearing for Next Week on Protecting Muslims' Civil Rights," *Washington Post*, March 22, 2011; Aliyah Shahid, "Katie Couric, CBS Anchor, Suggests America Needs a Muslim Version of 'The Cosby Show,'" *New York Daily News*, Jan. 1, 2011; Transcript of "Allah in the Family: Aasif Mandvi Hopes to Change America's Perceptions of Muslims by Starring in The Qu'osby Show," *The Daily Show with Jon Stewart*, Feb. 17, 2011; Christopher Morris (dir.), *Four Lions* (2010); Hajer Naili, "CNN Explores the Unwanted Neighbor Phenomenon," *Illume Magazine*, March 31, 2011.

CHAPTER 9: Trivializing National Security and Foreign Policy for Political Gain

This chapter draws on the following published sources: Thomas Kilgannon, "Senator Jesse Helms, RIP," *Freedom Alliance*, July 9, 2008; Michael Crowley, "Former Sen. Max Cleland: How the Disabled War Veteran Became the Democrats' Mascot," *Slate*, April 2, 2004; Don Gonyea, "Anger Over 'Betray Us' Ad Simmers on Hill," National Public Radio, Sept. 22, 2007; "MoveOn Vote: Clinton a 'No,' Obama a No-Show," *Huffington Post*, Sept. 20, 2007; "Gingrich Comment on Shutdown Labeled 'Bizarre' by White House," CNN, Nov. 16, 1995; Dan Gilgoff, "Mitt Romney on Obama's Cairo Speech: No Apologies," *US News & World Report*, June 2, 2009; Nile Gardiner and Morgan Roach, "Barack Obama's Top 10 Apologies: How the President Has Humiliated a Superpower," Heritage Foundation, June 2, 2009; Alex Altman, "Mitt Romney's No Apology," *Time*, March 3, 2010; "Fox Hosts Revive Fox-Manufactured Obama 'Apology Tour,'" *Media Matters*, June 3, 2009; Aaron Blake, "Tim Pawlenty to CPAC: Obama Should 'Stop Apologizing' for US," *Washington Post*, Feb. 11, 2011; Transcripts from "The American Conservative Union, CPAC Live," Washington,

DC, CPAC, Feb. 11, 2011; Rachel Weiner, "Tim Pawlenty Courts the Tea Party," *Washington Post*, March 1, 2011; Senator Jesse Helms (NC), "Order of Procedure," *Congressional Record,* 103rd Congress, 1st Session, Library of Congress, Sept. 14, 1993, S11665.

CHAPTER 10: Economic Collapse and the Loss of International Focus
This chapter draws from the following town hall meetings: Jackson County Listening Session, Lincoln Elementary School, Merrillan, WI, Jan. 16, 2010; Richland County Listening Session, Richland Center High School, Richland Center, WI, July 18, 2009; Walworth County Listening Session, Lions Field House, Williams Bay, WI, Jan. 24, 2009; Brown County Listening Session, Ashwaubenon Village Hall, Ashwaubenon, WI, March 28, 2009; Manitowoc County Listening Session, Manitowoc Public Library, Manitowoc, WI, April 17, 2009; Crawford County Listening Session, Gays Mills Community Center, Gays Mills, WI, July 18, 2009; Waushara County Listening Session, Wild Rose Lions Club Building, Wild Rose, WI, July 25, 2009; Iron County Listening Session, Mercer Community Center, Mercer, WI, Aug. 19, 2009; Vernon County Listening Session, Chaseburg Village Hall, Chaseburg, WI, Aug. 1, 2009; Waukesha County Listening Session, Waukesha County Technical College, Pewaukee Campus, Pewaukee, WI, Jan. 11, 2010; Marquette County Listening Session, Ada Mills Donner & Melvin R. Donner Civic Center, Endeavor, WI, June 27, 2009; Winnebago County Listening Session, EAA Museum, Oshkosh, WI, April 1, 2002; Door County Listening Session, Brussels Town Hall and Fire Station, Brussels, WI, Sept. 16, 2006; Ozaukee County Listening Session, Port Washington Senior Center, Port Washington, WI, Jan. 14, 2007; 2007 Listening Sessions of the Year Report; 2008 Listening Sessions End-of-the-Year Report; 2009 Listening Sessions End-of-the-Year Report; 2010 Listening Sessions End-of-the-Year Report.

This chapter draws on the following published sources: Ben Smith, "Health Reform Foes Plan Obama's 'Waterloo,'" *Politico*, July 17, 2009; "Rick Santelli's Shout Heard 'Round the World," CNBC, Feb. 22, 2009; "Is Congress Getting the Message? 12 News Investigates Best Way to Reach Representatives, Senators," WISN, Feb. 11, 2010; Bob MacGuffie, "Rocking the Town Halls—Best Practices: A Political Action Memo," Right Principles.

CHAPTER 11: Members of Congress Engaging Other Countries

This chapter draws on the following published sources: Transcript of the Senate of the Federal Republic of Nigeria, Votes and Proceedings, 5th National Assembly, 4th Session, No. 3, June 13, 2006, pp. 57–58; "The Santa Cruz Massacre, Nov. 12, 1991," ETAN; "Timorese Remember Cemetery Massacre," BBC News: Asia-Pacific, Nov. 12, 1999; Shirl McArthur, "King Abdullah Gets Royal Reception in Washington," *Washington Report on Middle East Affairs,* July–August 1999; "Bush's State of the Union Speech," CNN, Jan. 28, 2003; "Bush and Iraq: Follow the Yellow Cake Road," *Time,* July 9, 2003; Chris Frates, "Pakistan's Man in Washington," *Politico,* May 6, 2011; Senator Russ Feingold (WI), "Egypt," *Congressional Record,* 111th Congress, 2nd Session, Library of Congress, May 24, 2010, S4141; Eric Lichtblau, "Arab Unrest Puts Their Lobbyists in Uneasy Spot," *New York Times,* March 1, 2011.

CHAPTER 12: Americans Reaching Out to the Rest of the World

This chapter is based on interviews with the following people: Robyn Lieberman, March 25, 2011; John McCarthy, April 20, 2011.

This chapter draws on the following published sources: Brian Harper, "Where in the World Is . . . Tunisia?" *Marquette Tribune,* Feb. 3, 2011; "Al-Qaeda Claims Tunisia Attack," BBC News: Middle East, June 23, 2002; Senator Russ Feingold (WI), "Statements on Introduced Bills and Joint Resolutions," *Congressional Record,* 110th Congress, 1st Session, Library of Congress, May 23, 2007, S6557; press release of "Introduction of Global Service Fellowship Program Act of 2007," Office of US Senator Russ Feingold, May 23, 2007; Press Release of "International Service Volunteer Leaders Join Forces at Conference in Washington," Partners of the Americas, Dec. 1, 2009; "Rising Environmental Concern in 47-Nation Survey: Global Unease with Major World Powers," Pew Global Attitudes Project, June 27, 2007; James Miles, "The Pyongyang Concert 2008," *Economist,* Sept. 10, 2008; Mission Statement, Peace Corps.

CONCLUSION

The conclusion draws on the following published sources: Winston S. Churchill, *While England Slept: A Survey of World Affairs 1932–1938* (New York: G. P. Putnam's Sons, 1938); John F. Kennedy, *Why England Slept* (New York: Wilfred Funk, 1940); Shadi Hamid, "Al-Qaeda Losing Relevance," *USA Today,* May 4,

2011; Charles Kurzman, "Why Is It So Hard to Find a Suicide Bomber These Days?" *Foreign Policy*, September–October 2011; Peter Beinart, "The War on Terror Is Over," *Daily Beast*, May 1, 2011; Greg Miller, "US Officials Believe Al-Qaeda on Brink of Collapse," *Washington Post*, July 26, 2011; Associated Press, "US Counterterror Chief: Al Qaeda Now on the Ropes," Fox News, Sept. 1, 2011; Craig Whitlock, "Panetta Appears to Link Al-Qaeda Presence with Iraq Invasion," *Washington Post*, July 11, 2011; Global Security Newswire Staff, "Qaeda WMD Threat Remains after Bin Laden's Death, Ex-Official Says," *National Journal*, July 29, 2011; Senan Murray, "Suicide Bomber Attacks U.N. Building in Nigeria," *New York Times*, Aug. 26, 2011; Martin Crutsinger and Christopher S. Rugaber, Associated Press, "Obama Feels Heat of Cooling Economy," *Milwaukee Journal Sentinel*, June 8, 2011; Transcript of *Morning Joe*, MSNBC, May 2, 2011; Transcript of *Morning Joe*, MSNBC, May 6, 2011.

INDEX

ABOUT THE AUTHOR

RUSS FEINGOLD represented the state of Wisconsin in the United States Senate from 1993 to 2011. Since leaving the Senate, he has been a visiting professor at Marquette University Law School in Milwaukee, Wisconsin, and the inaugural Mimi and Peter Haas Distinguished Visitor at Stanford University. In February of 2011, Feingold founded Progressives United, an organization devoted to challenging the dominance of corporate money over our American democracy. Feingold, a Rhodes scholar, is an honors law graduate of both Harvard Law School and Oxford University and earned his bachelor of arts with honors from the University of Wisconsin–Madison. He is the recipient of the 1999 John F. Kennedy Profile in Courage Award and the 2011 Franklin D. Roosevelt Four Freedoms medal.

Russ Feingold is available for select readings and lectures. To inquire about a possible appearance, please contact the Random House Speakers Bureau at rhspeakers@randomhouse.com or 212-572-2013.